HITLER
AND THE
HOLOCAUST

Modern Library Chronicles

Robert S. Wistrich

Hitler and the Holocaust

A MODERN LIBRARY CHRONICLES BOOK

THE MODERN LIBRARY

NEW YORK

Published by arrangement with Weidenfeld & Nicolson,
a division of Orion Publishing Group Ltd.

LIBRARY OF CONGRESS CATALOGING-IN-PUBLICATION DATA
Wistrich, Robert S.
Hitler and the Holocaust / Robert Wistrich.
p.   cm.—(Modern Library chronicles)
Includes index.
ISBN 978-0-812-96863-7 (pbk.)
1. Holocaust, Jewish (1939–1945)   I. Title.   II. Series.

D804.3 .W469 2001
940.53'18—dc21
2001030835

Modern Library website address: www.modernlibrary.com

149137329

To my mother, Sabina,
who lived through it all without losing faith

CONTENTS

INTRODUCTION

> The missionaries of Christianity had said in effect: You have no
> right to live among us as Jews. The secular rulers who followed
> had proclaimed: You have no right to live among us. The German
> Nazis had at last decreed: You have no right to live.
>
> RAUL HILBERG, *The Destruction of the European Jews* (1961)

The Holocaust was an unprecedented crime against humanity that aimed at the annihilation of the entire Jewish population of Europe, down to the last man, woman, and child. It was the planned, deliberate policy decision of a powerful state, the Nazi Reich, which mobilized all of its resources to destroy an entire people. The Jews were not condemned to die for their religious beliefs or for their political opinions. Nor were they an economic or military threat to the Nazi state. They were killed not for what they had done but for the simple fact of their existence.

To be born a Jew, in the eyes of Adolf Hitler and the Nazi regime, meant that one was a priori not a human being and therefore unworthy of life. There were other innocent victims of Nazi racial ideology: Gypsies, who were considered racially impure, were sent to the gas chambers; Russians, Poles, and other occupied peoples in eastern Europe were reduced to slavery; even those ethnic Germans who were branded as mentally or physically defective were put to death until a public outcry moderated this policy. We know that under the Nazi regime, the SS, the Einsatzgruppen (mobile killing units), the Wehrmacht, the Order Police, and the guards in the death camps practiced brutality on a hitherto unknown scale; that they mowed down row upon row of shivering, half-naked adults and smashed the heads of Jewish infants without pity or remorse; that they built a vast system of concentration camps and death camps, the purpose of which was the production of corpses on an industrial scale.

The central unanswered question is why? Why were Jews worked to death on senseless, unproductive tasks, even when the Reich was experiencing an acute labor shortage? Why were skilled Jewish armament workers killed in the camps despite the pressing military needs of the Wehrmacht? Why did the Nazis insist they were fighting an omnipotent "Jewish" power even as their mass murder of the Jews revealed the powerlessness of their enemy?

At the heart of this seeming mystery lay a millenarian weltanschauung (worldview) which proclaimed that "the Jews" were the source of all evils—especially internationalism, pacifism, democracy, and Marxism; that they were responsible for Christianity, the Enlightenment, and Freemasonry. They were branded "a ferment of decomposition," formlessness, chaos, and "racial degeneration." The Jews were identified with the fragmentation of urban civilization, the dissolving acid of critical rationalism, and the loosening of morality. They stood behind the "rootless cosmopolitanism" of international capital and the threat of world revolution. In a word, they were the *Weltfeind*—the "world enemy" against which National Socialism defined its own grandiose racial utopia of a Thousand-year Reich.

In Hitler's genocidal, racist ideology, the redemption (*Erlösung*) of the Germans and of "Aryan" humanity depended upon the "Final Solution" (*Endlösung*) of the "Jewish question." Unless the demonic *Weltfeind* was annihilated, there would be no "peace" in a Europe that was to be united under Germanic leadership so that Germany could fulfill its "natural destiny" by expanding to the east to create *Lebensraum* (living space) for its people. The Second World War, which Hitler initiated, was simultaneously a war for territorial hegemony and a battle against the mythical Jewish enemy.

War made the Holocaust a concrete possibility. The victories of the Wehrmacht brought millions of Jews under the heel of German power for the first time. The task of annihilating them in cold blood was delegated by Hitler to the SS, under Reichsführer Heinrich Himmler and his closest subordinate, Reinhard Heydrich. As early as 1939, a so-called euthanasia program, directly responsible to Hitler and the Führer Chancellery, had been initiated to eliminate nearly ninety thousand ethnic Germans who were deemed "unfit to live" because they were physically or mentally "defective." This program, halted temporarily in 1941, proved to be a training ground for the "Final Solution." In late 1941, its personnel, apparatus, and experience in killing by poison gas was transferred to death camps in Poland to be used against the Jews.

The Holocaust required more than an apocalyptic ideology of anti-Semitism in order to be implemented. It was equally the product of the most modern and technically developed society in Europe—one with a highly organized bureaucracy. The streamlined, industrialized mass killings carried out in death camps such as Auschwitz-Birkenau and Treblinka were of a form unknown in European and world history. But millions of Jews were also killed by the Germans and their helpers via more primitive, "archaic" methods in Russia, eastern Europe, and the Balkans. The Einsatzgruppen and police battalions hunted down Jews and executed them in gruesome pit killings, in forests, ravines, and trenches. Russians, Poles, Serbs, and Ukrainians, although not earmarked for *systematic* mass murder, were also decimated in large numbers. Three million Soviet prisoners of war died in German captivity.

Some, such as Daniel Goldhagen, have argued that the Germans carried out these murders because they were

Germans; their political culture and mind-set, grounded in a nationalist pride in their *Volk,* had been preprogrammed by an "eliminationist anti-Semitism" that had existed since at least the mid-nineteenth century. But before Hitler, *völkisch* racist anti-Semitism had not made great inroads in Germany, though it was far from negligible. Anti-Semitism had been much stronger and more influential in Tsarist Russia, Romania, or in the Habsburg Monarchy and its successor states, especially Poland, Slovakia, and Austria. Germany before 1933 was still a state based on the rule of law, where despite long-standing prejudice Jews achieved remarkable economic success, were well integrated into society, enjoyed equal rights, and decisively shaped its modernist culture.

Hitler's rise to power would not have been possible without the carnage of the First World War, the traumatic impact of German military defeat, the humiliation of the Treaty of Versailles, the economic crises of the Weimar Republic, and the fear of Communist revolution. Anti-Semitism, while central to Hitler, Joseph Goebbels, Himmler, Jules Streicher, and other Nazi leaders, was not the main vote-getter of the movement. But once racist anti-Semitism became the official state ideology of the Third Reich, reinforced by an extraordinarily powerful propaganda apparatus and a barrage of anti-Jewish laws, its impact was devastating.

It is, however, important to realize that the receptiveness of Germans (and other Europeans) to the demonization of the Jews owed a great deal to the much older tradition of Christian anti-Judaism. The Nazis did not need to invent the images of "the Jew" as a usurer, blasphemer, traitor, ritual murderer, dangerous conspirator against Christendom, or a deadly threat to the foundations of morality. Both secular rulers and Christian churches had ensured that (until the French Revolution) Jews were pariahs in European society, condemned to positions of inferiority and subordination. Racism had been used in Catholic Spain in the fifteenth century, for example, to justify the removal of even converted

Jews from public functions and positions of economic influence.

The Protestant Reformation, especially in Germany, brought little improvement in the status of the Jews. Martin Luther's anti-Jewish diatribes would moreover become a contributing factor in the complicity of so many German Protestants with Hitler's deeds during the Third Reich's anti-Semitic persecutions. Catholics, too, were increasingly implicated in anti-Semitic political movements in France, Austria, Hungary, Slovakia, Poland, and other European states in the nineteenth and twentieth centuries. During the Holocaust, many Catholic clerics, like their Protestant counterparts, were often indifferent or even hostile to Jews. The deep ambivalence of the Vatican and the Christian churches cannot, however, be understood without taking into account the long-standing "teaching of contempt," which had deep roots in the New Testament itself and in the teachings of the Church Fathers. Nazism, though ultimately determined to uproot Christianity, built on the negative stereotypes about Jews and Judaism that the churches had disseminated for centuries.

The Germans did not carry out the Holocaust alone, although under Nazi rule they were undoubtedly its spearhead and driving force. When it came to killing Jews, they found many willing collaborators and "helpers" among Lithuanians, Latvians, Ukrainians, Hungarians, Romanians, Croats, and others. Austrians (who had been annexed to the German Reich in 1938) formed a wholly disproportionate number of the SS killers, death-camp commandants, and personnel involved in the "Final Solution." Even official France "collaborated" eagerly, not in the killing of Jews but in their deportation eastward and in the passage of draconian racist legislation.

The Holocaust was a *pan-European* event that could not have happened unless millions of Europeans by the late 1930s had wished to see an end to the age-old Jewish presence in their midst. This consensus was especially strong in the countries of east-central Europe, where the bulk of Jewry lived and retained its own national characteristics and cultural distinctiveness. But there was also a growing anti-Semitism in western Europe and America, tied to the hardships caused by the Great Depression, increased xenophobia, fear of immigrants, and the influence of fascist ideas.

This hostility was evidenced by the unwillingness of British and American decision-makers to undertake any significant rescue efforts on behalf of European Jewry during the Holocaust. Already in the 1930s, the quota system in the United States had precluded any mass immigration of Jews from central and eastern Europe, which might have relieved some of the enormous pressures on Jewry. British concerns about Arab unrest in Palestine, following increased Jewish immigration in the 1930s to their "national home," led to another major refuge being denied them. Hitler duly noted these responses and the appeasement policy of the West before 1939 and drew his own conclusions: his expansionist ambitions could be pursued without too great a risk, and the West would not interfere with his increasingly radical anti-Jewish measures.

The Jews of Europe, on the eve of the Holocaust, found themselves in a trap from which there appeared to be no escape. They were faced with the most menacing and dangerous enemy in their history—a dynamic power in the heart of Europe that openly sought their destruction. Its influence was felt in neighboring states, especially to the east and southeast, which were passing laws of their own to restrict Jewish rights and pushing for the removal or emigration of their Jewish populations. Moreover, the three million Jews in Communist Russia were cut off from the rest of the Jewish world; yet the identification of Jews with Bolshevism had become a highly dangerous political myth that would eventually fuel the mass murders carried out by the Nazis and their allies on the eastern front after June 1941.

The Jews of America were limited in what they could do for European Jewry by a combination of their own insecurity, their fears of anti-Semitism, and the reality of American isolationism prior to late 1941. The Jews of Palestine were still a relatively small community under British control and faced with a hostile Arab majority. The Zionist movement, while growing, was too fragmented politically and fractious to be effective.

The Nazi myth of the Jews as a well-organized, international power with clearly defined goals and common "racial" interests could not therefore have been further removed from reality. The Jews were in fact disorganized, relatively powerless, and lacking in solidarity or any agreed political agenda. Before and during the Holocaust they did not have a state, an army, a common territory, or a flag, let alone a coherent organizational center.

Except in rare cases, such as Denmark, Finland, Italy, and Bulgaria (which had relatively small Jewish populations), the Jews would moreover be cruelly disappointed by the lack of solidarity shown them by most of their Gentile neighbors once the dark night of persecution descended upon them. Even more bitter was the ease with which the protection of European states and governments was withdrawn and their rights were sacrificed as if they were absolute pariahs, beyond the pale of civilization. Hitler's war thus found many Jews trapped and virtually defenseless against a ruthless enemy bent on their total destruction in a world largely indifferent to their fate.

From this searing and potentially shattering trauma, the Jewish people nonetheless rose up after the Second World War to establish their own independent state. Other nations and minorities also learned the price of powerlessness after the Second World War and have fought to achieve their freedom from totalitarian tyranny and foreign oppression. But the Holocaust also has more universal lessons: it reminds us that xenophobia, racism, and anti-Semitism can lead to group violence and atrocities on an unimaginable scale; and that any society—however culturally, scientifically, and technologically advanced—can become totally criminal once it loses its ability to distinguish between right and wrong. The Holocaust underlines the danger of trusting in the idolatry of power without ethical restraint. It drives home the lesson that each individual is responsible for his or her own conscience and fate. It is a warning from history that obeying orders can be no excuse for criminal acts.

If there is a general lesson, then, it is that we must learn that evil can and must be resisted in its early stages; that we always have choices; and that there can be no place for racism and anti-Semitism in a civilized society. Thinking about the Holocaust is like staring into an abyss and hoping it will not stare back. It is the ultimate extreme case, a black hole of history that not only challenges our facile assumptions about modernity and progress but questions our very sense of what it means to be human.

1

A̲N̲TI̲-̲S̲E̲MITISM
A̲N̲D̲ T̲H̲E̲
J̲EWS

After Satan Christians have no greater enemies than the Jews.... They pray many times each day that God may destroy us through pestilence, famine and war, aye, that all beings and creatures may rise up with them against the Christians.

ABRAHAM A SANCTA CLARA
Viennese Catholic preacher (1683)

I hold the Jewish race to be the born enemy of pure humanity and everything noble in it. It is certain that it is running us Germans into the ground, and I am perhaps the last German who knows how to hold himself upright in the face of Judaism, which already rules everything.

RICHARD WAGNER (1881)

Jewry is one of the great negative principles of world history and thus can only be understood as a parasite within the opposing positive principle. As little as Judas Iscariot with his thirty silver coins ... can be understood without the Lord whose community he sneeringly betrayed ... that night side of history called Jewry cannot be understood without being positioned in the totality of the historical process where God and Satan, Creation and Destruction confront each other in an eternal struggle.

WALTER FRANK, "German Science in Its Struggle against World Jewry,"
German radio broadcast, 11 and 13 January 1939

Throughout recorded time, there have been countless massacres, some on religious grounds, others for political or territorial reasons. Native peoples have been exterminated in colonial wars. Millions of Africans were sold into slavery. The colonization of North America, Australia, Africa, and other parts of the globe by expanding Western societies involved constant displacement, despoliation, and sometimes even the genocide of indigenous populations in the name of empire, plunder, and "progress." The Turkish massacre of more than a million Armenians during the First World War marked a new scale of brutality.[1] However, if the number of victims alone were to be our point of departure, then we should look to those unfortunate Soviet citizens who were shot, starved, or worked to death in the gulags of Stalinist Russia as "enemies of the people," in the name of Marxist ideology.[2] The victims of this "autogenocide," which a totalitarian regime inflicted on its own subjects, numbered at least twenty million. (While staggeringly high, this was a much lower percentage of all Soviet citizens than the one third of all Jewish people in the world who were killed by the Nazis.) Even higher casualties were registered in Maoist China (the full story has yet to be told) and, on a much smaller scale, in Communist Cambodia during the 1970s. The slaughter in Rwanda and "ethnic cleansing" in the former Yugoslavia in the 1990s demonstrate that the genocidal chapter in human history is far from over.

Even during the Second World War, several genocides occurred, though of different magnitudes. Approximately three million Polish Gentiles fell victim to the Nazis, as did a similar number of Russian POWs who were starved to death by the Germans. Both groups were used as guinea pigs at Auschwitz-Birkenau before the gassing of Jews began. The German war in the east involved much more than exterminating the Jews: it was initially conceived of as part of a larger design for a radical racial restructuring in which Poles, Russians, and Ukrainians would be expropriated, deported, or killed.[3] Gypsies, too, were earmarked for destruction; between 250,000 and half a million Gypsies were sent to their deaths between 1939 and 1945, coterminous with the Jewish Holocaust. Gypsies (Roma and Sinti) did not, of course, hold the same place either in Christian consciousness or in the Nazi worldview as did Jews or Judaism, but prejudice and hostility toward their nomadic way of life was nonetheless widespread and in some ways comparable to the perception of Jews as alien to Christian Europe.[4]

The Nazis were particularly hostile toward the Gypsies as an "antisocial" element and as "people of different blood" who fell under the Nuremberg race laws of 1935. (Heinrich Himmler's decree of December 1937 permitted their arrest on the extremely elastic grounds of asocial behavior, even without the commission of any criminal act.) As early as 1936, some groups of Gypsies were sent to the Dachau concentration camp. Further legislation in 1938 to deal with the "Gypsy plague" aimed at a strict separation between "pure" (Sinti and Lalleri) and "mixed blood" Gypsies, as well as between Germans and Gypsies.[5] According to the Nazi Office for Racial Hygiene and Population Biology, more than 90 percent of the German Gypsies were defined as non-Aryan "mixed bloods," the favored government policy toward which was sterilization. During the war, Nazi policy became even more radical, and in the fall of 1941, five thousand Austrian Gypsies were deported to the Lódz ghetto. Then, in early 1942, some Gypsies were murdered along with Jews in the Chelmno death camp. Gypsies started arriving in Auschwitz-Birkenau on 26 February 1943; a great many died from hunger, disease, and "medical experiments." In 1944, women and children were gassed. In the Baltic states and the Soviet Union, Gypsies were murdered by the Einsatzgruppen; in Yugoslavia, they were killed by the Pavelić regime; in Hungary, they were persecuted and rounded up by Arrow Cross fascists. In France, they were interned and later sent to camps in Germany. Two thirds of the Polish Gypsies died under Nazi occupation.

The Nazis regarded "the fight against the Gypsy Menace" after 1935 as "a matter of race" and insisted on the need to "separate once and for all the Gypsy race (*Zigeunertum*) from the German nation (*Volkstum*)," to prevent the danger of miscegenation. In that respect, there was an ideological link between the murder of Jews and Gypsies in the Nazi vision of radical ethnic cleansing or "purification" of the *Volksgemeinschaft* (people's community). Indeed, the settlement of the "Gypsy question" was conceived from the outset in the framework of "knowledge stemming from ethnological research" under the jurisdiction of Heinrich Himmler as Reichsführer SS and chief of the German police. The fate of the Gypsies, as Himmler made clear in September 1942, was not a matter for the law or the courts, any more than was that of the Jews. Hence, they were totally at the mercy of the police and the SS and were liable to be thrown at any time into concentration camps. The accusations against them of hereditary racial inferiority, economic parasitism, or sexual "immorality," all of which were seen as threatening to the general German population, overlapped with the demagoguery of anti-Semitism.[6] The Gypsies, however, were deemed a "social menace," not a total and universal enemy like the Jews, engaged in a universal conspiracy against Germany and the "Aryan" world. The "Gypsy question" had, for example, only marginal importance in the Nazi political agenda, and Hitler himself referred publicly to Gypsies on only two occasions, in stark contrast to his relentless obsession with the Jews.[7] Moreover, those Gypsies who were considered "racially pure" were never regarded as a danger to the

German people and were even thought of as having noble blood. Thus, the horrible crime against the Gypsies as a social group did not aim in principle at their *total* annihilation.

The Jewish Holocaust was unprecedented—as compared to other genocides—because it was the planned, deliberate policy decision of a powerful state that mobilized its resources to destroy the *entire* Jewish people. In this diabolical aim, the Germans were almost successful in Europe, and only their military defeat prevented its gruesome completion. By 1945, two thirds of European Jewry had been wiped out by the Nazis, leaving only a remnant of the ancient Jewish culture that had existed on European soil for nearly two millennia. One of the more remarkable aspects of this mass murder was that Jews never constituted (except in the paranoid Nazi mind-set) any economic, political, or military threat to the German state. On the contrary, had there been a Nobel Prize for passionate identification with German language and culture before 1933, the Jews would surely have won it. During the First World War, many made great efforts to demonstrate their patriotic loyalty and validate their Germannness (*Deutschtum*) on the battlefield. Before the rise of Hitler, they had felt very much at home in what they regarded as a well-ordered state, based on the rule of law.

If anything, there were striking affinities between Germans and Jews that seemed to augur well for their common future: a great respect for education, hard work, the importance of the family, and a marked talent for abstract, speculative thinking. Both Germans and Jews were considered highly musical and often regarded by others as being both indispensable and troublesome, aggressive and prone to self-pity. *Judenhass* (Judeophobia) and *Deutschenhass* (Germanophobia) had more than a few attributes in common. But, as Freud shrewdly observed, the "narcissism of little differences" can produce great hatreds; proximity, affinity, and assimilation may in certain circumstances give rise to an intense and irrational backlash. The German "Jewish question" of the nineteenth and twentieth centuries was precisely such a case, amalgamating false perceptions, stereotypes, and delusions from many sources: Christian anti-Judaism, neo-Romantic *völkisch* mysticism, and a racist obsession with Jews and other "aliens" that assumed a special virulence in Nazi ideology.[8]

This shadowboxing with imaginary demons and projective angst persuaded the novelist Jakob Wassermann that Judeophobia was *the* German national hatred—a self-induced pathological delusion that was not only irrational but impenetrable. Germans, he concluded in 1921, were emotionally resistant to accepting Jews as their equals and given to scapegoating them for every crisis, setback, or defeat. Hatred of the Jews could encompass every conceivable sexual frustration, social anxiety, jealousy, animosity, bloodlust, and greedy instinct that Germans were otherwise unable to exorcise.[9] Thirty years earlier, the German philosopher Friedrich Nietzsche had been equally severe, heaping aristocratic contempt on the anti-Semites of the 1880s as *Schlechtweggekommene*— life's losers and born misfits; bungled, botched, and envious creatures, eaten up with neurotic *ressentiment*.[10] This verdict was all the more remarkable since Nietzsche had at one time been under the spell of the composer Richard Wagner—the *fons et origo* of modern German anti-Semitism. Moreover, to compound the irony, his own rhetoric about the *Übermensch* (superman), the "blond beast," and the "will to power" would later be eagerly annexed by fascists and Nazis. Indeed, Nietzsche's relentless assault on Judeo-Christian morality did provide one of the deeper sources of inspiration for the Nazi revolution. It was, after all, Nietzsche who had branded priestly Judaism and the teachings of the Gospels as the beginning of "the slave-revolt in morals." The Jews, he explained with oracular certitude, had engineered the greatest transvaluation of values in world history, two thousand years earlier in Roman-occupied Palestine. It was a most fateful and catastrophic event, responsible in his eyes for all the "decadent" modern ideologies of liberalism, rationalism, socialism, and leveling mass democracy.[11] In the 1930s, it would not be difficult for fascists and Nazis—intoxicated with self-deification—to adapt these Nietzschean ideas to their own totalitarian-nihilist agenda.[12]

It mattered little that few Nazis had actually read Nietzsche or paid attention to his contempt for Germans and admiration for Jews. The attraction lay in the prospect of transgression on a grand scale, the Nietzschean smashing of those taboos that still reined in the barbarian warrior-lust lurking under an increasingly thin "civilized" veneer. Nazism, (mis)understood as a Nietzschean experiment, seemed to be offering to the German people a Faustian pact. In return for destroying traditional Christian moral restraints, they might be granted future hegemony over the earthly kingdoms that other European powers had already partitioned among themselves.

The demonization of the Jews and Judaism assumed immense symbolic importance in this endeavor. The Nazi leaders (and especially Hitler) were obsessed with the idea of a "chosen people" and its imagined secret power. They read into it a prefiguration of their own will to set the races apart under an iron law until the end of time.[13] The singularity of the Jews, and the mystery of their survival over thousands of years, was treated as if it were a vindication of the eternal truths of blood and race.[14] Nazi racism can indeed be seen as a blasphemous gloss or perhaps even as a grotesque parody of Judaic chosenness. To put it bluntly, there could not be two chosen peoples. The character of Hitler's messianic pretensions necessitated the removal of that very people who had embodied chosenness for three millennia. The Jews were responsible (or, rather, guilty) in his eyes for having *invented* the very notion of a moral conscience, in defiance of all healthy, natural instincts.[15] They had bequeathed this noxious ideal to Christianity and Communism, with their contending dreams of the brotherhood of man, human equality, and justice. Though outwardly incompatible, these worldviews were for the Nazis two sides of the same Judaic coin: egalitarian ideals that had caused endless suffering, persecution, and intolerance. Moreover, the Jews were accused of having deliberately encouraged the mixing of races, as well as inventing doctrines of democracy, which could only destroy the foundations of human culture itself. For the Nazis, the world had to be liberated from such "evil" principles so that mankind could return once more to its pristine natural order. Thus the planned, systematic eradication of Judaic values was the necessary prerequisite of the physical annihilation of the Jewish people.

In its own perverse way, Nazism did indeed grasp something fundamental about Judaism and the Jews. For at the heart of Judaism stood the belief in a single, all-powerful deity who had created the universe and installed humanity at its heart to uphold moral law. The revelation of the divine law and the Ten Commandments at Mount Sinai had made the biblical Israelites into a covenanted people, who believed themselves to be chosen by God for a distinctive ethical mission; not to conquer an empire but to embody a divine revelation which affirmed that humanity was created in the image of its maker; that each human being carried a divine spark; and that each life was sacred. "Thou shalt not kill" rang out as the clarion call for any civilized moral code (one that Nazism would exactly invert), along with injunctions against adultery, theft, blasphemy, and the worship of false gods. In the Mosaic teaching, special attention was paid to the rights of the weak and oppressed, the orphan, the widowed, the enslaved, and the stranger within the gates. Judaism was in that respect the antithesis of the xenophobic racist nationalism espoused by fascists and Nazis. At the heart of the Torah (the five books of Moses) was the demand for "justice, and only justice." The cry of Amos: "Let justice roll down as waters, and righteousness as a mighty stream," is the leitmotif of biblical prophecy. The Amidah prayer of Rosh Hashanah (the Jewish New Year) makes the fulfillment of God's kingdom in this world conditional on the disappearance of arrogance, injustice, and oppression. In the Judaic conception, it is *that* ideal which is the ultimate goal of human history, one wholly incompatible with the Nazi vision of the world. The Torah (completed by the Talmud and rabbinical teachings through the centuries) became the constitution and "law of life" of the Jewish people, holding them together through two millennia of dispersion. It was their "portable homeland," in the profound words of the German-Jewish poet Heinrich Heine, and also the mark of their vocation as a distinct people among the nations.

Only in the era of emancipation in the nineteenth century (primarily in the democratic societies of the West) did Jews begin to redefine themselves as a denationalized *religious* group, comparable in certain respects to Catholics or Protestants.[16] Yet the bulk of the Jewish diaspora, concentrated as it was in eastern Europe, continued to preserve its distinct language (Yiddish), social code, value system, customs, and laws, as well as separate religious beliefs. The Jewish self-understanding of being a "people apart" was further reinforced by a strong sense of continuity with past glories. At the same time, the Jews were acutely conscious of the unceasing chain of persecutions to which they had been subjected during their long exile, following the destruction of the Second Temple (C.E. 70). Thus, a sense of being linked in a common community of suffering and fate reinforced their diasporic identity.

Even before the loss of national independence nearly two thousand years ago, Jews had already displayed formidable powers of resistance and survival against the sway of vast ancient empires such as Egypt, Assyria, Babylon, and Persia. Under Judah Maccabee and the priestly clan of the Hasmoneans, they had revolted against the cultural and political yoke of an all-conquering Hellenism, leading in 142 B.C.E. to the brief reestablishment of Jewish political sovereignty in Judea. Subsequently, the Jews rose in a series of unsuccessful revolts against the military might of Imperial Rome, preferring martyrdom to the betrayal of their heritage and faith. It was in this messianic atmosphere that Christianity emerged in first-century Palestine, as the teaching of a dissident sect of Judaism. Not only Jesus of Nazareth but his mother, Mary, all of his disciples, and the Apostle Paul were born as Jews. The new faith that grew out of the teachings of Jesus (as recounted in the Gospels) was to have a powerful influence on the subsequent fate of the dispersed and exiled Jewish people in what would become, after Constantine the Great, an increasingly Christian Europe from the fourth century C.E.[17] On the one hand, Jews were permitted to exist with some protection from the church and secular rulers in the Middle Ages; the other side of the same coin was their abject theological status as an "accursed people" and "murderers of God."[18]

In the New Testament there are a number of references to "the Jews" as children of "your father the Devil" or to the "synagogue of Satan." Nor is it an accident that Judas, the disciple alleged to have betrayed Jesus for filthy lucre, eventually emerged as a synonym for the Jewish people, or that his name became a universal byword for treachery and cowardice. In the writings of the Church Fathers from the fourth century onward, Jews are consistently and malevolently depicted as "murderers of the prophets," "adversaries and haters of God," "enemies of the faith," and "advocates of the Devil"; they were portrayed as vipers, slanderers, scoffers, and "leaven of the Pharisees"; carnal, sensual, dissolute, mercenary, and corrupt; they were supposedly driven exclusively by sex, money, and power—the things of *this* world that Christianity professed to despise.[19] This invective echoed down the centuries, with greater or lesser intensity according to country and circumstances, throughout most of the lands of Christendom. The main effect of these savage polemics was to humiliate, discredit, and delegitimize the Judaic parent religion from which Christianity itself had sprung.[20] Such a comprehensive negation demonstrated that Judaism had no raison d'être after the appearance of Christ, for the church had now become the "true" Israel and repository of the new covenant. The divine blessings and promises given to the Israelites in the Hebrew Bible (appropriated as Christian Holy Scriptures and revered as the anticipation and validation of the Gospels) were reserved for the church itself and for "God's people" (the Gentile Christians). Curses and maledictions were applied to the reprobate Jews. Had they not been abandoned and punished by God with permanent wandering and exile for their blindness in failing to recognize Jesus as Messiah? Would they not continue to be persecuted until they converted to the true faith?

After the First Crusade of 1096 (when crusading armies massacred Jews in the Rhineland as "infidels" and "Christ killers" before slaughtering both Muslims and Jews during their conquest of Jerusalem), the theological charge of deicide became increasingly explosive, blending with irrational popular superstitions.[21] The so-called blood libel that spread from Norwich in England (in the eleventh century) to the Continent was based on the pure fabrication that Jews required the fresh blood of Christian children to make their *matzot* (unleavened bread) at Passover time, which usually coincided with the Christian Easter.[22] The unexplained disappearance of any Christian child near Easter could, as a result, provoke suspicions that it had been kidnapped and killed by Jews. Such counterfactual myths produced ritual murder trials, pogroms, and violence against Jewish communities even in the nineteenth and twentieth centuries. No less destructive was the irrational fantasy that Jews deliberately and malevolently pierced holy communion wafers to make them bleed (the so-called desecration of the host), as if they were compulsively reenacting the crucifixion of Christ. Other ominous medieval accusations included the allegation that Jews poisoned wells in order to provoke the bubonic plagues that decimated European society in the fourteenth century. Jews in the Middle Ages were also persistently depicted as bloodsucking usurers, sorcerers, blasphemers, insatiable enemies of Christ, and agents of the Devil, secretly plotting the downfall of Christendom. Only on a soil watered for centuries by such fearsome demonology could the Holocaust have been conceived, let alone carried out with so little opposition.[23]

Even the great German Protestant reformer, Martin Luther, despite his devastating assault on the corruption, falsehoods, and superstitions abounding in the papal Rome of his day, was not free of the demonic conception of the Jews that he had inherited from the medieval church.[24] In his diatribe of 1543, "Concerning the Jews and Their Lies" (cynically used to justify the Nazi burning of synagogues in 1938), Luther reiterated the traditional Christian view of the Jews as a "damned" and "rejected" people. His "honest advice" to German rulers was to set Jewish houses of worship on fire, to break down their homes, deprive them of prayer books, forbid their rabbis to teach ("under threat of death"), and confiscate their passports and traveling privileges. The Jews had to be "stopped from usury" by being made "to earn their bread by the sweat of their noses" through hard labor in the fields. Luther proposed that the secular rulers of German principalities follow the example of France, Spain, and Bohemia by expropriating the property of the Jews, to "drive them out of the country for all time." This program of "severe mercy" (as Luther called it) "ought to be done for the honour of God and of Christianity in order that God may see that we are Christians, and that we have not wittingly tolerated or approved of such public lying, cursing, and blaspheming of His Son and His Christians."[25]

Like medieval Catholicism, Luther's Protestant Reformation in Germany created a powerful arsenal of myths, images, and fantasies on which Nazi anti-Semitism could build. Long before the Nazis, the Jews were the most potent and hated collective "other" against which Christian Europe could define itself.[26] At times, they seemed to have been raised to the status of a metaphysical abstraction, embodying the most sinister forces of heresy, carnality, and black magic.

"The Jew" resembled a creature of a different order, scarcely human at all. Nazism secularized and sharply radicalized this image but invented relatively little at the level of basic stereotypes.

The biological racism of the Nazis did introduce a relatively new element into Judeophobia, though this apparent innovation also had Christian precedents. For example, in fifteenth-century Spain, Catholic "purity of blood" statutes had been introduced to distinguish "Old" from "New Christians" (*conversos*, or Jewish converts) and to help root out "Judaizing" influences.[27] The manic hunt by the Spanish Inquisition for crypto-Jews, the violent pogroms that began in the late fourteenth century, the auto-da-fés, and the terrifying persecution that led to the mass expulsion of 150,000 Jews in 1492, were early modern foregleams of the Nazi genocide.[28] It was surely significant that this witch-hunt occurred in precisely that European society where Jews had enjoyed the most remarkable "golden age," a success story that anticipated the German-Jewish "symbiosis" of the nineteenth and twentieth centuries. In medieval Spain, too, Jews had already gone far down the road of acculturation, social integration, and extensive conversions. They had attained remarkable heights in literature, philosophy, commerce, the professions, and even in government. The prosperity and success of the Spanish Jews and "New Christians" aroused the envy of their rivals as well as the hostility of the Catholic Church, which feared the seeds of heresy. No less important, the decision to exclude both Jews and Muslims provided a way for Spain's ambitious rulers to proclaim the unity of a nation that had completed its "reconquest" from Islam under the banner of the Catholic faith. As elsewhere in Europe, the prospect of expropriating substantial Jewish wealth also provided a decidedly material incentive for both rulers and populace alike.

In contrast to the expulsions of Jews from England (1290), France (1306, 1332), the German principalities, and then from Spain and Portugal (end of the fifteenth century),

Poland was initially very welcoming to the Jews as an urban, commercial element who could help rebuild its shattered economy after the Mongol invasions. From the fourteenth century until the partitions of Poland in the late eighteenth century, Jews enjoyed an unprecedented degree of autonomy under charters of liberty guaranteed by successive rulers. They were frequently employed by the Polish nobility as estate managers and tax collectors, often served as middlemen between landowners and peasants, and played similar intermediary roles as traders and craftsmen. Poland became a leading center of Ashkenazi Jewish scholarship and spirituality. On the other hand, the massacres associated with Bogdan Chelmnicki, leader of a Ukrainian peasants' revolt in 1648–1649, were a frightening reminder of the vulnerability of the Jews' position in the Polish lands. Between one quarter to one third of the Jewish population in the Ukraine and southern Poland were slaughtered as "Christ killers" and as middlemen serving the interests of the hated Polish landlords.[29]

In western Europe, Jews finally began to enter the modern era with the French Revolution of 1789. By sweeping away all the feudal privileges of the ancien régime (including the special position of the Catholic Church), the French National Assembly for the first time established Jewish civic equality in Europe. The revolutionary generation that emancipated the Jews in 1791 had been influenced by universalist Enlightenment ideals, an optimistic faith in reason, a generally cosmopolitan outlook, and the belief that human beings could be perfected through education and change in social conditions. The more radical strand of the Enlightenment offered to the Jews the promise of a new beginning, as long as they were willing to throw off the shackles of their own Judaic tradition. Count de Clermont-Tonnerre pointedly told the French National Assembly, "The Jews should be denied everything as a nation, but granted everything as individuals.... If they do not want this ... we shall then be compelled to expel them."[30]

Many Jews of France and western Europe were ready to accept this emancipation contract (Orthodox Jews were an exception) although it involved abandoning a separate identity. The attractions of unrivaled individual opportunities, freedom of movement, new career prospects, and untrammeled entry into a modern, secular society proved difficult to resist.

By the end of the nineteenth century, however, there was a distinct backlash by conservative forces in France against the legacy of the 1789 revolution and its emancipation of the Jews. The Catholic Church linked the Jews with the secular, anticlerical Third Republic that had become dominant, especially after 1880. The Monarchists (who dreamed of a Royalist restoration), aristocratic army officers bitter at their defeat by Prussia in 1870, and a motley crew of anti-Semites and nationalists hoped to overthrow the hated republic. Their best opportunity came when a Jewish army officer from Alsace, Alfred Dreyfus, was accused in 1894 of betraying French military secrets to the Germans. Dreyfus's guilt became a dogma not only for intransigent anti-Semites, convinced that every Jew was a potential "Judas," but also for those on the Catholic and nationalist right who believed that there had been a deliberate conspiracy to destroy the French nation.[31] The plot had supposedly been hatched by all-powerful Jews (embodied by the Rothschild family and by "Jewish" international high finance), helped by Freemasons, Protestants, anticlerical republican radicals, and socialists. The Dreyfus affair provided an ideological matrix for the emergence of such ultranationalist and protofascist ideas.[32] It was also a kind of dress rehearsal for the mob politics of Nazi-style anti-Semitism.

The term *anti-Semitism* had been coined by the radical German journalist Wilhelm Marr in 1879 to mark it off from more traditional Christian forms of animosity toward Judaism. Indeed, Marr's "anti-Semitism" was also noticeably hostile to supranational Catholicism and to monotheistic religion in general. In a mediocre if sensational pamphlet, he claimed that German society had already become "Judaized" (a code word for the victory of materialism, Mammon, and laissez-faire capitalism); gloomily, he asserted that the Jews had conquered Germany by seizing control of its press and stock exchanges.[33] Similar charges were made in the same year by the Protestant court preacher, Adolf Stöcker, a powerful orator who had just founded the lower-middle-class Christian-Social Party in Berlin; and by the illustrious Prussian conservative historian Heinrich von Treitschke, who came up with the notorious slogan (much favored by the Nazis) that "the Jews are our misfortune." Between 1880 and 1914, imperial Germany emerged as the favored laboratory for ideological anti-Semites, both Christian and anti-Christian.[34] While this Judeophobia was by no means "eliminationist," its extent and obsessive quality played a part in preparing the way for the outrages to come.[35]

There were other full-fledged racist propagandists, such as the anticlerical Theodor Fritsch (1852–1933), whose *Handbook on the Jewish Question* was familiar to the young Hitler in Vienna before 1914. Fritsch was an indefatigable publicist, active in Saxony, who had founded the Hammer Publishing House for anti-Semitic literature in 1883 and a decade later produced a popular racist decalogue ("Ten Commandments for an Antisemite").[36] His catechism sternly warned Germans against having social, sexual, business, or professional intercourse with Jews or consuming any Jewish writings, "lest their lingering poison may unnerve and corrupt you and your family." Fritsch's handbook went through more than forty editions, inspiring a number of Nazis, who later honored him as an elder statesman. Other pre-1914 ideological anti-Semites highly regarded in the Third Reich included the orientalist scholar Paul de Lagarde (advocate of a virile Germanic and de-Judaized Christianity), who denounced the evils of Western liberalism, capitalism, and parliamentarism;[37] and Eugen Dühring, a former socialist and a vehement anti-Christian, who demanded radical measures to return Jews to the ghetto by subjecting them to a discriminatory aliens' legislation. Dühring insisted that the Germanic-Nordic race could fulfill its evolutionary destiny only after it threw off the yoke of a "Semitic" Judeo-Christianity.[38] Even more influential was the expatriate Teutomaniac Englishman, Houston Stewart Chamberlain, whose bestselling book, *The Foundations of the Nineteenth Century* (1899), greatly appealed to the bombastic imperialism of the German emperor, Wilhelm II. Chamberlain, a passionate Wagnerian and philosophical dilettante, lived long enough to hail Hitler in 1923 as the future "saviour" of Germany.[39]

Despite the growing influence of anti-Semitic ideologies in imperial Germany, the Second Reich still appeared to most Jews as a stable, prosperous, and highly cultured society where their civil rights were respected. Similarly, for Jews in the rest of western and central Europe (including the more than two million Jews in Austria-Hungary), the prospects of integration seemed promising before the First World War. Yet for many Jews, the war and its consequences had cruel repercussions. The Jews in Galicia and those along the Russian front soon found themselves fleeing for their lives, often punished as spies and traitors by the tsarist high command or deported into the Russian interior. In Poland, at the end of the war in 1918, the proclamation of national independence was accompanied by jarring pogroms against Jews, especially in places of mixed population, where their loyalties were arbitrarily deemed by Poles to be suspect.[40] Although the German Army on the eastern front treated Jews reasonably well, a special census (*Judenzählung*) of Jewish soldiers engaged in active duty at the front was undertaken in 1916. This was supposedly intended to verify rumors of shirking and black marketeering. The results were never published, though twelve thousand German Jews laid down their lives for the fatherland, and a relatively high number won awards for bravery on the battlefield. Such sacrifices did not prevent the pernicious legend from circulating that Jews (and Marxists) had "stabbed Germany in the back" during the war—a myth that became a powerful propaganda weapon for Hitler and the entire German nationalist right after 1918.

In November 1917, two events of decisive importance for modern Jewish history took place. The Bolshevik revolution in Russia overthrew an all-too-brief experiment in parliamentary democracy, led primarily by moderate Russian liberals and socialists. Although it consolidated the emancipation of Russian Jewry granted ten months earlier with the fall of tsarism, the immediate consequences of this revolution were disastrous for Jews: the worst pogroms hitherto recorded in Jewish history, with more than one hundred thousand fatalities among the Russian and Ukrainian Jewish population between 1918 and 1921.[41] Most of the atrocities were committed by the anti-Bolshevik White reactionaries and by the Ukrainian nationalist army, for whom Jews had become synonymous with the Communist Revolution. Though this amalgam was plainly a myth, there were a disproportionate number of leading Bolsheviks of Jewish origin in key positions during the early days of the revolution. None of these "non-Jewish" Jews identified in any way with Judaism, Jewish nationalism, or Russian Jewry.[42] Similarly, most Russian and Ukrainian Jews did not sympathize at all with Communism, but the anti-Semitic savagery of the anti-Bolshevik pogromists eventually drove them into alliance with the Reds.[43] The impact of the Bolshevik specter on Germany was to prove particularly fateful. After 1919, the newly created Nazi Party, along with other right-wing forces in Germany (and far beyond its borders), assiduously propagated the myth of a Jewish-Bolshevik conspiracy to destroy Germany and Western Christian civilization. This ideological fantasy was to become a central driving force of the Holocaust.

Almost simultaneously with the Bolshevik triumph in Russia, the British government (through its foreign secretary, Lord Balfour) issued on 2 November 1917 what came to be known as the Balfour Declaration. The announcement that the British government publicly favored "the establishment in

Palestine of a national home for the Jewish people" had coincided with the conquest by British troops of Palestine, formerly held by the Ottoman Turks. It laid the foundations
for what would officially become the British Mandate for
Palestine in 1922 and eventually the State of Israel in 1948.
Through the Balfour Declaration, the Zionist movement
gained its greatest success yet on the international stage,
achieving political recognition by what was then the leading
imperial power in the world. Ironically, this anticipation of a
restored Jewish statehood for the first time in nearly two
thousand years occurred at the same historical moment when
unprecedentedly large numbers of Jews were killing one another in the trenches of the First World War. Zionism, however, offered the prospect of a new centripetal force that
might yet transcend the centrifugal and disintegrating influences of modernization on traditional Jewish society.

The attitude of Nazis, nationalists, and anti-Semites in
Germany and elsewhere to the Zionist experiment was more
ambivalent than it was toward Communism. At one level,
Zionism could appeal to anti-Semites as a movement that
would encourage Jewish emigration. Palestine even appeared
to be a convenient dumping ground for unwelcome Jews, in
the eyes of the Nazi regime between 1933 and 1939. However, there was also a more sinister view of Zionism as a political tool in the Jewish bid for "world domination," put
forward in the 1920s by Hitler and the leading Nazi ideo-
logue, Alfred Rosenberg.[44] Thus, Zionism also reinforced
anti-Semitic notions of Jewish dual loyalties and fed the conspiracy myth of an insatiable Jewish lust for domination.

After 1918, with the breakup of the Ottoman, Russian,
Austro-Hungarian, and German empires, the map of Europe
changed irrevocably. Independent nation-states such as
Poland, Czechoslovakia, Yugoslavia, Romania, Hungary, and
the Baltic states emerged or were restored. Most of them contained numerous ethnic and religious minorities as well as
sizable Jewish populations. These nations spawned fiercely

exclusivist ethnic nationalisms and increasingly illiberal authoritarian regimes, deeply suspicious of Jews as "outsiders." Not only were Jews still regarded as "different" and as having group loyalties of their own, but they were seen either as unwelcome economic competitors or as dangerously subversive radicals. In Poland, Romania, and Hungary (which between them contained 4.5 million Jews in the 1930s), harsh quotas were soon introduced to restrict Jewish attendance at universities. Jews found themselves squeezed by government fiscal policy, subject to discrimination in employment, and vulnerable to the effects of the Wall Street crash and the Great Depression of the 1930s.[45] The subsequent impoverishment of the Jewish masses reinforced the effects of hostile legislation and nourished the increasingly nationalist and anti-Semitic climate that sought to exclude the Jews as much as possible from economic life.

Among the nations in interwar Europe most eager to encourage a massive removal of Jews from their midst was Poland. Biological and racist anti-Semitism of the pseudoscientific kind was admittedly less prevalent in Catholic Poland than in neighboring Nazi Germany. Equally, violence against the Jews was frowned upon. But once Hitler had come to power in 1933, the mood against Jews in Poland became more bellicose, especially on the nationalist right (among the "National Democrats" or Endecja) and in the ranks of its fascist hooligan offshoots.[46] By the late 1930s there were mini-pogroms in the countryside, and "ghetto benches" reserved for Jewish students at Polish universities.[47] Worse still, there was a growing competition among Polish politicians to see who could propose a more far-reaching solution to the "Jewish question" whether through economic boycott, social exclusion, legal discrimination, or mass expulsion. In October 1938, the Polish ambassador to Great Britain proposed that Polish Jews be allowed to go to Northern Rhodesia and similar colonies at a rate of one hundred thousand a year; otherwise, he declared, the Polish government would feel itself "inevitably forced to adopt the same kind of policy as the German government."

Polish anti-Semitism, despite some similarities, did in fact differ from the Nazi variety in a number of significant ways. In the first place, the "Jewish question" existed in Poland as a genuine minorities problem in an insecure, multiethnic state where in 1931 Poles made up less than 65 percent of the population.[48] Furthermore, threatened by such powerful neighbors as Germany and Bolshevik Russia, many Poles developed decidedly paranoid sentiments about ethnically non-Polish groups in their recently restored state, viewing them as a potential fifth column. Jews, who accounted for between one quarter and one third of the population in the large cities of Warsaw, Lódz, Lwow, Cracow, and Lublin, were particularly suspected of disloyalty or indifference to Polish national interests.[49] To the nascent Polish middle class, the Jews were dangerous business competitors; in the eyes of the dominant conservative and clerical elites, they were invariably seen as crypto-Bolsheviks; to the peasantry and small traders, they were alien exploiters.[50] For the Primate of Poland, Cardinal August Hlond (speaking in 1936), it was allegedly a fact that "Jews oppose the Catholic Church, are steeped in free-thinking, and represent the avant-garde of the atheist movement, the Bolshevik movement and subversive action." Nor did Cardinal Hlond fail to mention the classic allegation that Jews engaged in "white slavery," dispensed pornography, committed fraud and usury, as well as undermining Christian morality in general.[51]

Not only in Poland but also in Romania, Hungary, Slovakia, and even in Italy in the late 1930s, steps were being taken to restrict Jews in the professions and reduce them to second-class citizenship. This was an ominous sign of things to come. The Jews found themselves increasingly powerless against this pan-European trend to strip them of their hard-won civic and political rights. Massive pressure was building to impose a sweeping *numerus clausus* that would block their educational

and economic opportunities, effectively forcing them to emigrate in large numbers.

The relative feebleness of the Jewish response reflected a
long-standing disinclination and inability to act politically in
an organized and effective way to defend their vital interests
as a group. In the West, the politics of the emancipation contract (and subsequently of assimilation) permitted individual
lobbying and philanthropic activity but no self-assertive ethnic politics. The Jewish national movement, which advocated
precisely such a course, remained a minority force in the Jewish world, at least until the success of Hitler began to vindi-
cate many Zionist arguments. By then, however, it appeared
to be too late to do anything positive beyond desperately organizing a legal (or illegal) immigration to British-controlled
Palestine. Decision-making in the Middle East still rested,
however, in the hands of a British elite preoccupied with its
own considerations of imperial expediency.[52] They were
faced in Palestine with a well-organized Jewish community,
but one which still lacked a sovereign state, army, or clearly
agreed set of political objectives. The Palestine Yishuv (Jewish community) was numerically small, economically weak,
divided into warring political factions, dependent on British
goodwill, and facing a hostile Arab majority.

Even American Jewry, though by 1939 the richest, largest,
and strongest Jewish community in the world, was still far
from being the organized, vigorous, disciplined, cohesive
lobby of the postwar era, able to influence the foreign policy
of the U.S. government. On the contrary, it was so lacking in
unity or self-confidence and seemingly so cowed by the rise
in American anti-Semitism during the Depression years that
it was unable to seriously challenge the draconian immigration restrictions that helped to seal the fate of European
Jewry.[53] Much the same could be said of the smaller Anglo-
Jewish community (330,000), even though a few individual Jews did achieve prominence in British public life
during the interwar years.[54]

Equally powerless were the more than three million Polish Jews, despite their organized representation at local and national parliamentary levels in Polish society. Polish Jewry was a microcosm of the wider Jewish world with its turbulent, fractious, ideologically polarized politics—replete with internecine quarrels between right and left, religious and secular, Zionist and anti-Zionist extremes. The "nationality" politics of Polish Jews had little effect in the face of Gentile hostility, though there was an energetic defense against anti-Semitic violence by the Jewish Socialist Bund.[55] But whether they were law-abiding or revolutionary, nationalist or integrationist, central and eastern European Jews before 1939 had little chance of warding off the rising anti-Semitic tide. After 1939, the unequal struggle became increasingly hopeless, with one side (the Germans) heavily armed and the other (the Jews) essentially defenseless. This huge disparity in strength, if anything, increased the sadism of the Nazis, who claimed to be fighting against an omnipotent enemy, yet one that was manifestly not equipped to protect itself.

The powerlessness of the Jews was exacerbated after 1939 by the hostility of local populations, especially in eastern Europe, and their readiness to collaborate with the Germans in the "solution to the Jewish question." This was true even in Poland, which fought the Nazis from the first to the last day of the war, produced no Quislings, and developed the largest resistance movement in Europe. There were some Polish anti-Semites who not only fought against Hitler but even rescued Jews, though this was an act punishable by death. But though the scale of Polish suffering was second only to that of the Jews under Nazi occupation, the Poles, too, were hostile, indifferent, or else committed hideous acts against their Jewish neighbors—as did Lithuanians, Latvians, Estonians, Ukrainians, Belorussians, Romanians, Hungarians, and many other Europeans.

Writing in 1944, while hiding on the "Aryan" side of the Warsaw ghetto, the Polish-Jewish historian Emanuel Ringelblum bitterly observed: "Last summer, when carts packed with captive Jewish men, women and children moved through the streets of the capital, was it really necessary for laughter from wild mobs to resound from the other side of the ghetto walls …?"[56] Already in October 1940, he had confided to his diary that there were "a considerable number of anti-Semitic elements who collaborated with the Germans in waging war on the Jews."[57] The German-controlled radio, public-loudspeaker system, special exhibitions, brochures, leaflets, and posters spread a message of hate that struck a powerful chord with the local population, already intoxicated by the anti-Semitism of the Polish-language "reptile press."[58]

Mordekhai Tenenbaum, commander of the Jewish Fighting Organization in the Bialystok ghetto, was even more critical about Polish behavior as the death trains rolled to Treblinka and other places of slaughter. Had it not been for the passive and active aid of Poles, he maintained, "the Germans would never have been as successful as they were" in locating Jews. "It was the Poles who called out 'Yid' at every Jew who escaped from the train transporting him to the gas chambers, it was they who caught these unfortunate wretches and who rejoiced at every misfortune."[59]

The Polish Catholic courier Jan Karski, in a report to the Polish government-in-exile, had observed in 1940 that the "Jewish question" was like "a narrow bridge upon which the Germans and a large part of Polish society find themselves in agreement."[60] Zofia Kossak-Szczucka, a Catholic member of the Council For Aid to the Jews (Zegota) founded in late 1942, was profoundly shocked by the demoralization created in Polish ranks by the "universal, ominous silence" surrounding the massacre of millions of Jews. She also noted with horror the lack of protests in England, in America, in the international Jewish organizations, and in the Catholic Church, but it was above all for the soul of Poland that she worried. "The compulsory participation of the Polish nation in the bloody spectacle that is taking place on Polish soil can easily breed indifference to crime, sadism and above all the perilous conviction that it is possible to murder one's neighbour without punishment."[61]

Murder most foul is exactly what the Polish population of Jedwabne (about one hundred kilometers from Bialystok) perpetrated against nearly all of their 1,600 Jewish neighbors on 10 July 1941, shortly after the German invasion of the Soviet Union. While the Germans looked on and limited themselves to filming the proceedings for propaganda purposes, the Polish villagers slaughtered Jews with axes, poles, knives, and nail-studded clubs. Men had their tongues or eyes cut out, women were raped and murdered, babies were thrown to the ground and trampled to death. Jews, after being savagely beaten, were lined up in the market square and forced to sing that they "had caused the war"; other groups of Jews were forced to undress, sing, dance, and perform "insane exercises" while Polish peasant onlookers, including women and children, applauded. A group of young Jews was ordered to lift a giant statue of Lenin (from the time of the Soviet occupation) and drag it to the Jewish cemetery, where they were promptly butchered. All the remaining Jews, reeling from savage blows, were then forced into a nearby barn, which was set alight with kerosene, so that they burned alive.[62]

The ordinary Poles who carried out these barbarities, described in Jan Gross's harrowing book on Jedwabne, were no different in their brutal sadism from the German perpetrators analyzed by Daniel Goldhagen. Resentment against the Soviet occupiers who had fled Eastern Poland in June 1941 following the German advance—and the stereotypical identification of the Jews with Communism—was more likely an exacerbating factor than the real cause of the massacre.[63] More important was the potent cocktail of prewar anti-Semitism embedded in the radical nationalism of the Endecja and a deeply reactionary, primitive Catholicism, mixed with sheer greed and the desire to plunder Jewish property, opened up by the German war against the Soviet Union.[64] Similarly bestial pogroms were carried out by rural Poles elsewhere in the Bialystok region, with enthusiastic spectators laughing loudly and applauding as Jews fell under the merciless blows of murderers. As one eyewitness put it: "The seed of hatred fell on well-nourished soil, which had been prepared for many years by the clergy. The wild and bloodthirsty mob took it as a holy challenge that history had put upon it—to get rid of the Jews. And the desire to take over Jewish riches whetted their appetites even more."[65]

This was already the Holocaust in miniature, revealing the more archaic layers of the monstrous enterprise and its use of primitive, ancient weapons. It was but one small episode in the murderous war of Hitler against the Jews, but similar scenes would soon occur all over Europe.

2

FROM WEIMAR
TO HITLER

As for the final goal and mission of the Germanic *völkische* movement, as far as the Jews are concerned,... it is to wipe out the East European and vermin Jew with an iron broom. A perfect job needs to be done.

Völkische Beobachter editorial, 10 March 1922

We want to point the finger at the Jew as the inspirer, the originator, and the beneficiary of this terrible catastrophe [the Spanish civil war].... This is the enemy of the world, the destroyer of cultures, the parasite among the peoples, the Son of Chaos, the incarnation of evil, the ferment of decomposition, the plastic demon of the decay of humanity.

JOSEPH GOEBBELS, Nuremberg Party Congress, September 1937

And when I heard that the Jews were being driven from their professions and homes and imprisoned in ghettos, the points switched automatically in my mind.... It was only "the Jew" who was being persecuted and "made homeless."

MELITA MASCHMANN, head of the League
of German Girls in the Hitler Youth

The ill-fated Weimar Republic was established after 1918 in the wake of unparalleled national traumas. The unexpected defeat in the First World War, the abdication of the emperor, the threat of Communist revolution, the humiliation of the Versailles Treaty, and the prospect of huge reparations payments to the Western Allies weighed heavily on Germans. The specter of economic and political chaos could only benefit the enemies of the republic, especially those on the nationalist right.[1] They damned the government with the responsibility for signing a treaty that had accepted German "war guilt," and blamed it for the substantial loss of territory, the "shame" of an emasculated army, and the dependence on foreign loans. While the Communists were forcibly put down in 1919, a further blow to the republic came with the massive inflation of 1923 and the consequent monetary collapse, which had a devastating effect on the working classes as well as on many in the middle strata of German society who lost their life savings. Although the Weimar Republic enjoyed a brief period of economic and political stability between 1924 and 1928, important changes beneath the surface were already weakening the middle ground in German politics. More liberal parties, such as the Democrats and the German National People's Party, were steadily losing support. So, too, were the conservative nationalists whose share of the vote by 1928 had declined from 20 percent to 14 percent. The Social Democrats, the dominant party in the early years of the republic, also began to lose votes—mainly to the Communists, who never forgave them for 1919.[2] For its part, the Catholic Center Party, whose electoral base remained stable, was no longer willing to form a coalition with the socialists and began to move to the right.

German Jews, who numbered slightly more than half a million, were less than 1 percent of the population in the 1920s, and clearly oriented to the liberal-left wing of German politics. They had little political influence, despite anti-Semitic legends to the contrary, but they were disproportionately prominent in publishing, journalism, the arts, the free professions, trade, private banking, and commerce, including the ownership of department stores, which began to develop at this time. In 1933, Jews were 11 percent of Germany's doctors and about 16 percent of its lawyers—a degree of visibility that was even more pronounced in the big cities. Middle-class anti-Semitism in Germany—especially rampant among doctors, lawyers, shopkeepers, artisans, small businessmen, academics, and students—was undoubtedly stimulated by professional jealousy and envy.[3] It was also nourished by the intensive post-1918 propaganda of *völkisch* anti-Semitic organizations that branded Jews with the stigma of wartime profiteering, black-market dealings, stock-exchange speculation, and responsibility for defeat in the war. The economic and political crises between 1918 and 1923 exacerbated these embittered feelings.[4]

A constant refrain of the political right was the singling out of radical socialists and Communists of Jewish origin for their roles in the abortive revolutions of 1918 and 1919, thus accrediting the idea that Jews were inclined toward subversive activity and revolution. And indeed, the Spartacist revolt in Berlin (a Communist uprising) was led by the Polish-born internationalist Rosa Luxemburg, who, like a number of the early leaders of the KPD (German Communist Party), was Jewish, though thoroughly alienated from her origins. In the Bavarian capital, Munich, after the downfall of the Wittelsbach dynasty, the first Independent Socialist prime minister, Kurt Eisner, was not only a Jew but also a bohemian intellectual, a Berliner, and a pacifist who had published documents attributing responsibility for the First World War to Germany.[5] These attributes made him an almost perfect target for the hate of the conservative and antirepublican elements in Bavarian society. The middle classes were even more panic-stricken when in 1919 a Munich Soviet Republic was established that featured a number of Russian Jews in leading positions. It was soon crushed by the local Freikorps (on instructions from the Social Democrats), who exacted a murderous revenge. Over the course of 1918 and 1919, some of the most prominent Jewish revolutionaries, including Luxemburg, Eisner, Gustav Landauer, Eugen Leviné, and a number of other radical Jews like the Independent Socialist Hugo Haase were either brutally assassinated or shot—a fate that also befell the Spartacist leader Karl Liebknecht, who was not a Jew.[6] This wave of assassinations culminated in the killing of Germany's first ever Jewish foreign minister, the highly assimilated and versatile industrialist Walther Rathenau, by youthful right-wing nationalist fanatics in 1922. Rathenau, an ardent Prussian patriot who had contributed much to the efficiency of the Germany economy during the war, was demonized as an "Elder of Zion" and a "Jewish Bolshevik" by his blond, blue-eyed killers. Rathenau's murder was a worrying omen for German Jewry.[7]

The stream of impoverished Polish Jews arriving in Berlin in the early 1920s was another troubling development to some Germans. These Ostjuden (eastern Jews) were frequently unemployed and disoriented by the postwar upheavals and revolutions in eastern Europe. Moreover, they were cultural outsiders and an easy target for xenophobic accusations (made also by Social Democrats) of economic parasitism. In the Weimar Republic, they made up approximately one fifth of the Jewish population. The more assimilated and established members of German Jewry tended to believe that the revival of anti-Semitism was directed primarily or even exclusively against the Ostjuden, but this turned out to be a tragic self-deception.

The most militant of the many disparate *völkisch* anti-Semitic sects that mushroomed in the aftermath of the war was the National Socialist German Workers Party (NSDAP, or Nazi Party for short), founded in Munich in 1919. Its official party program of 24 February 1920 stood for "the uniting of all Germans within one Greater Germany" on the basis of national self-determination. The party called for the annulment of the Treaty of Versailles, demanding more land and soil for the German population; it advocated that the "yoke of interest-capital" be broken, favoring widespread nationalizations as well as profit sharing, land reform, the communalization of department stores, and other radical-sounding measures. Article 4 of the NSDAP program made it clear that only "persons of German blood" could be nationals (*Volksgenossen*) and therefore citizens. This automatically excluded Jews, who in the future, they hoped, would be permitted to live in Germany only as guests "subject to legislation for Aliens." Article 23 insisted that publishers, journalists, and "all editors and editorial employees of German-language newspapers must be German by race." It also called for laws against "trends in art and literature that have a destructive effect on our national life" (an implicit reference to Jews). Article 24 observed that the NSDAP stood for "positive Christianity" and fought "against the Jewish-materialistic spirit *within* and *without* us."[8]

Until 1930, the Nazi Party remained a minor although highly vocal *völkisch* grouping that continued to advocate (without much success) a nationalist form of socialism underpinned by strong anti-Semitic foundations. Between 1919 and 1924, it remained confined to Bavaria, appealing mainly to ex-soldiers, anti-Communists, anti-Semites, and a hodgepodge of déclassé elements that were attracted to the vague slogans of a "national revolution." Nevertheless, its leader, Adolf Hitler, a raucous, spellbinding Austrian agitator who had been a corporal in the German Army during the First World War, had already attracted some national attention. On

8 and 9 November 1923, the thirty-four-year-old Hitler, together with the old war hero General Erich von Ludendorff, had attempted to seize power in Bavaria, hoping eventually to march on Berlin and overthrow the Weimar Republic. The putsch failed miserably when Hitler and his followers were fired on by the Munich police while marching through the city center. The putschists dispersed in some confusion. Following his arrest, Hitler managed, with the help of a sympathetic judge, to turn his trial into a harangue against the "traitors of 1918," a public indictment of Weimar democracy, and a platform for his own extreme nationalist and anti-Semitic views. Though guilty of high treason, he was sentenced to a mere five years' imprisonment, of which he served just nine months in Landsberg prison, where he wrote *Mein Kampf* (My struggle). This sprawling, poorly written, primitive book was to become the Bible of the Nazi movement and a core anti-Semitic text as well.

As a political autobiography, *Mein Kampf* offers us vital insight into Hitler's background and the formative influences on his worldview. Hitler had been born in the small town of Braunau on the Inn, which lay on the border between Austria and Bavaria, on 20 April 1889. In his adolescent years, spent partly in Linz, he had come under the influence of the Pan-German ideology of Georg von Schönerer, the leading German nationalist in Austria, who advocated the *Anschluss* (union) of the two German states into one German Reich. (Hitler fulfilled this dream in 1938.) The rancorous Schönerer passionately hated the cosmopolitan Habsburg ruling dynasty of Austria, the Czechs, and other neighboring Slavs who threatened German hegemony, the Roman Catholic Church, and especially Jews.[9] Schönerer had in 1885 proclaimed anti-Semitism the "main pillar of a true folkish mentality, and thus ... the greatest achievement of this century."[10] Schönerer turned his advocacy of "Germandom" into a matter of faith and early in his political career had added an "Aryan" clause excluding even the most ardent German nationalist Jews from membership in his movement. Hitler fully accepted Schönerer's intransigent ethnic anti-Semitism (rooted in blood and race), adopted his hatred of the "Jewish press" and the "Jewish-led Social Democracy," and shared his loathing for universal suffrage. He was no less scathing about parliamentarianism, liberal democracy, and the House of Habsburg, which he held responsible for betraying the German *Volk*. The young Hitler learned to identify with the Germanic cult of the *Führer* (leader) and adopted Schönerer's German greeting of "Heil!"[11]

Another important Austrian role model for the young Hitler, to whom he devoted many pages in *Mein Kampf,* was the extremely popular and elegant mayor of Vienna, Karl Lueger, leader of the Christian-Social Party. He had come to power largely through the skillful, demagogic use of anti-Semitism, focusing his attacks on the prominent role of Viennese Jews in the liberal press, in the stock exchange, and in banking and industrial capitalism.[12] In his propaganda, he fused Catholic prejudice against the "Christ killers" with the more modern anticapitalist resentments of a lower middle class facing economic crisis. Lueger cleverly mixed this with the xenophobic feelings of many Viennese toward the Ostjuden, who by 1900 already formed about 25 percent of Vienna's 175,000-strong Jewish community. Hitler greatly admired Lueger and absorbed from him the lesson that anti-Semitism could be an extremely effective instrument of mass mobilization in crystallizing the resentments of the "little man."[13] But he disliked the easygoing opportunism behind Lueger's policy toward Jews and Slavs, the Viennese mayor's refusal to embrace the racial principle, and his tight alliance with the Catholic Church, though he did appreciate the tactical shrewdness behind this strategy in prewar Austria. According to Hitler, Lueger, who still allowed Jews the escape route of baptism, was simply not radical enough. "Lacking was the conviction that this was a vital question for all humanity, with the fate of all non-Jewish peoples depending on its solution."[14]

The other great influence on Hitler's view of the Jews was the German nationalist composer Richard Wagner, whose operas he knew by heart and whose diatribes against the corrupting role of Jews in music and art he avidly consumed at an early age.[15] The intensity of Hitler's emotional identification with Wagner gave special weight to this connection. Those passages in *Mein Kampf* which claim that Jews have never produced any creative art—least of all in music (!) and architecture—and which portray their "parasitic" cultural activity in exceptionally malevolent language could have been lifted verbatim from Wagner's writings.[16] For Wagner, the Jews represented the "evil conscience of our modern civilization" or, in a phrase much repeated by the Nazis, "the plastic demon of the decline of mankind."[17]

Nevertheless, there were distinctive features to Hitler's anti-Semitism. One element, which he himself directly related to "the visual instruction of the Vienna streets," derived from his stylized encounter with the caftan-wearing Orthodox Galician Jews from eastern Europe. The way he tells it, this "apparition in a black caftan and black hair locks" first made him wonder about the foreignness of the Jew and whether this strange being could possibly be a German.[18] The impact was apparently instantaneous: "For a few pennies, I bought the first anti-Semitic pamphlets of my life." Once he had begun to take cognizance of the "Jewish question," Hitler tells us that wherever he went he "began to see Jews, and the more I saw, the more sharply they became distinguished in my eyes from the rest of humanity."[19] The climax of this psychodrama, which turned him (by his own somewhat hysterical account) from a "weak-kneed cosmopolitan" into a "coldly rational" anti-Semite, was the realization that the internationalist Austrian Social Democracy was "Jewish" in character: "When I recognized the Jew as the leader of the Social Democracy, the scales dropped from my eyes. A long soul struggle had reached its conclusion."[20]

Of course, Hitler's account need not be taken literally. No

doubt he had an interest in rationalizing his anti-Semitism, demonstrating its iron logic and continuity. We know that Hitler did in fact mix quite freely with Jews in prewar Vienna and relied on them to sell his picture-postcard sketches and paintings.[21] Yet much of what he writes still rings true and reflects the greater salience of the "Jewish question" and of anti-Semitism in the Austrian capital, especially compared to imperial Germany. The repressed sexual dimension to Hitler's Judeophobia also seems striking: "With satanic joy in his face, the black-haired Jewish youth lurks in wait for the unsuspecting maiden whom he defiles with his blood, thus stealing her from her people. With every means he tries to destroy the racial foundations of the people he has set out to subjugate."[22] Hitler drew a direct parallel between this highly personal racist fantasy, drawn from the back streets of imperial Vienna, and the postwar occupation of the Ruhr by black French colonial troops. In both cases, he saw a Jewish conspiracy: "It was and it is Jews who bring the Negroes into the Rhineland, always with the same secret thought and clear aim of ruining the white race by the necessarily resulting bastardization."[23]

Mein Kampf is permeated by obsessions with "racial purity" as well as by the Social Darwinist principle of a relentless battle of each nation for its own self-preservation. In the case of the German *Volk*, its foremost vital need, Hitler wrote, was to acquire more *Lebensraum* in the east, at the expense of Soviet Russia, the menacing citadel of international Communism. Thus, for ideological, economic, and geopolitical reasons, Hitler called for an all-out war against "the Jewish doctrine of Marxism." Its egalitarian doctrines contradicted "the significance of nationality and race," denied the value of personality, and negated the "eternal laws of nature."[24] In an apocalyptic prophecy of the kind that he was to invoke frequently after 1939, whenever he referred to the "Final Solution" of the "Jewish question," Hitler wrote in

Mein Kampf: "If, with the help of his Marxist creed, the Jew is victorious over the other peoples of the world, his crown will be the funeral wreath of humanity.... Hence today I believe that I am acting in accordance with the will of the Almighty Creator: by defending myself against the Jew, I am fighting for the work of the Lord."[25]

Though Hitler had abandoned the simple Catholic faith of his boyhood, one can find in these and other passages crude echoes of popular Christian beliefs, transmuted into the new "political religion" of National Socialism.[26] In claiming divine sanction for his fight against the Jews and "Jewish Marxism," Hitler was signaling that he considered this political battle to be a crusade or holy war in which there could be no compromises. The "war against the Jews" was an existential matter of life and death, an "either-or" question in which the future of civilization itself was at stake.[27] There were also other related themes that in retrospect seem to prefigure the Holocaust, such as the statement that twelve to fifteen thousand "Hebrew corrupters" ought to have been gassed in the First World War, so that "the sacrifice of millions at the front would not have been in vain."[28] This does not necessarily mean that Hitler envisioned gassing the Jews in 1924, but it is important to understand his peculiar logic in order to grasp its full implications. Like many demobilized soldiers of his generation, he was convinced that the German Fatherland had been betrayed in 1918 by pacifists and Marxists, deliberately incited by the Jews. This "betrayal" must never be allowed to recur, as Hitler made abundantly clear to the Czech foreign minister in early 1939: "We are going to destroy the Jews. They are not going to get away with what they did on 9 November 1918."[29] The ninth of November symbolized for Hitler not only the disgrace of the German defeat and surrender but the chaos of Communist revolution and the advent of the hated "Jewish Republic." He had entered politics to make sure this would never happen again. By implication, only the preventive gassing of the Jews could forestall a repetition of "the stab in the back" and ensure a future German victory.

War, revolution, and the Jews were inseparably locked together in Hitler's mind. Revealingly enough, his first known statement about political affairs comes in a letter on the "Jewish question" dated 16 September 1919, in which he defines Jewry strictly as a "racial," not a religious, group. He describes its actions in a horrifying metaphor as resulting "in a racial tuberculosis of peoples."[30] Rejecting mere pogroms as a purely "emotional" response to the Jewish problem, Hitler called instead for a "rational anti-Semitism" that would revoke the Jews' "special privileges." The final objective, he wrote to his correspondent, "must be the complete removal [*Entfernung*] of the Jews."[31] This ambiguous term could mean either their forced emigration, their extermination, or perhaps a mixture of both.

Hitler's speeches of the early 1920s, like those of other leading Nazis in southern Germany such as Alfred Rosenberg, Julius Streicher, and Hermann Esser, constantly hammer away at the need to take ruthless, systematic measures against the Jews; to remove them from all government employment, newspaper offices, theaters, and cinemas; to "eliminate" their "spirit" from German culture and the economy; and to break their imagined political power by sweeping away the Marxist parties. In *Mein Kampf* as in many of his speeches, Hitler conjured up the specter of Bolshevik Russia, where "the Jew" (frequently compared to a vampire or giant parasite) had "killed or starved about thirty million people with positively fanatical savagery, in part amid inhuman tortures, in order to give a gang of Jewish journalists and stock exchange bandits domination over a great people." In his unpublished *Secret Book* of 1928, Hitler elaborated still further on the meaning of the "Jewish-Bolshevik" tyranny: "The end of the Jewish world struggle therefore will always be a bloody Bolshevization. In truth this means the destruction of all the intellectual upper classes linked to their peoples so that he can rise to become the master of a mankind become leaderless."[32]

Marxism was thereby reduced to a weapon of terror that the Jews had ruthlessly used to destroy an "inherently anti-Semitic Russia" and to extirpate the Russian national intelligentsia along with the Russian upper classes. The massive atrocities in "this Jewish struggle for hegemony in Russia amounted to 28–30 million people in number of dead. This is fifteen times more than the world war cost Germany."[33] The Bolshevik Revolution had not only destroyed marriage, sexual morality, and the bonds of social order, it had deliberately created a "chaotic bastardization" that left the Jews as its "only intellectual cement." Hitler's unbending conclusion from this so-called Jewish-Bolshevik genocide—which he regarded as the "most terrible crime of all times against mankind"—was that only the National Socialist movement could prevent a similar victory for Jewry in the bitter struggle that "is being waged in Germany at the present time."[34] For Hitler, in other words, Germany was the pivotal land that would determine whether Communism (and Jewry) would triumph or not. The problem was that even the bourgeois parties were tools of Jewry. Behind "the Jew" stood not only Marxism, democracy, and "the so-called Christian Center" but also "the bourgeois national parties of the so-called national fatherland leagues"—in short, the entire parliamentary political spectrum. Hence, National Socialism in its *total war* against the Jews would have to completely destroy the Weimar "system" and replace its rotten foundations with a ruthless racist dictatorship.

It is evident that the Nazi discourse on these issues had qualitatively moved some distance beyond the familiar themes of pre-1914 anti-Semitism, whether Christian or anti-Christian. Hitler had adopted a political conception of Jewry that was ultimately derived from the war; he had embraced a mental universe of *Sieg oder Untergang* (victory or downfall) in relation to Communism and the Jews. Moreover, the latter were consistently dehumanized in zoological language either as an inferior race or as "vermin" to be cleansed or else as germs, bacilli, and microbes that attack and poison organisms unless they are eradicated.[35] Jewry is presented as the equivalent of a bubonic plague in the Middle Ages, only the medical metaphors in this case invoke more modern diseases like cancer and tuberculosis. "The Jew" was invariably referred to in Nazi discourse as a type to which *all* Jews conformed, whether western or eastern, men or women, secular or religious, assimilated or unassimilated, bourgeois or proletarian. Even baptized Jews were irrevocably tainted in Nazi ideology by the stigma of degenerate blood. Jews as a "counter-race" were perceived as the polar opposite to the German "Aryans," being inherently destructive, parasitical, and agents of decomposition (*Zersetzung*).[36]

By virtue of their abstract intellect, mercenary egoism, and corrupt mentality, the Jews were a special danger to German women. Julius Streicher in *Der Stürmer*, the most pornographic of all Nazi anti-Semitic publications, specialized (much to Hitler's delight) in elaborating on the presumed sexual pathology of the "Jewish peril." Streicher regularly accused Jews of rape and of exploiting German girls for prostitution; he revived the medieval blood libel that Jews abducted German children for ritual murder purposes; he even claimed that Jews deliberately sought to poison the blood of German women through sexual intercourse.[37] *Der Stürmer* reveled, for example, in the absurd theories put forward by the racist author Arthur Dinter in his bestselling novel, *The Sin Against the Blood* (1918). Dinter had claimed in all seriousness that if a German woman had ever engaged in sexual relations with a Jew, she would transmit Jewish hereditary characteristics even to children conceived with German fathers. For Hitler, who had gnawing doubts about the possible taint of Jewish blood in his own family background, such obsessions had a special significance.[38] Intense, guilt-ridden sexual puritanism, the deeply rooted desire to avenge himself for early deprivations and social humiliation, together with a morbid fixation on blood and race heightened the irrational extremism of his Judeophobia.

But how far could such personal obsessions be shared by other groups in German society? To what extent, if any, did paranoid anti-Semitism help Hitler to win power? It is probably impossible to measure its impact on Germans in any convincing way. We do know that the consequences of the First World War encouraged many disillusioned former soldiers not only to despise the postwar republic and its democratic politicians but also to blame the Jews for the debacle. Rightwing nationalists, conservative monarchists, and members of the old elites, frightened by the Bolshevik Revolution in Russia and the prospect of an encore in Germany, were often receptive to the myth of a Jewish conspiracy. Among the lower classes, many did indeed believe that Jews had profiteered from the war or the reparations. There were others, too, who resented Jewish immigration from the east or believed that the stock exchange and banking capital were mainly in the hands of Jewish financiers. Such arguments were hardly new. They had long attracted impoverished artisans, craftsmen, and small traders.[39] But now, in the overheated atmosphere of the early postwar years, extreme anti-Semitism did seem to burst through traditional restraints. It extended from the semi-respectable DNVP (Deutschnationale Volkspartei, the German National People's Party) to the student fraternities, where it was especially violent; it penetrated the churches and found an echo in Communist efforts to play the nationalist card by denouncing "Jewish finance capital."[40] The notorious Russian anti-Semitic forgery, *The Protocols of the Elders of Zion*, translated into German shortly after the war, briefly became a bestseller.[41] By 1933, there were more than four hundred anti-Semitic associations and societies in Germany, along with some seven hundred anti-Jewish periodicals. Some of the scurrilous pamphlets portrayed the Jews in the hysterical tones reminiscent of *Der Stürmer.* More respectable conservative opinion deplored the permissive mores, modernist culture, and radical politics of Berlin in the 1920s, which was attributed to Jewish and Marxist influence.[42]

On the other hand, throughout the 1920s the Nazi vote remained modest. Even in the 1928 Reichstag elections, they obtained only eight hundred thousand votes and a mere twelve seats in parliament. National Socialist success in using anti-Semitism seemed limited outside of regions where there was a preexisting historical tradition or local factors favoring it. Thus, anti-Semitism resonated in Franconia, Hesse, Westphalia, and some areas of Bavaria but was relatively muted in the Rhineland, Baden, Württemberg, and Schleswig-Holstein. Even among ordinary Nazi Party members, only a hard-core minority (though a very vocal one) regarded anti-Semitism as the critical issue. It was evidently less important than anti-Communism, nationalism, or the woes of unemployment in attracting new adherents to the movement. Nevertheless, in Nazi agitation among high-school and university students, anti-Semitism was undoubtedly a crucial weapon in recruitment, helping the Nazis to "capture" a commanding position at German universities by 1930.[43] Similarly, they had achieved some success among professional associations of physicians and teachers in spreading the anti-Jewish message. Since Jews in the Weimar Republic were well represented in the free professions, the universities, and cultural life, it was relatively easy to ignite competitive envy against them in these sectors.

Nazi penetration of the countryside and of urban middle-class groups just as the Great Depression began to bite in Germany after 1929 helps to explain the remarkable increase in their vote in the September 1930 elections. The movement leaped dramatically from 12 to 107 seats (18.3 percent of the total) in the Reichstag, making it the second largest party. In July 1932, the Nazis definitively emerged as the biggest party in the Reichstag, with 37.3 percent of the vote (230 seats), which was their peak performance under strictly democratic conditions. The staggering shift in their fortunes had coincided with their emergence as a catchall party appealing to the unifying ideal of *Volksgemeinschaft* (national community). They appeared to be a movement that, unlike all its rivals, was able to transcend regional, class, religious, and party barriers. Though the Nazis made little impact on the solid electoral base of the Catholic and socialist parties, it did win over much of the youth vote, the disaffected *Mittelstand*, disillusioned supporters of the weakened middle-class parties, some sections of the unemployed, unskilled workers, and much of the farming constituency.[44] To achieve such a broad appeal, Hitler focused his message more intensely around integral nationalism. Between 1930 and 1933, he temporarily toned down the full-blooded anti-Semitism that lay at the core of his worldview.

Hitler had no difficulty in tailoring Nazi propaganda in order to attain power by legal means, once he recognized that anti-Semitism was not his most effective issue or central to the electorate. Instead, he underlined his unswerving rejection of a parliamentary democracy that had palpably failed. He acknowledged the urgent need to regenerate economic life in the face of mass unemployment and adapted his message to the longing for stability, law, and order felt by so many ordinary Germans. Hitler knew how to play with uncanny skill on the chord of wounded German pride and national humiliation while holding out the promise of a redemptive reawakening that would lift Germans from their despair. Anti-Semitism in this political context was a crucial policy adjunct, but it was not decisive. Nonetheless, it was employed with great effectiveness to exacerbate local grievances, to satisfy the radical anticapitalist urges of the SA (storm troopers) rank and file, and to reinforce street campaigns against the Marxist parties. Hitler was far too shrewd to allow it, though, to interfere in the complex political game that would bring him power in January 1933.

For a brief moment after the Nazi vote declined in the November 1932 elections, reducing their representation to 196 seats in the Reichstag, it seemed that they might have passed their peak. It was the backstage maneuverings of authoritarian conservative politicians, wealthy industrialists, and army leaders that unexpectedly opened the door to Hitler.[45] This conservative camarilla hoped to manipulate the Nazis for their own narrow purposes and dreamed of dealing the deathblow to the Weimar parliamentary system and finally smashing the left-wing parties. They unwisely gambled on their ability to control events. These reactionary elites who had always despised the republic thought they could tame Hitler and convince him to do their bidding. Especially naïve in this respect was the former chancellor and Catholic Center Party politician Franz von Papen. He desperately needed Hitler's electoral appeal to further his ambitions, since he lacked any popular support himself. Determined to take revenge on his hated rival, General Kurt von Schleicher, and to remove him from the chancellorship, Papen was eager to promote a coalition of nationalists and Nazis. He persuaded the aging President Paul von Hindenburg to accept this coalition.

On 30 January 1933, Hitler became chancellor and Papen his deputy in a cabinet that contained eight conservatives and only two Nazi ministers. But in the new age of mass politics, such cabinet arithmetic counted for relatively little. During this realignment, the Nazi "war against the Jews"—not for the first or the last time—was temporarily suspended. The "Jewish question," so central to Hitler's own concerns, was quietly subordinated to the immediate task of seizing power. But any illusions that the assumption of office might moderate Nazi policy toward the Jews were to be swiftly and cruelly dashed.

Hitler's accession to power marked the end of Jewish emancipation in Germany. In the next six years, a whole century of Jewish integration into German society and culture would be comprehensively and brutally reversed. From the outset, the Nazis instituted terroristic policies directed against political opponents and Jews, who were subjected to random violence by marauding gangs of SA thugs. On 1 April 1933, the German government officially proclaimed a one-day economic boycott of Jewish shops and businesses, organized by the fanatical Julius Streicher. It was ostensibly designed as a form of "self-defense" and a response to anti-German "atrocity stories" allegedly inspired by Jews abroad. Propaganda Minister Joseph Goebbels asserted that the boycott was a "spontaneous," grassroots action, but this was belied by the public response of Germans, which was decidedly mixed. For German Jews, it was, however, a tremendous shock to suddenly become the targeted victims of government-inspired hate and to be turned into hostages whose safety would henceforth be conditioned on the "good behavior" of their coreligionists in the outside world. Within less than a week, the new Law for the Restoration of the Professional Civil Service pensioned off civil servants of "non-Aryan" origin. In deference to President Hindenburg's sensitivities as a field marshal and war hero, Jewish war veterans (whose relatively large number appears to have surprised the Nazis) were temporarily exempted from this legislation. Separate laws disbarred 1,400 lawyers as well as 381 Jewish judges and state prosecutors. By the end of 1934, 70 percent of all Jewish lawyers and 60 percent of all Jewish notaries had been dismissed. By mid-1935, more than half the Jewish doctors in Germany had been removed from their profession. Within less than five years, the medical purge became total.[46]

Goebbels moved rapidly against thousands of Jewish academics, artists, journalists, and writers, some of whom were Nobel laureates or enjoyed international reputations. Albert Einstein was only the most celebrated among the many prominent scientists and intellectuals who emigrated. No fewer than two hundred Jewish academics followed suit in 1933 alone. Altogether in the first year of Nazi rule, about forty thousand Jews left Germany, those who were young and single having the best chance to begin a new life abroad. The purges in the artistic and cultural spheres were especially swift. The new Chamber of Culture, established by Goebbels in September 1933, immediately excluded Jews from employment in theater, film, and music, and a National Press Law likewise prevented Jews from being journalists. The result was an unprecedented hemorrhaging of talent, with Germany's loss a gain for the Western democracies, especially for Britain and America. This was not, however, the way the Nazis saw it. On 6 April 1933, Hitler had told representatives of the medical association in Berlin that the claim of Germany "to its own peculiar intellectual leadership must be met by the early elimination of the surplus Jewish intellectuals from cultural and intellectual life."[47]

In May 1933, as if to underline the point, Goebbels solemnly declared at a book-burning ceremony in the capital that "the era of an exaggerated Jewish intellectualism is forever over." The books of leading writers, both Jewish and Gentile but all considered "decadent" or opposed to Nazi ideology, were consigned to the flames in city squares all over the country, before excited crowds of Germans, with university students especially at the forefront. Alongside such well-known "Jewish" subversives as Marx, Freud, Einstein, Kurt Tucholsky, Heinrich Heine, and Leon Trotsky, the writings of non-Jews such as Thomas Mann, Bertolt Brecht, Erich Maria Remarque, Erich Kästner, and H. G. Wells went up in smoke in a gigantic execution of what was now called "un-German literature." In contrast to the economic boycott, neither the book burnings nor the purges in the arts or sciences elicited any public protests. The cultural "Aryanization" policy appeared to be popular, echoing a long-standing belief among many Germans that Jews were overrepresented in these areas. It held out the tempting promise of new career opportunities for ambitious non-Jewish Germans.

Jewish responses to this assault varied greatly. For some, the sudden vehemence of German anti-Semitism after 1933 came as a total shock, and there were those who hoped that it would pass away like a bad dream. Optimists easily persuaded themselves that Hitler was but a temporary aberration, a freak phenomenon who either would not last in office or would soon be forced by his blue-blooded coalition partners to moderate his policies. There were those who had built up family businesses over generations or were too deeply attached to the German language and culture to envisage any alternatives. There were the elderly, for whom a fresh start seemed inconceivable. Then there were the excessively well established, who had too much property to lose. Even after six years of humiliating and degrading persecution, philologist Victor Klemperer, an assimilated, converted German Jew, could write the following in his diary.

> Until 1933 and for at least a good century before that, the German Jews were entirely German and nothing else. Proof: the thousands and thousands of half- and quarter-Jews etc. Jews and "persons of Jewish descent", proof that Jews and Germans lived and worked together without friction in all spheres of German life. The antisemitism which was always present is not at all proof to the contrary, because the friction between Jews and "Aryans" was not half so great as, for example, that between Protestants and Catholics, or between employers and employees, or between East Prussians, for example, and southern Bavarians, or Rhinelanders and Berliners. The German Jews were a part of the German nation, as the French Jews were part of the French nation etc. They played their part within the life of Germany, by no means as a burden on the whole. Their role was rarely that of the worker, still less of the agricultural labourer. They were, and remain (even though now they no longer wish to remain so), Germans, in the main intellectuals and educated people.[48]

For thoroughly Germanized Jews, the "Jewish question" was altogether artificial, based on a zoological concept of "blood purity" that had no connection with reality. Hence it is not surprising that Klemperer despised the Zionist solution to the Jewish problem as "something for sectarians," a historical throwback and absurdity that was "contrary to nature," not to say a crime against reason. "It seems complete madness to me," he observed, "if specifically Jewish states are now to be set up in Rhodesia or somewhere. That would be letting the Nazis throw us back thousands of years."[49]

But it was those like Klemperer, clinging on at all costs in Germany, who seemed increasingly out of touch with events. Nearly 10 percent of German Jews had already fled the country by the end of 1933, mostly to neighboring France, Belgium, Switzerland, and Holland, though these lands were themselves in the grip of economic depression, and Jewish refugees were not exactly welcomed. Moreover, as refugees, they had to forfeit much of their property, which had been confiscated by the German authorities, making emigration much more difficult. The Nazis cynically judged that the more destitute Jewish refugees appeared to be, the more of a burden they would become on potential host countries, thereby stirring up anti-Semitic sentiments there. The immigration quotas and closed-door policy of the United States and many other countries—including Canada, Australia, and South Africa, which had large territories and sparse populations within the British dominions—seemed to confirm their assessment. Nevertheless, about 200,000 Jews left Germany within the first six years of Nazi rule, and another 82,000 emigrated from Austria in 1938. Out of all these Jewish refugees, the largest single group (132,000) found new homes in the United States; 55,000 Jews emigrated to British-controlled Palestine, 40,000 to England, 20,000 to Argentina and Brazil; 9,000 went to Shanghai, 7,000 were accepted in Australia, and another 5,000 in South Africa. But the absolute figures are deceptive unless one takes into account the size, population, and resources of the host countries.

Palestine, as the "Jewish National Home" designated by the League of Nations, appeared for the first time to be an increasingly realistic prospect for many German Jews. By then, alternative options were shrinking fast. Jewish emigration to

Palestine was indeed initially encouraged by the Nazis as a way of making Germany *Judenrein* (free of Jews).[50] The Third Reich even signed a "transfer" agreement (*Ha'avara*) with the Zionist leadership of Palestinian Jewry (the Jewish Agency), which permitted Jews to take out a portion of their capital in the form of German goods. This much-criticized deal enabled thousands of German Jews to emigrate to Palestine, where they significantly strengthened the Jewish community through an influx of educated manpower and technical and organizational skills. Although the new immigrants received only a portion of their money, they were nonetheless better off than if they had emigrated to other destinations, where no such arrangements were in place. Above all, their lives were saved, since they were physically farther removed from the Reich than those in neighboring European countries were. Of course, had the British Eighth Army not defeated Rommel in late 1942 in the deserts of North Africa, even that outcome might have been less fortunate.

In the economic sphere, Hitler proceeded slowly against the Jews in the early years of Nazi rule, following the expert advice of Economics Minister Hjalmar Schacht.[51] He was well aware of Germany's financial vulnerability and the vital importance of overcoming mass unemployment. Hence, government legislation mainly targeted small Jewish traders and professional people rather than Jewish-owned banking houses, department stores, and companies that were important to the German economy. Nevertheless, by 1935 about one quarter of all Jewish businesses had been dismantled or "Aryanized" at knockdown prices. It was only after June 1938, when the German economic recovery had been fully achieved, that the systematic dispossession and expropriation of Jewish property was finally undertaken. This definitive elimination of the Jews from the German economy obliged about 120,000 Jews to leave the country, almost penniless, within just more than one year.

Hitler's anti-Jewish policy in the early years of Nazi rule

had to be relatively cautious on account of his domestic and international situation. He could not initially afford to ignore President Hindenburg and the more conservative ministers in the Cabinet, such as Papen, Alfred Hugenberg, Foreign Minister Constantin von Neurath, and Schacht, who expected him to preserve law and order while keeping in check the plebeian anti-Semitism of the more radical Nazis. The conservative nationalists were hardly "philo-Semites" or defenders of Jewish rights. They had no problem with the *numerus clausus* law, which had limited Jews to 1.5 percent of the places in high schools and universities, nor with the formal canceling of their citizenship on 23 March 1934. Strictly *legal* measures that aimed at isolating and excluding the Jews appeared acceptable to them, as they did to many Germans, including the leaders of the Protestant and Catholic churches.[52] Violent anti-Jewish street actions were another matter. Leading Nazi Party officials themselves euphemistically referred to such gangsterism as *Einzelaktionen*—the kind of SA rowdiness and sadistic hooliganism that was giving Germany a bad name abroad. Hence, Deputy Führer Rudolf Hess, citing Hitler's need to refute "allegations of atrocities and boycotts made by Jews abroad," gave a confidential order in April 1935 to party militants not to engage in acts of terror against individual Jews.[53] It was not easy, however, to pacify the Nazi rank and file, who could not understand why any Jewish banks, department stores, export houses, or industrial enterprises were permitted to function in a National-Socialist State that was reputedly at war with world Jewry.[54] The "little Nazis" greedily anticipated the liquidation or "Aryanization" of Jewish property, which they believed had been promised to them by the party program and by their leaders' anticapitalist demagogery. But while Hitler profoundly sympathized with the violent impulses of the more fanatical anti-Semites, he knew that the time was not yet ripe to implement a truly radical approach.

The Nuremberg Race Laws of September 1935 were a

kind of compromise between these countervailing pressures. The laws "for the Protection of German Blood and German Honour" formally stripped the Jews of their remaining rights as citizens.[55] They also forbade marriages and extramarital sexual intercourse between Jews and subjects of the state "of German or related blood"; they prohibited Jews from employing female German servants under forty-five years of age (presumably out of fear that Jewish men might seduce younger German women); they forbade Jews from flying the national flag (the swastika) or Reich colors. The Reich Citizenship Law also provided a new definition of who was, and who was not, a Jew. It differentiated among three categories: (1) full-blooded Jews, who were designated as persons descended from at least three fully Jewish grandparents, as were those who belonged to or had later joined the Jewish religious community, had two Jewish grandparents, or had married a Jew; (2) the *Mischlinge* (part-Jews or persons of mixed descent) "first degree," who had two Jewish grandparents but had not married a Jew or been a member of the local synagogue; (3) the *Mischlinge* "second degree," who had only one Jewish grandparent. According to the somewhat inflated Nazi statistics, in 1935 there were no fewer than 750,000 Germans who fell into the category of first- or second-degree *Mischlinge*, in addition to the estimate of 475,000 "full Jews" who practiced their religion and another 300,000 who did not. Thus, there were more than 1.5 million Germans of "Jewish blood" in 1935, according to the peculiar Nazi categorizations. Time would show that differences among these labels could become life-and-death issues.

The declared objective of the Nuremberg Race Laws, according to Hitler's own Reichstag speech, was "to find a separate secular solution [*eine einmalige säkulare Lösung*] for building a basis upon which the German nation can adopt a better attitude towards the Jews [*ein erträgliches Verhältnis zum jüdischen Volk*]."[56] The Nazi leader could simultaneously claim both that he was seeking to solve "the Jewish problem

by *legal* means" and that by disenfranchising the Jews, he was
finally fulfilling a cardinal point in the NSDAP program of
1920—namely, that no Jew could ever be a *Volksgenosse* (racial
comrade) or a *Reichsbürger* (citizen of the Reich). No less important, Hitler warned starkly that if workable arrangements
with the Jews broke down, he might have to pass a law "hand-
ing the problem over to the National Socialist Party for final
solution" (*zur endgültigen Lösung*).[57] Yet top Nazi officials, such
as Interior Minister Wilhelm Frick, also made more reassuring remarks at this time. In December 1935, Frick declared
that "the Jews will not be deprived of the possibility of living
in Germany."[58] The director of the German Press Agency
even suggested that "Germany is helping Judaism to
strengthen its national character and is making a contribution
towards improved relations between the two peoples."[59] The
correspondent of *The Times* of London summarized the official commentary on the Nuremberg Race Laws as follows:
"The members of the Jewish minority in Germany received
through the new legislation the right to live their own cultural and national life. They can have their own schools, the-
atres and sports clubs.... But the participation of Jews in the
political or social affairs of the German people is now and for
ever (says the commentary) prohibited." The correspondent
even noted that Hitler had informed party leaders that he was
against arbitrary "individual actions."[60]

Although German Jews had been reduced to second-class
citizens, many had not yet given up hope that they might still
find a niche within the Third Reich. They clutched at the
straw that racial separation might indeed stabilize their position, as some official rhetoric seemed to imply, by offering
them a "legally protected" framework.[61] German Jews had
been isolated from the rest of the population, but not all their
means of livelihood had yet been destroyed. Some German
Zionists also managed to find a few positive aspects to the
race laws, though for different reasons. They particularly
welcomed its contribution to the collapse of "assimilationist"

illusions. There were even those among them who misguid-
edly believed that the principle of racial separation offered
good prospects for increased and more intense Jewish cultural activity.[62] Ironically, this proved to be true for the brief
period before the radicalization of Nazi policy in 1938
brought the curtain down on any illusions of a semiau-
tonomous Jewish existence within the Third Reich.

The spectacular extravaganza of the 1936 Berlin Olympics
encouraged the hopes and delusions of German Jewry for a
little while longer, as the worldwide attention led to a toning
down of the more vicious abuse and a halt to more blatant
acts of anti-Semitic terror. The Nazis even permitted the
token participation of a few Jewish athletes on their Olympic
team to appease international criticism.[63] Germans were
ordered to be on their best behavior in order to radiate a
positive image abroad of the new Reich as a law-abiding,
peace-loving state. Significantly, Hitler postponed any act of
vengeance against German Jewry for the assassination in February 1936 of the Swiss Nazi Party leader by David Frank-
furter, a young Yugoslav Jew. But Hitler was only biding his
time. As he told an assembly of regional Nazi leaders on
29 April 1937, he had long ago made himself an "expert"
on the Jewish problem, and in the next two to three years it
would of course "be settled one way or the other."[64] Indeed, in
a secret 1936 memorandum on his Four-year Plan, he made it
clear that German Jewry would be expropriated in the event
of the Reich going to war, an eventuality for which he was already planning. Toward the end of 1937, with full employment achieved, the drive to completely eliminate Jews from
the German economy was noticeably accelerated. Not by accident, this coincided with the resignation of Schacht from
the Economics Ministry, followed in February 1938 by the removal of Neurath as foreign minister as well as the sacking of
War Minister von Blomberg and the chief of the Army High
Command, Werner Freiherr von Fritsch. At a stroke, the
Chancellor had rid himself of the last remaining representa-

tives of aristocratic conservatism in high positions, thereby gaining full control over the armed forces and foreign policy.

A month later, Hitler annexed his former Austrian homeland. Vienna, with its prosperous community of nearly two hundred thousand Jews, quickly became a model for the rapid forced emigration of Jewry from the Reich. After a particularly violent and brutal campaign of intimidation, Jews were forced by the SA to scrub the pavements of Vienna with small brushes, watched by crowds of jeering spectators. Jewish businesses were expropriated with electrifying speed, and Jewish homes shamelessly looted by Austrian Nazi thugs.[65] The Austrian tradition of anti-Semitism (which had molded the young Hitler thirty years earlier) flared up again with an intensity that caught even the invading Germans by surprise. The hysterical reception accorded Hitler on his triumphant return to Vienna in March 1938 provided the catalyst for this unprecedented outpouring of repressed hatred against the Jews.[66]

The Austrian model of radicalized anti-Jewish measures was immediately adopted in Germany itself. A full-scale "Aryanization" of the larger Jewish firms was initiated by Hermann Goering, the overseer of the Four-year Plan, as part of the broader policy of accelerated rearmament. A decree of 26 April 1938 obliged all Jews to report their total assets; in June 1938, drafts for the obligatory "Aryanization" of Jewish businesses were already in place. The mood in party circles and in the country was becoming more violently hostile to Jews. *The Times*'s correspondent noted that even in Berlin, hitherto "the most tolerant German city in its treatment of Jews," slogans such as "Germans must not buy from Jews" or "Out with the Jews" were becoming visible.[67] Storm troopers were seen picketing Jewish shops and roughly handling their owners. A campaign of arrests led to about one thousand Jews being taken off to concentration camps, originally established in 1933 for political opponents.

The flood of anti-Jewish legislation, the expropriations of businesses, and the general aggression of the regime had inevitably produced a new wave of Jewish emigration from Nazi Germany that began to alarm the democratic countries. At the initiative of America's president, Franklin D. Roosevelt, an international conference was convened in July 1938 in Evian, France, ostensibly to address the plight of the Jewish refugees being ousted from Germany and Austria.[68] The organizers preferred, however, to emphasize that the talks covered political refugees from all countries. In attendance were representatives from twenty-nine governments, including Great Britain and its dominions, most of the Latin American republics, France, Belgium, Holland, Switzerland, and three Scandinavian countries. The London *Daily Express* approvingly summarized some of the characteristic responses to the challenge of the hour made by individual delegates. The Australian minister for trade and customs explained that his country could do nothing more for Jewish refugees. Australia wanted only British immigrants, and they had no desire to import a "racial problem" by "encouraging any scheme of large-scale racial migration." The Canadian representative, whose country's record on Jewish immigration was abysmal, evoked economic uncertainties and unemployment problems. Argentina indicated that it was looking mainly for "experienced agriculturalists," which seemed to rule out most Jews. Belgium would not assume any international obligations "whose consequences she cannot foresee."[69]

Most disappointing of all was the refusal by the United States and Great Britain to contemplate taking in any substantial number of Jewish refugees. Indeed, once America, the sponsoring nation, made plain its unwillingness to open its own doors, it had virtually doomed the Evian Conference. In retrospect, the whole exercise seemed designed by the American State Department as a way to *divert* refugees from the United States and forestall any international pressure to liberalize its own immigration laws.[70] The British attitude was no less hypocritical. The Foreign Office successfully managed to keep Palestine off the agenda and blocked any denunciation of the Nazi government. The delegation pleaded lack of resources to explain its own refusal to take any more Jews, while vaguely promising to investigate whether a limited number of refugees could not be settled in its East African colonies. *The Times* of London in an editorial on 16 July 1938 praised this offer and commented: "The refugee problem can be solved only by a mixture of mercy and cool calculation, both of which were shown in excellent proportion at Evian."[71] Golda Meir, the future prime minister of Israel and an observer at the Evian Conference, took a very different view, writing in her autobiography, "I don't think that anyone who didn't live through it can understand what I felt at Evian—a mixture of sorrow, rage, frustration and horror."[72]

Most revealing of all as a response to this fiasco was Hitler's contemptuous reaction. Even before the results of the conference were known, he mocked the humanitarian pretensions of the Western democracies (especially Britain and America) that claimed to be so solicitous of "these criminals" (i.e., the Jews). In January 1939, he referred again to the charade: it had been a "shameful spectacle to see how the whole democratic world is oozing sympathy for the poor tormented Jewish people, but remains hard-hearted and obdurate when it comes to helping them—which is surely, in view of its attitude, an obvious duty."[73] Indeed, the Nazi leadership could only have felt bolstered in its increasingly brutal policy on the "Jewish question" by the results of the Evian Conference. The whole miserable farce had demonstrated that Western nations were not at all willing to open their doors and accept Jewish refugees or to commit themselves to rescue Jews. Nor were they ready to publicly criticize Nazi anti-Semitic legislation—preferring instead to view it as an *internal* German matter. Finally, there was another troubling implication, which was as yet only dimly visible on the horizon. If Nazi Germany could no longer expect to export, sell, or expel its Jews to an indifferent world that plainly did not want them, then perhaps they would have to do something even more drastic.

3

PERSECUTION

AND

RESISTANCE

All the Gestapo roads lead to Ponary and Ponary means death. Let us not be led like sheep to the slaughter. True we are weak and helpless, but the only response to the murders is self-defence. Brothers, it is better to die fighting like free men than to live at the mercy of the murderers.

ABBA KOVNER, *Manifesto of Zionist Youth*, Vilna, 31 December 1941

Why didn't we resist when they began to resettle 300,000 Jews from Warsaw? Why did we allow ourselves to be led like sheep to the slaughter?

EMMANUEL RINGELBLUM, *Diary*, 15 October 1942

In exile the Jews had always been in a minority; they had always been in danger; but they had learned that they could avert danger and survive destruction by placating and appeasing their enemies.... A two-thousand-year-old lesson could not be unlearned; the Jews could not make the switch [when their leadership realized] ... that the modern machine-like destruction process would engulf European Jewry.

RAUL HILBERG, *The Destruction of the European Jews* (1973)

In October 1938, seventeen thousand Jews of Polish origin hitherto residing in Germany found themselves brutally expelled en masse by the Nazi authorities. Dumped along the Polish-German frontier in appalling conditions, they were refused entry by the Polish government. Having previously rendering them stateless, Poland had already demonstrated its desire to rid itself of its Jewish citizens. Among the Polish Jews who were suddenly abandoned in no-man's-land was the Grynszpan family. Their seventeen-year-old son, Herschel, then living alone as an illegal and stateless immigrant in Paris, was outraged by the treatment of his parents and of the Jews in general. (He later told French investigators; "My people have a right to exist on this earth.")[1] In an act of anguished revenge, he shot Ernst vom Rath, the third secretary at the German embassy in Paris. The German diplomat died of his wounds on 9 November 1938. Grynszpan's action was immediately denounced by the Nazi propaganda machine as a "declaration of war" and part of a worldwide Judeo-Masonic conspiracy.

In response, the Nazis unleashed an unprecedented orgy of ferocious anti-Jewish violence and terror across Germany, euphemistically referred to as Kristallnacht (Crystal Night) after the crystal-like shards of glass from the shattered windows of Jewish shops across the land. All over Germany, more than four hundred synagogues burned, while more than 7,500 businesses and other properties owned by Jews were looted and ransacked. At least one hundred Jews were murdered, many more injured, and thirty thousand summarily packed off to concentration camps, where they were to suffer unspeakable indignities. Describing these events in Berlin on

10 November, the *Manchester Guardian* correspondent noted that the plundering and destruction of Jewish shops had been going on for nearly eighteen hours. "There are streets in the business quarters whole sections of which this evening are literally paved with broken glass, while in the kerbs and on the road are lying smashed office furniture, typewriters, telephones, bales of papers and other wreckage which had been hurled out of the windows by the wrecking squads."[2]

The British correspondent went on to recount how the wreckers "entered the synagogues, throwing petrol over the pews and setting the interiors on fire. As far as could be observed the work of the fire brigades was largely to stand by and keep an expert watch that the fires did not spread from the synagogue interiors to neighbouring buildings. . . . The crowds watched the burning of the synagogues with apathy."[3]

The American consul in Leipzig, David Buffum, who left one of the more graphic accounts of the pogrom, wrote that the barrage of Nazi ferocity "had no equal hitherto in Germany, or very likely anywhere else in the world since savagery began."[4] After describing the destruction and violation of property, he added, "The most hideous phase of the so-called 'spontaneous' action has been the wholesale arrest and transportation to concentration camps of male German Jews between the ages of sixteen and sixty, as well as Jewish men without citizenship. This has been taking place daily since the night of horror."[5] Such was the scale of the damage that, according to internal reports of the Security Services and other evidence, a significant number of Germans were shocked and even disgusted at such vandalism of property and brazen violations of public law and order.[6] On the other hand, not only ideological fanatics took part. Among the mindless mobs of looters, there were many ordinary Germans, incited to a fever pitch, who seized the opportunity to enrich themselves. Moreover, there was virtually no discernible public protest, not even from the churches, though Jewish houses of worship had been primary targets.

The pogrom had been incited and masterminded by Propaganda Minister Goebbels. It was he who had made the initial incendiary speech on 9 November in a Munich beer hall (commemorating the failed Nazi putsch of 1923) after news had come of vom Rath's murder. He called the diplomat's death the first shot in a new war between the Germans and Jews. His diaries reveal not only that the Führer was informed of every step but that Hitler explicitly wanted to make the Jews pay for the damage and to expropriate their businesses.[7] Publicly, however, the Führer preferred to distance himself, preserving an attitude of aloof detachment. Hitler's immediate concern was that the pogrom should be given the appearance of being a "spontaneous" expression of popular wrath against the Jews. The SS and SD (security services) leadership, which in principle rejected the methods of "rowdy anti-Semitism," quickly recovered from its initial surprise and found new opportunities in the aftermath to pursue its own agenda and establish a firmer grip on all policy-making that related to the "Jewish question."

Goebbels himself had been out of favor with Hitler since mid-1938 because of his messy affair with a Czech actress, a circumstance which may help to explain the particular zealousness he exhibited in calling for vengeance against the Jews. He, too, was eager to reestablish his own *locus standi* in Jewish policy but would certainly not have incited the pogrom without Hitler's prior authorization. Goering, on the other hand, who now supervised the "Aryanization" policy, was determined to keep the "Jewish question" as far as possible out of radical Nazi hands. Like Himmler and Heydrich, who respectively controlled the German police and the SD, he opposed methods of uncontrolled violence, preferring to tighten the net around German Jewry through administrative measures. Goering, in fact, considered actions like Kristallnacht to be serious public-relations blunders and deplorable lapses into "wild Aryanizations."[8] He wanted to seize Jewish property for the German state, not to see it destroyed by marauding mobs.

Moreover, he was initially alarmed at the insurance claims (estimated at 225 million reichsmarks) that could result. Himmler shared his disapproval, even writing in a memo that it was Goebbels's "megalomania" and "stupidity" that were primarily responsible for initiating an operation that could only exacerbate Germany's already difficult diplomatic relations. But whatever the policy differences and power struggles within the Nazi elite, there was no basic disagreement about the need for a "reckoning with the Jews."[9]

Kristallnacht was the most violent public display of anti-Semitism seen in German history since the Crusades. It also proved to be a significant turning point on the road to the Holocaust. Undoubtedly, the lessons that the Nazi leadership drew in its aftermath brought about a shift in its methods of persecution. At a marathon session in Goering's offices at the Reich Air Ministry on 12 November 1938, it was decided to levy a fine of one billion marks on German Jewry for what was styled its "hostile attitude" toward the German Reich and its people. After announcing the fine, Goering added cynically, "Moreover, I have to say once again that I would not wish to be a Jew in Germany."[10] The participants apparently felt that the public degradation they were inflicting in making Jews pay and even apologize for the huge damage caused by the Nazis, was not enough. Goebbels, Goering, and Heydrich took turns during the meeting in fantasizing about additional humiliations: that Jews should wear personal insignia, that they should have isolated compartments in trains or be forced to give up their seats to Germans, that they should be placed in forests alongside animals they resembled, and so on.[11] Goebbels suggested expelling Jewish children still in German schools, banning Jews from all public places, and imposing curfew restrictions. In the following month, the more concrete suggestions were promptly agreed to by Hitler; the momentum of the anti-Jewish campaign had indeed increased.[12]

The most practical outcome of the November 1938 meeting was the elimination of the Jews from the economy and the confiscation of all remaining Jewish factories and businesses. The department stores, major industrial concerns, and merchant banks that had been spared longest were now stripped, closed, or taken over.[13] An additional decree was issued to exclude Jews from the retail trade, crafts, and sales agencies, from managing firms, and from membership in any cooperatives. In a highly significant sentence at the outset of his remarks, Goering invoked directly the Führer's authority for these steps: "Gentlemen! Today's meeting is of a decisive character. I have received a letter written on the Führer's orders by [Martin] Bormann, the chief of staff of the Führer's deputy, requesting that the Jewish question be now, once and for all, coordinated and solved one way or the other" (*so oder so*).[14] *So oder so* was a key Hitler phrase in relation to the Jews—one that intimated that there would be no turning back. Nazi policy had clearly been radicalized by Kristallnacht. In its wake, all Jewish business enterprise, freedom of movement, and social intercourse with Germans was brought to a virtual end.[15] The scale and impunity of the violence had stigmatized the Jews, even more than before, as a pariah people, to be degraded at will, placed outside the ranks of society and the universe of moral obligation. Their existence on German soil was being torn up by the roots. Excluded from using public transport, from going to concerts, theaters, cinemas, shopping centers, beaches, and park benches and even from owning a dog, German Jews were not merely outcasts at the end of 1939: they were *socially dead* people. They could even lose their driving licenses because their presence on the roads might conceivably offend the "German traffic community." Three years later they would be obliged to wear the yellow stars that were to definitively seal their pariah status.

There was an immediate increase in the pressure on German and Austrian Jews to emigrate, which was still official Nazi policy. But there was also an upsurge in attitudes that hinted at what would eventually climax in the "Final Solution" a few years later. Thus, on 24 November 1938, the SS journal *Das Schwarze Korps,* under the heading JEWS, WHAT NOW? prophesied that Germans could not tolerate the presence of hundreds of thousands of Jewish "criminals" and "subhumans" much longer. Mocking the indifference and hypocrisy of the "civilized nations" and "the great screaming of world Jewry," it called for a solution that went beyond mere segregation. "We would be faced with the hard necessity of exterminating the Jewish underworld in the same way as, under our government of law and order, we are wont to exterminate any other criminals, namely by fire and sword. The result would be the factual and final end of Jewry in Germany, its absolute annihilation."[16] The mood was ripe for a revival of the apocalyptic anti-Semitism that identified Jews with the criminal "subhuman" underworld. Demonization had accompanied the Nazi campaign against Jewry since 1919, but now it seemed as if the Jews who were still left in Germany could more easily be branded as total outcasts and made to fit existing propaganda stereotypes. As Ian Kershaw has written, this depersonalization accentuated the numbing indifference of German popular opinion "and formed a vital stage between the archaic violence of the pogrom and the rationalised 'assembly line' annihilation of the death camps."[17]

Kristallnacht served another important function as a precursor for the dual war that Hitler was now feverishly planning. The conventional war for territorial hegemony and *Lebensraum* in the east and the "war against the Jews" entered a new phase of synchronization. Ever since 9 November 1918, the two themes had been closely connected in Hitler's mind. He told the Czech foreign minister in January 1939, "With us the Jews would be destroyed [*vernichtet*]; not for nothing had the Jews made November 9, 1918: this day will be avenged."[18] Now, on 9 November 1938, twenty years after the German surrender, the pogrom against the Jews was a means to psychologically prepare the German nation for a new European war. It was Hitler's way to disabuse the Germans of any idea that the Munich peace agreements two months earlier marked the end of the international political crisis.

Hitler's infamous Reichstag speech of 30 January 1939, delivered on the sixth anniversary of his accession to power, has to be seen in the context of a self-fulfilling prophecy and of a war that would have two faces.

> One thing I should like to say on this day which may be memorable for others as well as for us Germans: in the course of my life I have very often been a prophet, and have usually been ridiculed for it. During the time of my struggle for power it was in the first instance the Jewish race which only received my prophecies with laughter when I said that one day I would take over the leadership of the State, and with it that of the whole nation, and that I would then, among many other things settle the Jewish problem. Their laughter was uproarious, but I think that for some time now they have been laughing on the other side of their face. Today I will once more be a prophet: if the international Jewish financiers in and outside Europe should succeed in plunging the nations once more into a world war, then the result will not be the bolshevisation of the earth, and thus the victory of Jewry, but the annihilation of the Jewish race in Europe![19]

This was an extraordinary outburst from the leader of a great power and can hardly be reduced to a mere "metaphor" or a piece of utopian rhetoric, as the German historian Hans Mommsen has tried to do.[20] The vehemence with which Hitler delivered this particular section of his speech, and the frenzied applause of the Reichstag delegates, makes it plain that it was a deadly serious threat. But it has to be analyzed at several different levels. The most immediate target was world Jewry, which Hitler typically held responsible for the mounting criticism of his regime after Kristallnacht. He was warning those who did not yet comprehend what he already knew with inner certainty because it lay at the very heart of his personality and mission—namely, his will to exterminate the

Jews. But it was also a threat against the Western democracies. Had he not repeatedly declared his willingness to collaborate with other states in seeking an "international solution" to the "Jewish question"? In return, he had heard only the sanctimonious hypocrisy of the liberal democracies, complaining of "this barbaric expulsion from Germany of such an irreplaceable and culturally eminently valuable element."[21]

Hitler knew that neither British nor American politicians had been willing to put their reproving speeches into practice. Did the Evian Conference not conclusively demonstrate that in the wide empty expanses of the British empire, the United States, and Latin America, no room could be found for Jewish refugees? Hitler nevertheless dispatched former Economics Minister Schacht on one last trip to England, to see if he could not reach an agreement with the American negotiator, George Rublee, to ransom German Jewry.[22] The Nazi plan was that world Jewry and the democracies would bankroll the emigration of the German Jews through a loan of 1.5 billion Reichsmarks, to be repaid in ten years' time through German exports. Acceding to this blackmail would in effect have meant financially rewarding the Nazis for their expropriation and expulsion of the Jews, though Hitler did not see it that way. He had no reason to keep the Jews in Germany alive except as a bargaining chip in his cat-and-mouse game of war and peace with the West.

But there was yet another, more sinister level to this "prophecy," which can be better understood in the light of Hitler's earlier remarks to South African Defense Minister Oswald Pirow in Berlin on 24 November 1938. He had told his pro-German guest that "world Jewry" (which in this case seemed to refer primarily to American Jews) regarded their European coreligionists as "the advance troops for the Bolshevization of the world"; he had spoken heatedly of the Jewish "invasion" from the east and declared that his mind was irrevocably made up: "One day the Jews would disappear from Europe [*Die Juden würden... aus Europa verschwinden*]."[23]

In his Reichstag speech two months later, this prospect was more specifically linked to the outbreak of a world war. The prophecy of annihilation was impersonally couched, but it clearly related to the *physical* destruction of European Jewry, especially if there should be any involvement of the United States and American Jewry (linked in Hitler's mind to the international Jewish financiers "outside Europe"). The constant references during the war years to his January 1939 prophecy, especially after the "Final Solution" had begun, cannot be accidental. Twice in 1942 and three more times in 1943 he recalled his words, but each time he confused the date of his speech about "annihilation" (30 January) with the outbreak of war in September 1939.[24] Such a compulsively repeated "mistake" is in itself remarkable. For Hitler, the world war and the "war against the Jews" seem to have been one and the same confrontation. So, too, the "prophet" and the *Realpolitiker* were one and the same person. The prophet was there to give periodic expression to the dark fantasies of *Sieg oder Untergang;* the politician proceeded more pragmatically, with the requisite tactical flexibility, adapting himself to the shifting international and diplomatic constellation.

Between 1933 and 1939, Nazi policies on the "Jewish question" had been influenced, as we have seen, by many contradictory currents within the German state and society, as well as by forces beyond it. Although the Jews were perceived in unwavering terms by the Nazi leadership as a deadly "enemy" to be isolated and removed from Germany, there was as yet no clear plan to exterminate them physically. In retrospect, one can see that the measures of economic boycott, legal exclusion, and defamation had been carried out with some caution compared to the avalanche that followed. The Nuremberg Race Laws had marked an important advance in realizing the Nazi Party program, but they had not shattered the institutions and will to live of German Jewry or the foundations of its economic existence. At the same time, despite their massively discriminatory character, the racial laws did not encounter any significant opposition from the conservative elites, the churches, the business circles, the intellectuals, or the mass of the German population. Thus it would seem that at least until November 1938 (and possibly beyond) there was public consensus on the "Jewish question" within which the Nazi regime still operated.

The increasingly visible movement in 1938–1939 toward the more radical policy of expelling Jews entirely was an important qualitative change in this situation. It could doubtless be rationalized in bureaucratic logic as the next stage of squeezing the Jews out of Germany, without any clear notion of what should follow. But while the central role of the bureaucracy and of internal power struggles over the right to influence the anti-Jewish policy is apparent, one can hardly ignore the crucial part played by Hitler in providing the dynamics and the momentum. As Goering tersely put it: "In the last analysis, it is the Führer alone who decides."[25] This was especially true with regard to grave decisions, such as those of war and peace or concerning the when, where, and how of the Holocaust. Only in Hitler's mind were war and genocide so closely related. It was his apocalyptic perspective that presupposed the globalization of the "Jewish question" in 1939, in the context of a coming world war. Once Germany was engaged, after September 1939, in a war against Poland, Great Britain, and France that it seemed to be winning, the door was open for a complete "removal" of the Jews of Europe, though not yet their complete destruction. The invasion of the USSR in June 1941 would bring in its wake a more violent and far-reaching extension toward a comprehensive "solution," leading to the beginnings of a streamlined annihilation of European Jews. Finally, with the entry in December 1941 of the United States into the war, the last remaining constraints on the organizational coordination of this plan were removed, and it became fully operational. The conflict had truly become a *world war*, and there was no further point in holding

European Jews as potential hostages for the "good conduct" of their American coreligionists.

What linked these stages was the intense Nazi commitment to the ideological fantasy that they were fighting a "great racial war" in which either the "German-Aryans" or the Jews must prevail and eventually rule the world. The overall Nazi project remained the racial "purification" and reorganization of Europe along ethnic lines, involving the resettlement and relocation of entire populations.[26] Within that overarching biological-political framework, the Jews were, however, a special case. For the "Final Solution" did indeed suggest *finality:* it was a plan to hunt down and kill every Jewish man, woman, or child from Paris to Bialystok, from Amsterdam to Rhodes. The comprehensive totality of this genocidal project is what differentiated the Holocaust from the massive Nazi violence inflicted on Poles, Russians, Ukrainians, Serbs, and Gypsies, not to mention the so-called mercy killings of ethnic Germans and the starvation of millions of Soviet POWs, or the torture of Communists and persecution of homosexuals and Jehovah's Witnesses.[27]

The implacable nature of the Nazi campaign against the Jews derived from their special status as a *Weltfeind* (world-enemy). Implicit in this ideological conception was the proposition that even successfully solving the problem of German Jewry (for example by complete emigration) could never bring the "Jewish question" to a close. For at the core of the conflict was the demonic Jewish world power that would always seek to destroy Germany, National Socialism, and so-called Aryan civilization. The satanic quality of the adversary also meant that "international Jewry" would constantly seek to widen the war and intensify the struggle in order to spill ever more precious German blood on the battlefield. Within this phantasmagoric logic of racial war, the most extreme measures could therefore be justified in advance as actions of imagined self-defense. Yet the simple truth remained that

Jews as a group were weak, vulnerable, and at no time had harbored any aggressive designs against Germany.

There was, however, one empirical reality that the Nazis could not ignore. The military occupation of Poland had at one stroke added more than two million Polish Jews to the Jewish population at Hitler's mercy. (And as a result of the Nazi-Soviet pact, just over one million Jews in eastern Poland were to fall under Russian rule from September 1939 until June 1941.) This dramatic increase bedeviled the Nazis in their frantic efforts to create territories that were *Judenrein*. Each time they annexed or conquered an area, they acquired more Jews than they were managing to remove by encouraging emigration. Thus, after the *Anschluss* of March 1938, two hundred thousand Austrian Jews had entered the Reich. Following the rape of the Czech lands a year later, another 120,000 Jews came under Nazi control. After the collapse of Poland, further victories of the Wehrmacht in the West, and then the conquest of the Baltic states, White Russia, the Ukraine, Galicia, the Crimea, and other lands to the east hugely swelled the numbers of Jews in Nazi hands. What was to be done with them? In Warsaw alone, there were as many Jews in 1939 (about 330,000) as in the whole of the Reich. As Ostjuden, they had long been objects of German fear and prejudice. Nazi propaganda now made sure that no German would ever forget that they were permanent sources of dirt, infectious disease, criminality, and Bolshevism and were the heart of the "world Jewish problem." Goebbels, after visiting the Lódz ghetto, on 2 November 1939, wrote in his diary, "It's indescribable. These are not human beings any more, they are animals. Therefore, we have not a humanitarian task to perform, but a surgical one. One must cut here, in a radical way. Otherwise, one day, Europe will perish of the Jewish disease."[28]

Goebbels, like many radical Nazi anti-Semites, regarded the eastern Jew as the quintessential animal-like "other," symbolizing pestilence and life-threatening disease. He had visited the ghetto to supervise the production of the violently anti-Semitic film *The Eternal Jew*, eventually screened in 1940. In an earlier diary entry of 17 October 1939, Goebbels was even more explicit: "Pictures from the 'Ghetto' film. Such a thing never existed before. Scenes so dreadful and brutal in their details that one's blood freezes. One pulls back in horror at so much brutality. This Jewry must be exterminated."[29] It is almost as if Goebbels was unconsciously offering a preview of the mind-set behind the decision to launch the Holocaust. On the same day in his diary entry for 17 October, Goebbels notes that he had mentioned the film to Hitler, who "showed great interest."[30]

The German invasion of Poland immediately resulted in the sadistic humiliation of Polish Jewry (Orthodox Jews often had their beards and sidelocks ripped off) and the murder of some seven thousand Jews in the first three months of the campaign. On 21 September 1939, Heydrich set out the guidelines of SS policy in his instructions to the Einsatzgruppen. He distinguished between the "final aim" and the stages leading toward it, beginning with "the concentration of the Jews from the countryside into the larger cities." The points of concentration were to be cities with rail junctions "or at least located on railroad lines." He also ordered each Jewish community to set up a Council of Jewish Elders, an administrative body consisting of authoritative personalities and rabbis who would be responsible "for the exact and prompt implementation of directives already issued or to be issued in the future."[31]

The councils (*Judenräte*) would also be held responsible for the evacuation of Jews from the countryside, for housing, transport, tax collection, labor allocation, hospitals, schools, orphanages, sewage disposal, and other community functions. The councils were to become a kind of horrible caricature of Jewish government, mediating between the fearfully oppressed Jewish population (who often resented their power) and the Nazi authorities to whom they were wholly subordinate. The council leaders were under constant and tremendous stress, having to face daily pressures of Nazi extortion, reprisals, exactions, and levies, as well as the desperate anguish of the starving Jewish population.[32] Knowingly or unknowingly, they presided over doomed communities. The composition of the councils was usually middle class, selected from merchants, doctors, lawyers, and other professionals who had usually been active in Jewish public life before the war. Sometimes they were selected on Nazi orders by prominent persons in the community; at other times the selection was quite arbitrary. Refusal to serve more often than not meant death. For the Nazis, a *Judenrat* was an instrument for dominating and ruling the ghetto, a valuable executor of their policies, saving them the tasks of policing and enforcing their own decrees.

By making the councils responsible for life-and-death decisions, such as who would be handed over to the Germans for deportation to the death camps—the first of which had been established at the end of 1941—the Nazi rulers managed to implicate the Jewish leadership in the bureaucratic process of destruction. In effect, according to Raul Hilberg's highly critical view of their role, Jews ended up providing the Germans with administrative personnel that enabled the machinery of annihilation to function more smoothly. In his view, the Jewish response pattern, fashioned by two thousand years of ghetto history, was one of alleviation, evasion, paralysis, and compliance.[33] Prior to the Holocaust, Jews "could avert or survive destruction by placating or appeasing their enemies."[34] Confronted by Nazi terror, they could not adapt. Under such degrading conditions, some Jews even collaborated with the enemy. For example, the much-hated Jewish police force was directly responsible for physically rounding up deportees and pushing them onto trains, which made them accessories to the extermination of fellow Jews. They were part of a privileged power structure, which was bound to lead to corruption, as well as severely undermine Jewish solidarity.

But they, too, were coerced, often by means of the cruelest blackmail. Finally, Hilberg has argued that the councils induced a fatally illusory feeling of "normality" and submissive Jewish behavior that greatly facilitated the work of the Nazis.

Hannah Arendt went even further and regarded such collaboration as a symptom of the "moral collapse" that Nazism caused throughout respectable European society, among persecutors, bystanders, and victims alike. "The whole truth was that if the Jewish people had been disorganized and leaderless, there would have been chaos and plenty of misery but the total number of dead would hardly have been six million."[35] This highly simplistic verdict ignores not only the circumstances and context but also the wide range of responses among Jewish council leaders. Some were no doubt guilty of complicity or corrupted by their power, while others tried to protect Jewish interests as best they could. The head of the Warsaw *Judenrat*, industrial engineer Adam Czerniakow, who committed suicide in 1942 when the Nazis began to demand ten thousand "nonproductive" Jews per day for "resettlement," which invariably meant liquidation, was a good example of a council leader who desperately sought salvation for Jews. A courageous man, constantly intervening with the Germans to alleviate their inhuman regulations, Czerniakow in his diary conveys an overwhelming sense of powerlessness and failure.[36] By July 1942, more than one hundred thousand Jews in the Warsaw ghetto had perished as a result of starvation and disease, especially typhoid and dysentery.

Czerniakow despised his counterpart in Lódz, the "king" of the local *Judenrat*, Mordechai Rumkowski, as "self-important," arrogant, and stupid. Rumkowski, who flamboyantly rode in a horse-drawn carriage and issued banknotes with his portrait on them, had clearly developed megalomaniac tendencies. Yet Rumkowski pursued an identical strategy of "rescue through work" in the hope that economic rationality might win out over Nazi ideological fanaticism. Increased productivity became a goal in itself despite the starvation.

Rumkowski organized the 180,000 ghetto inhabitants efficiently and tyrannically, deciding who was to live and who to die. His reasoning illustrated the horror of the Jewish predicament: "I must cut off the limbs to save the body itself. I must take the children because if not, others will be taken, as well."[37] Like the chairman of the Vilna *Judenrat*, Jacob Gens, Rumkowski believed in the bargaining process, providing the Germans with all the Jews they demanded in the vain hope of thereby protecting and saving those who remained. Gens was no less authoritarian in his leadership style than Rumkowski and equally convinced that only his methods offered any hope for the constantly squabbling and fractious Jewish community. Opinions about his role remain divided, but the charge of collaboration is hard to refute. Gens was shot by the Gestapo a few days before the liquidation of the Vilna ghetto, while Rumkowski went to the gas chambers in 1944, along with most of the inhabitants of the Lódz ghetto after the deportations began in the middle of 1942.

Ghettos had been established throughout Poland from the end of 1939. The largest of them all was the Warsaw ghetto, which suffered from obscene overcrowding, holding as many as half a million Jews at its peak. Sealed off in November 1940 by barbed wire from the rest of the city (though there was an active smuggling route), the population was packed into 1.3 square miles, compared to the area of 53.3 square miles inhabited by fewer than one million Polish Christians. The gates to the ghetto were guarded by German, Polish, and Jewish police. Inside this living hell, Jews were forbidden to keep cash or merchandise. They lived in complete economic isolation from the outside world. When pressed into forced labor, the Jews were paid nothing or else a tiny sum, usually insufficient to buy even a loaf of stale bread. In the largest ghettos, Warsaw and Lódz, about one quarter of the Jews died from disease, starvation, and the inhumanly harsh conditions. The Nazis spuriously claimed that they had created the ghettos to prevent the spread of epidemics, but their insidious propa ganda goal was to mark off the Jews as people who were not only different but physically degenerate. By starving them, they could ensure that reality resembled the stereotype, even as they decimated them. A contemporary chronicler of the Warsaw ghetto, Chaim Kaplan, who wrote poignantly about "the gigantic catastrophe" that had descended upon Polish Jewry, commented in his diary on 10 March 1940 that the depth of Nazi anti-Semitic hatred went far beyond political ideology.[38]

> It is a hatred of emotion, whose source is some psychopathic disease. In its outward manifestation it appears as physiological hatred, which sees the object of its hatred as tainted in body, as lepers who have no place in society.... But the founders of Nazism and the party leaders created a theoretical ideology with deeper foundations. They have a complete doctrine which represents the Jewish spirit inside out. Judaism and Nazism are two attitudes to the world that are incompatible, and for this reason they cannot co-exist side by side. For 2,000 years Judaism has left its imprint, culturally and spiritually, on the nations of the world. It stood fast, blocking the spread of German paganism.... Two kings cannot wear one crown. Either humanity would be Judaic or it would be pagan-German. Up until now it was Judaic. Even Catholicism is a child of Judaism, and the fruit of its spirit.... The new world which Nazism would fashion, would be pagan, primordial, in all its attitudes. It is therefore ready to fight Judaism to the finish.[39]

Kaplan had grasped something of the violently pagan essence of Nazism while insisting on the extraordinary vitality of Judaism even in the midst of the inferno.

Though Polish Jewry outwardly lay crushed and broken amid the terrible suffering inflicted upon it by its Nazi conquerors, most Jews had not lost their vibrant will to live, love of life, or indomitable spirit. Kaplan records the extraordinary atmosphere a few months after the Warsaw ghetto was sealed: "In the daytime, when the sun is shining, the ghetto groans. But at night everyone is dancing even though his stomach is empty. Quiet, discreet evening music accompanies the dancing. It is almost a *mitzvah* to dance. The more one dances, the more it is a sign of his belief in the 'eternity of Israel'. Every dance is a protest against our oppressors."[40]

Despite their desperate situation, Jews managed to set up study groups, lending libraries, and underground schools in the ghettos. There were committees that provided child care and charity for the needy as well as a wide variety of cultural activities. Ghetto dwellers sought, despite the tragic circumstances, to preserve (as best they could) their fidelity to tradition and Jewish religious values. Torah scrolls were salvaged, and Talmud study, prayer, bar-mitzvah celebrations, and Hebrew-language classes continued. Chaim Kaplan wrote in his diary on 2 October 1940, on the eve of the High Holy Days: "Again: everything is forbidden to us; and yet we do everything! We make our 'living' in ways that are forbidden.... It is the same with community prayers: secret *minyanim* in their hundreds all over Warsaw hold prayers together and do not leave out even the most difficult hymns. Neither preachers nor sermons are missing; everything is in accordance with the ancient traditions of Israel."[41]

This was a spiritual self-affirmation no less significant than more obviously political and military forms of resistance. Despite the gnawing hunger and recurring outbreaks of typhus, the tenacity with which the intelligentsia in the Warsaw ghetto fought to keep alive the cultural heritage of such a highly diverse community was truly remarkable.[42] Concerts, seminars, literary evenings, and discussions were held regularly at the Judaic Library. There were festivals of Jewish culture and music. Poets and prose writers recited from their works, chamber music was played, plays were performed. The classics and more recent works of world literature were avidly read. Orphanages, too—like that of Janusz Korczak—ran cultural programs for the general public, reaching members of the Jewish community who had never previously attended such events.[43] There were so-called children's corners, where, apart from food, children were offered some form of education and entertainment.

Such intense cultural activities eloquently testify to the refusal of Polish Jewry to accept their degradation to the level of beasts, which the Germans tried by every conceivable means to impose upon them. Notwithstanding their awareness of impending catastrophe, they were determined to fight for their individual and collective Jewish identity, for their human dignity and some form of national survival, however remote the prospects might seem.[44] The common cliché that Jews did not resist their persecutors and simply went "like sheep to the slaughter" is neither an accurate nor a fair description, though in its original context the phrase was intended by the Jewish Resistance more as a call to arms. When presented as a blanket criticism, it overlooks the extraordinary lengths to which the Nazis went in disguising the genocidal intent of their policy toward the Jews. The perpetrators deliberately encouraged false hopes and the illusion that compliance and work might be the salvation of Jewry.

The slogan of "sheep to the slaughter" also overlooks the fact that the notion of total physical extermination was not only unprecedented but must have seemed to most Jews (and Gentiles) like the product of a diseased imagination. It underestimates the state of sheer exhaustion and demoralization in which the ghettoized Jews found themselves and the degree to which they were isolated and cut off from the outside world. It ignores the intimidating effects of collective punishment as practiced by the Nazis whenever they were faced with even the most trivial and minor acts of defiance. The knowledge that the Germans would exact terrible reprisals was a serious disincentive all over Europe to any armed resistance. There were relatively few efforts at revolt, for example, by the many well-trained Allied soldiers and the hundreds of thousands of Russian prisoners of war in German camps, though they were watched over by a fairly small number of guards. Charges of passivity have rarely been made against them. Yet Western prisoners were not subjected to the unrelenting dehumanization that was the common fate of the Jews in the ghettos and the Nazi camps.

The Jewish population, to a much greater extent than any other, had the terrifying experience of being hunted down like wild animals. To make matters worse, they found themselves—at least in eastern Europe—in a generally hostile and anti-Semitic environment. Even in the event of escape, Jewish men were still marked by circumcision, often easily identified by their beards and facial features or else by their distinctive garb. Despite these great obstacles, Jews did subsequently rebel in the ghettos of Warsaw and Bialystok, in the death camps of Treblinka, Sobibór, and Auschwitz, and took up arms with the partisans wherever they succeeded in escaping their tormentors. It was probably no accident that the progenitors of militant resistance came from Lithuanian Jewry, the first to be subjected to savage and massive killing conducted by the Germans, with enthusiastic participation from the local population.[45] It was as if they sensed that Lithuania was a kind of experimental laboratory for the "Final Solution." This realization gave birth to the armed struggle in the Vilna ghetto in January 1942. It was based on the prophetic insight of the Zionist Pioneer Youth Group (Hashomer Ha-Tsair) that "Hitler aims to destroy all the Jews of Europe" and that the Lithuanian Jews were "fated to be the first in line."[46] In his manifesto of 31 December 1941, Abba Kovner, the leader of the group, warned that only one quarter of the eighty thousand Jews of Vilna remained and that those taken from the ghetto would never return. It was in this context that he added, "Let us not be led like sheep to the slaughter. True we are weak and helpless, but the only response to the murders is self-defence."[47] The revolt was a desperate gesture of defiance that led to the formation of a United Partisan Organization, drawn from all groups in Jewish political life but principally Zionists, Bundists, and Communists. The Jewish youth groups were unburdened by family responsibilities and more receptive to revolutionary action. They instinctively opposed those *Judenräte* that advocated obedience and passivity in the vain hope of warding off greater evils. In the summer of 1943, some of the young Jewish fighters managed to escape from the Vilna ghetto, forming partisan units and contributing to the eventual liberation of their city.

Armed revolts also broke out elsewhere in at least twenty ghettos in eastern Europe, the best known of them being the uprising in the Warsaw ghetto, which lasted from 19 April until 15 May 1943.[48] It was the first armed rebellion by civilians anywhere in Nazi-occupied Europe, taking the Germans completely by surprise. The ghetto fighters consisted initially of the six-hundred-member Jewish Fighting Organization, led by twenty-four-year-old Mordechai Anielewicz, and the National Military Organization, which had four hundred men and women in its force. Armed with only a few machine guns and rifles and a larger number of grenades and Molotov cocktails, the ghetto fighters had little training and minimal help from the local Polish resistance. They had witnessed the disappearance of the bulk of the ghetto inhabitants, whether through deportations to the death camps or by death from starvation and disease. The remaining sixty thousand Jews in the ghetto, many of them teenagers, were the most able-bodied survivors, who had been left for last. When the SS entered the ghetto to round up more Jews for deportation, to their great astonishment they were met by bombs, shooting, and mine explosions. It eventually took three thousand troops under the command of SS General Jürgen Stroop, equipped with heavy machine guns, howitzers, artillery, and armored vehicles—subsequently reinforced by bombers and tanks—to overcome the hopelessly outgunned Jewish resistance. The Jews held on in the sewers until the ghetto had been totally razed by German forces, some of the fighters jumping from the burning buildings rather than surrendering to their oppressors. They knew from the outset that they were engaged in a hopeless battle, but they were determined to die with honor and dignity. In his last letter from the ghetto on 23 April 1943, Mordechai Anielewicz observed that "what happened exceeded our boldest dreams" and that "what we dared do is of great, enormous importance."[49] He had no illusions about his own fate or that of his comrades. What mattered most was that self-defense in the ghetto and Jewish armed resistance had finally become a reality. More than fifteen thousand Jews died in battle, and more than fifty thousand were captured and sent to death camps.

It is important to note that there were also revolts in the death camps themselves, including one at Auschwitz-Birkenau, where prisoners blew up one of the crematoriums, killing several SS guards; there was also a much bigger rising in Treblinka (August 1943). At Sobibór, on 14 October 1943, several hundred prisoners stormed the gates in a rebellion that led to the shutting down of the camp two days later. Though a majority of the prisoners perished in the breakout attempt, more than one hundred managed to escape, many joining partisan units in the forests. Tens of thousands of Jews across Nazi-occupied Europe took part in the various partisan or resistance movements, some to seek revenge on their murderous enemy, others to save their own lives and, where possible, those of their fellow Jews. Jewish partisans fought bravely in the forests of the Ukraine and Poland, in the Carpathian mountains, and in white Russia and Lithuania.[50] In eastern Europe, the partisan activity usually took place in exclusively Jewish units because of the open hostility from the local populations. Sometimes this antagonism extended to the anti-Nazi partisan groups, which in Poland and elsewhere were not infrequently riddled with anti-Semitism. The Jewish Brigade formed in the forests near Vilna under Abba Kovner was the most celebrated of all the Jewish partisan groups. Other focal points of Jewish resistance were in the areas of

Bialystok, Kovno, and Minsk, where Jews were prominent from 1943 in the multinational partisan units under Soviet control. The Soviet High Command, as a matter of principle, did not approve or permit the existence of separate Jewish partisan units.[51] In southern and western Europe, Jews faced a less overt form of hostility from the indigenous population and found it easier to operate as part of the national resistance movements in France, Belgium, Holland, Italy, Greece, and Yugoslavia (where about two thousand Jews fought in the ranks of Marshal Tito's guerrilla movement).[52] Despite the adverse conditions, Jews were also prominent among the founders of the partisan movement in Slovakia, with at least 2,500 Jews fighting in the Slovak national rebellion in the summer of 1944.

In France, Jews at one stage represented more than 15 percent of the resistance forces, more than twenty times their proportion of the total population. Their role in positions of leadership and command as well as in the rank and file of the resistance was outstanding. Half of the founders of *Libération* were Jews, and they were almost 20 percent of the members of the National Committee, the highest institution of the French underground. The founder of the Franc Tireurs et Partisans in the Paris region in 1942–1943 was a Jew, as were a disproportionate number of those who rallied to Charles de Gaulle's Free French forces in London. Often enough, the Jewish resistance fighters in France and western Europe suppressed the fact of their Jewishness. Sometimes this was for security reasons; others may have believed that it would not help the Allied cause, either because the Germans and their French collaborators at Vichy would exploit the fact or out of fear that it might arouse latent anti-Jewish feelings in the Resistance.[53] No doubt many also felt their French identity to be more important than their Jewish loyalties or origins. The relatively high number of Jews in the French Communist resistance was also downplayed, both by Jews themselves and by the Communist Party. Mostly this was for political and ideological reasons not dissimilar from those prevailing in the wartime Soviet Union and eastern Europe. One result of this discretion has been that the story of Jewish resistance in the Holocaust period is less known than it should be, except in Israel, where it assumed overriding importance, though the dominant narratives are often distinctly selective. If we also consider the heroism and skill of the more than half a million Jewish soldiers in the ranks of the Red Army, as well as the distinguished service of more than seven hundred thousand Jews in the British and American armies (not to mention other Allied forces), then the military contribution of Jews to the defeat of Nazi Germany was by no means negligible. Approximately 10 percent of world Jewry (1.6 million out of 16 million) actually fought in the war, including the thirty-five thousand Palestinian Jews who volunteered for the Jewish Brigade in the British Army.

Within Germany itself, there was virtually no armed resistance of any sort, and thus no armed Jewish resistance either. But a significantly high proportion of German (and Austrian) Jews who emigrated from the Reich before 1939 did become involved in Belgian, Dutch, Italian, and French resistance to fascism and in efforts to sabotage the German occupation. Those Jews who remained in Germany had no possibility of direct political resistance, but this did not deter either the rabbis or the official representatives of the German Jewish community from making dignified protests against the persecutions and the first deportations to the east.[54] Moreover, the Jewish press in the Third Reich, for as long as it survived, was without doubt the last enclave of liberal and humanist values. Between the lines, one can read many instances in its pages of veiled protest against the state-sponsored propaganda that mercilessly degraded Jews.[55]

Despite the totally isolated and vulnerable position of German Jewry in the Third Reich, there were probably between two and three thousand Jews, mainly young people, directly active in the German anti-Nazi underground.[56] This is a remarkably high number given that there were only two hundred thousand Jews left in Germany at the outbreak of war in September 1939. (The proportional equivalent of such a figure for the German population would have been about seven hundred thousand antifascist militants, of which there is certainly no evidence.) However, it needs to be remembered that the Jewish antifascists (mainly socialists and Communists) generally felt that their affinities and first loyalties were to the German workers' movement. Jews were especially numerous in the German Communist resistance, which included the wholly Jewish underground group led by Herbert Baum that was responsible for the courageous though ill-conceived and disastrous attack on the Nazi propaganda exhibition *Das Sowjetparadies* (the Soviet paradise) in the Berlin Lustgarten. The boys and girls of the Baum group were atheists, and their alienation from Jewry was fully reciprocated by Jewish communal feelings about Communist agitation.[57] It did not help that the Communists periodically indulged in crude propaganda against "Jewish capitalists," even after such a social group had ceased to exist in Germany. On the other hand, following Kristallnacht, the Communist underground press did display some real signs of solidarity with the persecuted Jewish population.[58] Despite the nondemocratic, totalitarian character of their organization and ideology, the Communists were particularly prominent among those who made the greatest sacrifices within the limited German resistance.

The Jewish youth movement in Nazi Germany (which reflected a diversity of cultural and political trends within German Jewry) was a favorable seedbed for antifascist activity. This derived partly from the strong socialist orientation of many of the Zionist youth groups, dating back to the days of the Weimar Republic. The movement led a unique existence under the Third Reich, preserving under the noses of the Gestapo the more humanistic aspects of the pre-1933 German culture, which were fast disappearing in society as a

whole. Until it was banned, the Jewish youth movement provided what Arnold Paucker has called "an oasis of free thinking in a totalitarian Germany" that continued to flourish and
stimulate anti-Nazi activity.[59] Later, during the terrible war
years, antifascist Jews in Germany and outside carried on
more dangerous illegal actions ranging from sabotage, assassination attempts, and pacifist propaganda to helping Allied
POWs to escape. These activities, like those of Jews in other
areas of the resistance, had many motivations and were not
always inspired by the "Jewishness" of the individual participants. Nevertheless, the prominence of many Jews in the resistance was not unconnected to their principled and strong
emotional identification as members of a specially persecuted minority group.

4

THE "FINAL SOLUTION"

If just once, at the beginning or during the course of the [First World] war, we had exposed twelve or fifteen thousand of those Hebrew corrupters of the people to poison gas ... the sacrifice of millions of men would not have been in vain. On the contrary, if we had rid ourselves of those twelve or fifteen thousand fiends, we might perhaps have saved the lives of a million good brave Germans.

ADOLF HITLER, *Mein Kampf* (1925)

And then they all come, those worthy eighty million Germans, and each one has his own decent Jew. Of all who talk that way, none of them has watched, none of them has gone through it. Most of you know what it means to see one hundred bodies lying there, five hundred lying there or one thousand lying there. To have gone through this and, aside from exceptions due to human weakness, to have remained decent, that has made us tough.

HEINRICH HIMMLER, *speech to higher SS and police leaders, Poznan,* October 1943

It is sometimes forgotten that Jews were not the primary target of the Nazis in the first eighteen months after the invasion of Poland in September 1939. The Germans, having decided in agreement with the Soviet Union on the destruction of the Polish state, proceeded to eliminate its elites, to "transfer" parts of its population eastward, to extinguish any manifestation of its national identity, and to reduce the mass of its people to helotry. In 1939 and 1940, close to ten thousand Polish intellectuals, members of the nobility, and clergy were killed by the Einsatzgruppen in a deliberate effort to crush resistance. In the wake of the killers came German economists, technical experts, and academic planners who calculated that much of Poland's rural population was "nothing more than dead weight," whose continued presence was an obstacle to industrial "development" and to Germany's economic interests. "Negative demographic policy"—a technocratic concept emanating from Goering's Four-year Plan Agency—envisaged organizing the deaths of millions of Poles (and later Russians) as a solution to problems of food supply as the war was extended.[1] It was no accident that two million Soviet prisoners of war were allowed to die of starvation in German camps before the end of 1941. Goering himself predicted in November 1941 that "twenty to thirty million people will starve in Russia." Perhaps, he cynically added, that was a good thing, "since certain people will have to be decimated." New strategies of racial reordering, in the name of "Germanization" and a settlement policy for the conquered territories, were being devised in the framework of Himmler's Generalplan Ost, which covered the whole area between Leningrad and the Crimea.[2]

During the 1939–1941 period, however, the Nazis had not worked out a clear, consistent policy with regard to Jews, Poles, or even the half-million ethnic Germans they had "repatriated" to German-annexed territory. On 25 May 1940, Himmler had submitted a secret memorandum, entitled "Reflections on the Treatment of the Peoples of Alien Race in the East," to Hitler. With regard to the non-German population as a whole, he made it clear that the sole aim of schooling the "subhuman people of the East" must be to teach them simple arithmetic, the ability to write their own names, and the inclination "to obey the Germans."[3] The Poles were to be treated as "a people of laborers without leaders" whose main task was to provide the Reich with migrant workers. Without any qualms, Himmler also advocated kidnapping "racially" valuable Polish "children of good blood" (blond, blue-eyed, and Nordic-looking) and sending them to the Reich to be brought up as "Aryans." At this early stage, Himmler explicitly rejected "as un-German and impossible the Bolshevist method of physical extermination of a people." Instead, he appeared to be relying on a mixture of "racial sifting," resettlement, and the splitting up of the different ethnic groups in eastern Europe "into as many parts and fragments as possible." He also hoped that "the concept of Jews will be completely extinguished through the possibility of a large emigration of all Jews to Africa or some other colony."[4]

Himmler was probably alluding to the idea being seriously considered in leading Nazi circles of deporting Jews en masse to the East African tropical island of Madagascar, then a French colony. In 1937, the Polish government had approached the French and British about sending a million Polish Jews either there or to southern Africa. Now, following the defeat of France, Franz Rademacher (the official responsible for Jewish affairs at the German Foreign Ministry) had drawn up a memorandum envisaging the deportation of four million Jews from Europe and their resettlement in Madagascar, once the island was transferred from French to German control.

The funds would naturally be provided by the despoiled Jews. They would supposedly enjoy nominal self-government in the administration of the law courts, culture, and economic life but would ultimately be under the "expert" control of the SS. Of course, the deported Jews would be stripped of German or any other European citizenships, becoming instead citizens of the "great ghetto" henceforth to be known as the Madagascar Mandate.[5] Rademacher even saw this project as a useful Nazi response to Zionist ambitions in Palestine: "This arrangement will prevent the possible establishment of a Vatican State of their own, in Palestine by the Jews, thus preventing them from using for their own purposes the symbolic value which Jerusalem has for the Christian and Mohammedan portions of the world."[6]

More ominously, Rademacher added that "the Jews will remain in German hands as a pledge for the future good conduct of the members of their race in America." The Rademacher plan had the approval of Foreign Minister Joachim von Ribbentrop and was taken seriously (with some modifications) by Heydrich and his SS bureaucrats, as long as their domination of the project could be assured. But the German failure to defeat Great Britain in 1940 meant that control of sea traffic in the Atlantic, which was essential to the success of the plan, could not be assured. Although the plan was still sometimes referred to by Hitler in conversations with Benito Mussolini and other foreign leaders, the African solution was soon quietly shelved. Formally, however, it was only on 10 February 1942 that Foreign Office departments finally received an official confirmation from Rademacher of what Hitler had decided several months earlier: "The war with the Soviet Union has in the meantime created the possibility of disposing of other territories for the Final Solution. In consequence, the Führer has decided the Jews should be evacuated not to Madagascar, but to the East. Madagascar need no longer therefore be considered in connection with the Final Solution."[7]

The German invasion of the Soviet Union in June 1941, code-named Operation Barbarossa, was indeed inextricably linked with the decision to implement a genocidal war against all the Jews of Europe. It also cost the lives of twenty million Soviet citizens (more than half of whom were civilians), including three million Red Army POWs. In this gigantic confrontation, which has been rightly called "the most savage military campaign in modern history," all traditional conventions of behavior, let alone ethical or legal restraints, were wholly abandoned.[8] In the so-called Commissar Order of 6 June 1941, the German Army was specifically told by its commanders not to show any mercy or "respect for international law" in the fight against Bolshevism, especially against "political commissars of all kinds." This Communist enemy allegedly employed "barbaric, Asiatic fighting methods" that necessitated the immediate execution of all Red Army political officers. Some six hundred thousand of these officers were summarily shot by the Wehrmacht in the first few months of fighting. Ruthless punitive action was also stipulated against partisans and anyone assisting them, as well as against Jews and members of the Communist Party. The Wehrmacht was ordered to provide close military and logistical assistance to the Einsatzgruppen of the SS, which would follow in its footsteps and the task of which was the murder of Jews and other Soviet citizens designated for elimination.

The four Einsatzgruppen battalions that operated on the vast Russian front from the Baltic to the Black Sea would, with the help of the Wehrmacht and Nazi police units, murder more than one million Jewish men, women, and children in the first eighteen months of the Russian campaign. In the Ukraine, beginning in Lvov, they found willing collaborators among local nationalists. A report for the period of 1–31 October 1941 dealt with the extermination in the Ukraine, including the notorious Babi Yar massacres of Jews just outside the capital city, Kiev.[9] The report noted cryptically:

The bitter hostility of the Ukrainian population against the Jews is extremely great, because it is thought that they were responsible for the explosions in Kiev. They are also seen as NKVD [Soviet secret police] informers and agents, who unleashed the terror against the Ukrainian people. All Jews were arrested in retaliation for the arson in Kiev, and altogether 33,771 Jews were executed on September 29th and 30th. Gold, valuables and clothing were collected and put at the disposal of the National Socialist Welfare Association (NSV), for the equipment of the *Volksdeutsche,* and part given to the appointed city administration for distribution to the needy population.[10]

The indescribable horror of this bloodbath against defenseless and wholly innocent men, women, and children is never, of course, remotely glimpsed in this sterilized accounting or in other German documents.

Some of the earliest massacres took place in the Baltic states, where the Einsatzgruppen were aided enthusiastically, especially by Lithuanians. Here is a typically stone-cold extract from a report by Karl Jäger, commander of Einsatzgruppe 3, on the extermination of Lithuanian Jews, dated Kovno, 1 December 1941:

I can confirm today that *Einsatz Kommando* 3 has achieved the goal of solving the Jewish problem in Lithuania. There are no more Jews in Lithuania, apart from working Jews and their families. These number: in Shavli about 4,500, in Kovno about 15,000, in Vilna about 15,000.

I wanted to eliminate the working Jews and their families as well, but the Civil Administration [*Reichskommissar*] and the Wehrmacht attacked me most sharply and issued a prohibition against having these Jews and their families shot. The goal of clearing Lithuania of Jews could be achieved only through the establishment of a specially selected Mobile Commando under the command of SS *Obersturmführer* Hamann, who adopted my aims fully and who was able to ensure the co-operation of the Lithuanian Partisans and the Civil Authorities concerned. The carrying out of such *Aktionen* is first of all an organisational problem. The decision to clear each sub-district systematically of Jews called for a thorough preparation for each *Aktion* and the study of local conditions. The Jews had to be concentrated in one or more localities and, in accordance with their numbers, a site had to be selected and pits dug.... The Jews are brought to the place of execution in groups of 500, with at least 2 kms distance between groups.... All the officers and men of my command in Kovno took active part in the *Grossaktionen* in Kovno. Only one official of the intelligence corps was released from participation on account of illness.

I consider the *Aktionen* against the Jews to be virtually completed. The remaining working Jews and Jewesses are urgently needed, and I can imagine that this manpower will continue to be needed urgently after the winter has ended. I am of the opinion that the male working Jews should be sterilised immediately to prevent reproduction. Should any Jewess nevertheless become pregnant, she is to be liquidated.[11]

The pattern described here was typical for the eastern front and a faithful reflection of the "ideological war" of extermination and enslavement that Hitler had ordered. The Wehrmacht, which objected in Poland and Lithuania to murdering valuable Jewish workers, did, however, actively participate in the killings of Jews in the Soviet Union. The commander of the Sixth Army, Field Marshal Walter von Reichenau, explained to his troops in an order issued on 10 October 1941 what the rationale for their conduct in the war against Bolshevism had to be:

The essential goal of the campaign against the Jewish-Bolshevik system is the complete destruction of its power instruments and the eradication of the Asiatic influence on the European cultural sphere.... In the East the soldier is not only a fighter according to the rules of warfare, but also a carrier of an inexorable racial concept [*völkischen Idee*] and the avenger of all the bestialities which have been committed against the Germans and related races.

Therefore the soldier must have *complete* understanding for the necessity of the harsh, but just atonement of Jewish subhumanity. This has the further goal of nipping in the bud rebellions in the rear of the Wehrmacht which, as experience shows, are always plotted by the Jews.[12]

On 20 November 1941, General Erich von Manstein, commander of the Eleventh Army and one of Germany's most brilliant generals, elaborated on this theme.

Since 22 June the German *Volk* is in the midst of a battle for life and death against the Bolshevik system. This battle is conducted against the Soviet army not only in a conventional manner according to the rules of European warfare.... Jewry constitutes the mediator between the enemy in the rear and the still fighting remnants of the Red Army and the Red leadership. It has a stronger hold than in Europe on all key positions of the political leadership and administration, it occupies commerce and trade and further forms cells for all the disturbance and possible rebellions.

The Jewish-Bolshevik system must be eradicated once and for all. Never again may it interfere in our European living space. The German soldier is therefore not only charged with the task of destroying the power instrument of this system. He marches forth also as a carrier of a racial conception and as an avenger of all the atrocities which have been committed against him and the German people.

The soldier must show understanding for the harsh atonement of Judaism, the spiritual carrier of the Bolshevik terror.[13]

Such ideological statements by top German field commanders, exhorting their troops to ever greater ferocity against the "racial" and political enemies of the Reich, were becoming commonplace. The military leaders spoke, like Colonel-General Hoth, commander of the Seventeenth Army, on 25 November 1941, of "our mission to save European culture from the advancing Asiatic barbarism"; of the German sense of "honor" and race when confronting the

Jewish-Bolshevik "disregard of moral values." Not only the commanders but also the combat troops accepted this Nazified view of the war as an ideological struggle for survival against demonic Jewish-Bolshevik enemies. As Omer Bartov has pointed out, Wehrmacht soldiers serving on the Russian front were young men "who had spent their formative years under the Third Reich and were exposed to large doses of indoctrination in Nazified schools and especially in the Hitler Youth and the Reich labour service."[14] Their education and socialization had instilled in them the mind-set requisite for a genocidal task.

More specifically, the *Vernichtungskrieg* (war of destruction) that the army waged against the Soviet Union, "Judeo-Bolshevism," and the "Asiatic hordes" in the east provided the precondition for the "Final Solution" of the "Jewish question" in Europe. On this issue, Hitler knew that his conservative, anti-Bolshevik generals were in broad agreement with his views, just as they had no difficulties with starving or working to death Slav *Untermenschen,* or reducing them to a reservoir of slave labor for the German *Herrenvolk* (master race). Operation Barbarossa had opened up new vistas for the Nazi elite in terms of "solutions" to a series of long-range problems they had hitherto postponed or held on ice. Ever since the 1920s, Hitler had dreamed of a war against the Soviet Union, to establish *Lebensraum* to the east in a Greater German Empire. But this would have to be a *Weltanschauungskrieg* (war of ideologies) to destroy international Communism, which was itself regarded by the Nazis as the main political arm of Jewry—the expression of its will to dominate the world.[15]

As the gigantic battle with the Soviet Union approached, it is striking how Hitler began to return to the language of *Mein Kampf* and the anti-Semitic racial eschatology of his early days as an agitator in Munich. At a preparatory conference on 30 March 1941, Hitler had emphatically informed his military commanders that war with the Soviet Union would be "a struggle between two opposing world outlooks" (*Kampf zweier*

Weltanschauungen gegeneinander)—a race war totally different from the confrontation in the West.[16] His guidelines for the ruthless elimination of Bolshevik commissars, partisans, and Jews were then carried out to the letter in the field.

It is important to grasp the qualitative leap that was now taking place along the continuum of murderous actions which taken together comprised the Holocaust. The period from the conquest of Poland until June 1941 can in retrospect be seen as a "testing laboratory" for Hitler's racial and imperial ambitions. Soviet Russia, on the other hand, became the arena for the final struggle, "the prelude to the millennium," to borrow Lucy Dawidowicz's pregnant phrase for the Nazi apocalypse.[17] In Poland, the racial policies designed to expel Poles and Jews from areas annexed to the Reich and to replace them with "racially pure" Germans and *Volksdeutsche* had enjoyed only limited success. The civilian Governor-General in conquered Poland, Hans Frank, was constantly complaining that his fiefdom had become a vast dumping ground for Jews from Germany, Austria, and the other annexed Polish territories, overburdening his administration. In the ghettos, as a result of deliberate German cruelty, there were acute overcrowding, chronic shortages of food, and a complete absence of sanitation, leading to outbreaks of typhus and other infectious diseases. Though hundreds of thousands died in these appalling conditions or in the labor camps, and Jews were brutally and randomly killed, systematic mass murder was not yet the German policy.

All of this swiftly changed after the invasion of Soviet Russia. On 31 July 1941, almost six weeks after the invasion began, Heydrich received an order from Goering "to carry out all preparations with regard to the organisation, the material side and financial viewpoints for a total solution (*Gesamtlösung*) of the Jewish question in those territories of Europe which are under German influence." He was further instructed to submit a draft "showing the administrative, material and financial measures already taken for the execution of the intended final solution (*Endlösung*) of the Jewish question."[18] In mid-June 1941, Heydrich had given the higher SS and police leaders in the east open-ended orders about killing Jews, saboteurs, subversives, and Comintern officials. His instructions did not, however, go much beyond the Commissar Order that had preceded the invasion. But under the cover of protective security measures against partisans in the occupied territories, it was easier—as Hitler himself pointed out in a planning conference on 16 July 1941—"to wipe out anyone who gets in our way."[19] Eichmann himself during his interrogation by the Israeli police in 1960 affirmed categorically that in August 1941 he had heard point-blank from Heydrich, "The Führer has ordered physical extermination."[20] He assumed that the order must have come down through Himmler and would never have been put into writing, on which point he was probably correct.

In September 1941, as German forces became increasingly bogged down in their military campaign, the killing of Soviet Jews increased greatly. Significantly, Hitler had indicated on the evening of 2 October 1941 that these accelerating massacres in the east enjoyed his full approval. Recalling yet again his Reichstag prophecy of January 1939 that "the Jew would disappear from Europe," he cynically told Himmler and Heydrich, "It's not a bad idea, by the way, that public rumour attributes to us a plan to exterminate the Jews. Terror is a salutary thing."[21] This statement occurred just over a month after Himmler had informed the Gauleiter of the Wartheland, Arthur Greiser, that it was "the Führer's wish that the Altreich and the Protectorates [Bohemia and Moravia] should be cleared of Jews from west to east. I am therefore doing all I can to see that the deportation of the Jews ... into the territories assimilated into the Reich during the past two years is completed during this year as a first stage, preparatory to their being sent further east early in the new year."[22]

Hitler's September 1941 order for the "removal" of Jews from the Reich to the east went beyond the geographically limited killing of Soviet Jews toward a pan-European solution of the "Jewish question." Heydrich, at a conference in Prague on 10 October 1941, spoke of "the Führer's wish that German Jews be deported to Lódz, Riga, and Minsk by the end of the year, if possible."[23] This formula of "the Führer's wish" (*des Führers Wunsch*), deployed by both Himmler and Heydrich, came to assume a life of its own during the Holocaust, as one of those key code terms (like *evacuation, resettlement, transport to the east*) that covered or disguised the horrible reality of mass murder. The circular of 23 October 1941 from Gestapo chief Heinrich Müller (issued in Himmler's name) banning "all further Jewish emigration, with immediate effect," was one more decisive pointer to the emergence of a new phase.[24] For where would the Jews go if they could no longer emigrate or stay where they were? This question was all the more acute as the Russian winter set in and heavy German losses were for the first time being sustained at the hands of the "Jewish-Bolshevik" enemy.

There were also other significant indicators regarding a decision for genocide around September and October 1941. The brutality of face-to-face mass shootings on the eastern front were beginning to take their psychological toll on the Einsatzgruppen, and Himmler (after witnessing one such execution) had become more "sensitized" to the needs of his troops and the desirability of a so-called humane method of killing. By September 1941, Einsatzgruppe C was in possession of a truck that used exhaust gases to kill trapped Jewish victims. In October 1941, plans for the construction of gassing apparatus had been discussed by Adolf Eichmann, Alfred Wetzel (the Jewish expert of the Ostministerium), and Viktor Brack, the supervisor of the euthanasia program in the Führer Chancellery.[25] They agreed that "there is no reason why those Jews who are not fit for work should not be removed by the Brack method [i.e., gassing].... The work-worthy on the other hand will be transported to the East for labour."[26]

Riga and Minsk were mentioned as destinations for deported German Jews. The Germans had, of course, no intention of feeding the new mass influx; and once they were incapable of hard labor, these Jews had few prospects of survival. Moreover, now that a technology (the "gas vans") had been decided upon, it remained only to find the sites and construct the "annihilation camps" (*Vernichtungslager*). The first death camp was built at Chelmno (Kulmhof) in Poland, where the gassing of Jews began on 8 December 1941.[27] It appears that Himmler had been given a special authorization to have one hundred thousand Jews killed there. (About this time, gas trucks were also being used by the Germans to kill Jews in Semlin, Serbia.)[28] This was followed in March 1942 by Belzec in eastern Poland (near the former Soviet border), the first extermination camp equipped with permanent gas chambers. By then, Auschwitz-Birkenau in Silesia, which became the biggest of all the death camps (though it was a concentration and industrial labor camp as well), was also operational, though the gassing of Jews did not begin until two months later.[29] Sitting astride the major railway artery from Vienna to Cracow, this huge complex of camps—known commonly as Auschwitz (Oswiecim in Polish)—ultimately became the most notorious embodiment of the Holocaust as an assembly-line process of mass murder. It is estimated that 1.2 million Jews died in the gas chambers of Auschwitz-Birkenau, along with a much smaller number of Poles, Gypsies, and Soviet POWs. Similar killing facilities were constructed at other death camps in Poland—Sobibór (May 1942), Treblinka (July 1942), and Majdanek (autumn 1942)—the sole purpose and product of which was mass murder.

Toward the end of 1941, pressures for the physical elimination of the Jews were building from many sides, especially in that strange no-man's-land known as the Polish General Government. Governor-General Hans Frank, in a notorious speech of 16 December 1941 in Cracow, could not have been more explicit about his intentions: "One way or another—I will tell you that quite openly—we must finish off the Jews. The Führer put it into words once: should united Jewry again succeed in setting off a world war, then a blood sacrifice shall not be made only by the peoples driven into war, but then the Jew of Europe will have met his end."[30] Hitler's *so oder so* ("one way or the other"), mimicked here by Frank, was becoming the Nazi signature tune for the Holocaust.

Frank then referred dismissively to "criticism" of the cruelty and harshness of measures "now applied to Jews in the Reich." In language that was again unmistakably reminiscent of Hitler, he ranted that one could have pity "only for the German people and for nobody else in the world." If European Jewry survived the war, he declared, while Germans had sacrificed "the best of our blood" for Europe, this would be at most a half success. His confident expectation was, however, that "the Jews will disappear," and hence he intended to send a representative to Reinhard Heydrich's upcoming January 1942 Wannsee Conference in Berlin. Frank then reported to his audience what he had been told on a recent visit to Berlin: instead of making trouble by refusing to have more Jews thrown into his territory, he would do better to "liquidate" them himself. There was no room for sentimentality or compassion, he concluded.

We must destroy the Jews wherever we meet them and whenever the opportunity offers so that we can maintain the whole structure of the Reich here.... The Jews batten on to us to an exceptionally damaging extent. At a rough estimate we have in the Generalgouvernement about 2.5 million people [Jews]—now perhaps 3.5 million who have Jewish connections and so on. We cannot shoot these 3.5 million Jews, we cannot poison them, but we can take measures that will, one way or the another [*so oder so*], lead to extermination, in conjunction with the large-scale measures under discussion in the Reich.[31]

The measures to which Frank so vilely alluded were to be spelled out in some detail at the notorious ninety-minute Wannsee Conference of 20 January 1942, held in the serenity of an elegant suburban villa in Berlin. It was organized by Reinhard Heydrich in his capacity as chief of the security police and the SD but, more important, as the designated "Plenipotentiary for the Preparation of the Final Solution of the Jewish Question." Heydrich, the most "Aryan"-looking of the Nazi leadership and a fanatical anti-Semite (despite misleading rumors about his partly Jewish ancestry), was determined to push the meeting forward in brisk and businesslike fashion.[32] The conference was to have been held originally on 8 December 1941 and had already been delayed for six weeks. Its ostensible purpose was to coordinate a general plan among the various Reich ministries and service chiefs to exterminate (though the word was naturally avoided) *all* of European Jewry. There were five representatives of the SS and police present, including Gestapo chief Heinrich Müller and the conscientious Adolf Eichmann (from the Reich Main Security Office), who took the minutes. The nine civilians represented the Ministry of the Interior (Dr. Wilhelm Stuckart), the Ministry of Justice (Dr. Roland Freisler), the Reich Chancellery (Wilhelm Kritzinger), the Ministry of the Occupied Eastern Territories (Drs. Meyer and Georg Leibbrandt), the office of the Four-year Plan (Erich Neumann), the office of the Governor-General (Dr. Bühler), the Party Chancellery (Gerhard Klopfer), and the Foreign Ministry (Dr. Martin Luther).

Heydrich opened the meeting by referring to commissions he had received from Goering in September 1939 and July 1941 to prepare a practical organizational plan for "the final solution of the European Jewish Question." This task demanded "prior joint consideration by all central agencies directly involved in these questions with a view to maintaining parallel policy lines." With evident relish, he emphasized that the responsibility for handling the "Final Solution" would be centralized in the hands of Himmler and himself. Heydrich then briefly reiterated two key elements in the struggle so far: namely, the "forcing of the Jews out of the living space (*Lebensraum*) of the German people" and out of the various areas of its life (*Lebensgebiete*).[33] Accelerated emigration of the Jews had until recently been vigorously pursued "as the only possible provisional solution." Heydrich recalled some of the difficulties encountered along this road, including restriction or canceling of entry permits by foreign governments, lack of shipping space, and financial obstacles. Nonetheless, in eight years of Nazi rule—from 30 January 1933 until 31 October 1941, when Himmler had banned emigration because of wartime conditions and new "possibilities in the East"— 537,000 Jews had been "sent out of the country." That total comprised 360,000 from Germany proper, 147,000 from Austria (after March 1938), and about 30,000 from Bohemia and Moravia. The wealthy Jews and major foreign Jewish organizations had been made to finance this emigration. But this was past history, a mere prelude to the great tasks ahead.

In place of emigration, there was now a new prospect, namely "the evacuation of the Jews to the East in accordance with the prior approval of the Führer [*nach entsprechender vorheriger Genehmigung durch den Führer*]." This "evacuation" was only a temporary expedient prior to "the coming final solution of the Jewish question [*die kommende Endlösung der Judenfrage*]." But to use Heydrich's technocratic jargon, "practical experience of the greatest importance" had already been acquired. Presumably, Heydrich was referring elliptically both to organizational experience in deportations and to the lessons learned in shooting, gassing, and other killing techniques that had been tried out in the east during the preceding six months.

According to the overblown estimates of the Reich Main Security Office, the "Final Solution" of the European "Jewish question" would encompass no fewer than eleven million Jews. (Heydrich implied that even this calculation might be on the low side, since he believed foreign countries only partially applied racial principles, thus underestimating the true number of Jews.) His target list included 330,000 English Jews, 4,000 Jews from Ireland, and Jews from neutral Sweden (8,000), Switzerland (18,000), Spain (6,000), and the European portion of Turkey (55,500), none of whom would suffer German occupation. Estonia was the one country already listed as *Judenfrei*. Particularly high population estimates were quoted for the Soviet Union (5 million Jews), the Ukraine (2.99 million), and unoccupied France (700,000). According to Heydrich, Europe was "to be combed from West to East," with the Reich (Germany, Austria, Bohemia, and Moravia) receiving priority "because of the housing problem and the socio-political needs." In reality, the Holocaust proceeded somewhat differently.

Heydrich envisaged some difficulties in Hungary and Romania, which he regarded as corrupt, even asserting that "in Hungary it is imperative that an advisor in Jewish questions be pressed upon the Hungarian government without too much delay." On the other hand, in Slovakia and Croatia he believed that "the most essential problems in this field have already been brought near to a solution." Heydrich did not expect too many difficulties "in registering Jews for evacuation" in occupied or unoccupied France; however, he spoke only of "preparatory steps to settle the question in Italy." Chillingly deceptive was his casual mention of the "five million Jews in European Russia," without so much as a hint that Soviet Jews in their hundreds of thousands had already been massacred. Instead, he gave a distorted occupational breakdown of Russian Jewry, adding cynically: "The influence of the Jews in all walks of life in the USSR is well known."

The timing of each "evacuation" project would, he claimed, be "determined chiefly by the military developments." In territories or areas influenced by the Reich, competent Foreign Office people were expected to confer with the relevant SD officials. The zealous Foreign Office representative, Martin

Luther, a relentless bloodhound in "Jewish affairs," drew attention to likely problems with the Scandinavian countries, but, given the small number of resident Jews there, he suggested deferring the "evacuations" there.[34]

Heydrich then briefly detailed the "special administrative and executive measures" that were to apply to the conscription of Jews for labor (*Arbeitseinsatz*) in the eastern territories. Despite Heydrich's laborious euphemisms, it must have been clear to all present that most of the deported Jews would certainly be "unfit for labor" and therefore could expect to be disposed of immediately. For those who were fit, he envisaged large gangs (with the sexes separated) used for road building "in which task a large part of them will undoubtedly fall out through natural elimination [*durch natürliche Verminderung ausfallen wird*]." Those Jews who survived this nightmare scenario would not, of course, be allowed to go free. They would have to receive "special treatment [*Sonderbehandlung*]," since they represented the most physically resistant, "a natural selection of the fittest," a "germ-cell [*Keimzelle*] of a new Jewish revival." This, according to Heydrich's way of thinking, was proven by "the experience of history."[35] These work projects, similar to those in the Stalinist gulags, never came to fruition, apparently vetoed by Hitler, who temporarily preferred at this point to use the available manpower for other ends.

Finally, the Wannsee meeting devoted considerable time to the question of *Mischlinge* and mixed marriages, a fact that has puzzled some historians—especially since the lengthy and abstruse discussions did not seem to produce any conclusive result. For the Nazis, however, this was an issue of real importance and conceptual difficulty.[36] No fewer than seventy-five thousand persons had been defined as first-degree *Mischlinge* (two Jewish grandparents) and between 125,000 and 130,000 as second degree (one Jewish grandparent). It was crucial for German officials to know who should be treated as a Jew, since the Nuremberg Race Laws in principle remained valid for the implementation of the "Final Solution." *Misch-*

linge of the first degree were, as before, to be treated as Jews, and those of the second degree as Germans. But there were some exemptions. For instance, the children of a first-degree "mixed blood" in a marriage with a "person of German blood" were regarded "essentially as Germans." Their "mixed blood" parent would also be exempt from "evacuation." Similarly privileged would be those cases of "*personal* merit" involving a first-degree *Mischling* previously exempted by the highest party or state authorities. But even the exceptions would have to undergo "voluntary" sterilization if they wished to stay in the Reich. It was a hopelessly entangled bureaucratic thicket of racist insanity, but for the Nazis these were deadly serious issues. Heydrich and the Reich Main Security Office could be well satisfied with their results in most areas. They failed, however, to stiffen and unify the convoluted legislation on half and quarter Jews. Partly they were blocked by bureaucrats like Stuckhart, by the Führer Chancellery, and possibly by Hitler himself, until he reversed his position in 1944.

In the concluding session of the Wannsee Conference, it was notable that Undersecretary of State Bühler insisted that the "Final Solution" should first of all be implemented in the General Government, where he claimed that "the Jews represented an immense danger as carriers of epidemics" and were permanently undermining the economic system through black-market operations. Echoing the demands of the absent Hans Frank, he declared that the majority of the 2.5 million Jews were "*unfit for work*"—tantamount to passing a collective death sentence on them in this context. The protocol states laconically: "He had this one request only, namely that the Jewish question in this territory be solved as quickly as possible." In fact, with the exception of Galicia, where German massacres of Jews had already started in October 1941, no systematic extermination in the General Government began until the spring of 1942.[37]

The historic significance of the Wannsee Conference is clear. Despite its sanitized language, the record of it does reveal a general and centrally organized plan for the massacre of European Jewry in its entirety, and it is the only surviving official document that does so in such detail. It is the text that definitively revealed the fates of western and central European Jews, as well as those of the millions of Polish and Russian Jews, whose murder was already under way. The Wannsee gathering also demonstrated that the German state bureaucracy had no serious objections to the genocidal plans of Heydrich's Reich Main Security Office, with the exception of some anticipated difficulties and reservations concerning *Mischlinge.* By implication, it was also evident that the vast majority of German Jews (except for certain carefully defined categories) were doomed to suffer the rigors of the "Final Solution."

The first deportations of German Jews in mid-October 1941 had not always resulted in instant death. An element of uncertainty about how to deal with them is suggested by a letter in December 1941 from Wilhelm Kube (General Kommissar of Byelorussia and a longtime party member) to Heinrich Lohse, Reich Commissar for Ostland, describing the condition of German Jews who had been sent to Minsk and asking for clear directives. Kube observed that these Jews included First World War heroes decorated with the Iron Cross, war invalids, and half and even three-quarter "Aryans." He asserted that they differed sharply from Russian Jews in their skills, productivity, and "personal cleanliness." These German Jews were "people who came from our own cultural sphere," not at all like "the brutish hordes in this place." Kube asked if the proposed slaughter was to be carried out by Lithuanians and Latvians, "themselves rejected by the population here," and respectfully requested that "the necessary action be taken in the most humane manner."[38] He did not want, however, to give an order for liquidation on his own responsibility.

Kube's misgivings make it clear that the application of the genocidal plan to German Jews was not immediately self-evident, even for some hardened party members. This fact was reflected in the delay—until late 1941—in requiring Jews of the Reich (Germany, Austria, and the Czech Protecktorat) to wear the yellow star or in finally completing the deportations from Germany. Indeed, the German Reich was not declared *Judenrein* until June 1943. The Nazi regime proceeded more cautiously in this area, since the forcible removal of German Jews could not be concealed from the population and might provoke uncomfortable questions.

An even more serious potential obstacle to a speedy and comprehensive elimination of the Jews arose from the usefulness to the German military machine of industrious Jewish workers in the eastern territories. The SS was determined to overrule, wherever possible, such pragmatic considerations. This would be made crystal clear in reply to the important query raised on 15 November 1941 by Lohse, who had written to the Ministry of Occupied Eastern Territories concerning Jewish workers. He wished to know if there was "a directive to liquidate all the Jews in *Ostland*."[39] Was this to be done "regardless of age, sex, and economic requirements (for instance, the Wehrmacht's demand for skilled workers in the armament industry)?" Lohse was all in favor of "the cleansing of *Ostland* of Jews," but he was also sensitive to the needs of the armament plants and repair workshops. In the Baltic states, as in Poland and the western lands but unlike in the Soviet Union or Yugoslavia, the army did not see itself as engaged in the murder of Jews. To deprive the factories of Jewish workers "through their liquidation" when they could not yet be replaced by local personnel did not seem sensible to Lohse. The reply he received, signed by liaison officer Otto Bräutigam, was significant: "The Jewish question has presumably been clarified meanwhile by means of verbal discussion. In principle, economic considerations are not to be taken into account in the settlement of the problem. It is further requested that any questions that arise be settled directly with the Higher SS and Police Leader."[40]

It is evident from such correspondence that the implications of the "Final Solution" were not always apparent to those in the field who were expected to implement it. Undoubtedly, there was much chaos and administrative confusion, and many clashing interests and logistical problems that needed improvised solutions. But that does not mean that the mass murder of European Jewry was something that the Nazis simply stumbled into, without any centralized control or ideological guidelines. Undoubtedly, for Hitler, the *Endlösung* was a matter of grand policy, though he left the execution of its details to trusted subordinates such as Himmler and Heydrich.

An illuminating example of Hitler's vision of the "Final Solution," not long before the Wannsee Conference, is revealed in his conversation of 28 November 1941 with the Grand Mufti of Jerusalem, Haj Amin el-Husseini—the exiled leader of the Palestinian Arabs, then living in Berlin. Ever since 1933, Haj Amin had eagerly sought to win Nazi support for his Palestinian nationalist and pan-Arab aims, with somewhat mixed results. Like many Arab nationalists in the 1930s, he ardently admired the order and discipline of the Reich, looking to Hitler to overthrow British imperialism in the Middle East and to help him destroy the "Jewish National Home" in Palestine.[41] At their meeting in Berlin, the Mufti emphasized that the Arabs had the same enemies as Nazi Germany, "namely the English, the Jews, and the Communists." The Arab world, he declared, was ready to cooperate with the Reich by acts of sabotage and revolt, as well as by raising a Muslim Arab legion to fight in the Balkans. In exchange, the Mufti desired a public declaration by Hitler in favor of Arab national goals and the liberation of Palestine from the Zionist Jews.

Hitler was cautious regarding such a commitment. He reminded the Mufti that he was speaking "as a rational man, and primarily as a soldier," who believed that the fate of the Arab world would be ultimately decided by the "very severe battles going on in the Soviet Union." On the other hand, he was positively effusive in explaining to the Palestinian leader the rationale for the anti-Jewish crusade that he was conducting. He told the Mufti that "Germany stood for uncompromising war against the Jews [*Deutschland trete für einem kompromisslosen Kampf gegen die Juden ein*]." He was resolved, "step by step, to ask one European nation after the other to solve its Jewish problem, and at the proper time to direct a similar appeal to non-European nations as well."[42] At the same time, he spelled out the *ideological* meaning of the Second World War in terms formulated more sharply than in any other single German diplomatic document. "Germany was at the present time engaged in a life and death struggle with two citadels of Jewish power: Great Britain and Soviet Russia." Hitler conceded that "theoretically there was a difference" between English capitalism and Soviet Communism. But in practice, he observed, "the Jews in both countries were pursuing a common goal."[43] However, the hour of "reckoning with the Jews" was now fast approaching. "This was the decisive struggle," Hitler informed his Arab guest. Politically, the war was mainly "a conflict between Germany and England," but ideologically "it was a battle between National Socialism and the Jews [*weltanschaulich sei es ein Kampf zwischen den Nationalsozialismus und dem Judentum*]."[44]

Hitler also asked the Mufti to lock "in the uttermost depths of his heart" the information that "he would carry on the battle to the total destruction [*Zerstörung*] of the Judeo-Communist empire in Europe."[45] This was a decidedly heavy hint of the massive annihilation of Jewry, which was already under way and would soon be greatly accelerated. Moreover, the war against the Jews would not be confined to the European continent, once the German armies had reached the exit of the Caucasus and stood poised on the northern edge of the Middle East. Hitler also reassured the Palestinian leader that he was actively opposed to the Jewish National Home as "a state centre" [*ein Staatlicher Mittelpunkt*], the influence of which could be only destructive. More important still, he promised that when the hour of Arab liberation struck, the sole German objective in the Middle East would be "the destruction of the Jewish element residing in the Arab sphere under the protection of British power [*die Vernichtung des in arabischen Raum unter der Protektion der britischen Macht lebenden Judentums sein*]."[46]

Hitler had revealed the global vision behind his genocidal project, encompassing even the Middle East and "extra-European" peoples. It is not confined to European Ashkenazi Jews but also includes "the Jewish element residing in the Arab sphere."[47] It is directed against "Jewish" capitalism in Great Britain no less than against Judeo-Communism in the Soviet Union. The imminent entry of the United States into the war (within fewer than two weeks) was to highlight even more the globalization of the conflict and its "Judaization."

German historian Christian Gerlach recently argued that Hitler's decision to irrevocably destroy the Jews of Europe was made formally as late as 12 December 1941, one day after his declaration of war on the United States. His most important evidence (from Goebbels's notes) consists of remarks made by Hitler in his private residence that very afternoon, before the assembled Nazi Party Gauleiters and Reich leaders.[48] Hitler returned once more to his famous prophecy of destruction, uttered nearly three years earlier, about what would happen "if the Jews again provoked a world war." He solemnly warned that these were not "vain words," since the war had now arrived and "the destruction of the Jews must be the necessary result." There was no room for sentimentality regarding the Jews, since the German people had "already sacrificed 160,000 dead on the Eastern front." Hence those who were "truly responsible for this bloody war" (i.e., the Jews) should pay for it with their lives.[49]

This was open incitement to mass murder, all the more significant in view of the forum in which it was made. Almost all the top party leadership and most of the decision makers who would have to implement the "Final Solution" in their fiefdoms were present. Moreover, with American entry into the war, the Jews of Europe had lost whatever role they might still have had (in Nazi minds) as bargaining chips with which to affect the behavior of the United States. Nazi Germany would henceforth be at war with three global powers (the United States, the Soviet Union, and the British Empire)—a fact that strengthened the Nazi vision of Germany as the protectionist guardian of the *European* continent. Jews, in this context, could be all the more easily demonized as the threatening "fifth column," the revolutionary subversives and plotters against whom European nations had to unite under Nazi leadership.

However, there are solid grounds on which to believe that the "Final Solution" was decided upon well before December 1941. Plans for gassing Polish Jews were already under way by then, and earlier statements by Goebbels, Rosenberg, Heydrich, and Hitler himself had clearly pointed in the direction of genocide. For instance, in a letter of 6 November 1941, Heydrich had written to Otto von Stülpnagel of the German High Command in Paris explaining why he had authorized the bombings of seven Parisian synagogues on 2 October.[50] Heydrich said that he had acted only "from the moment when, at the highest level, Jewry had been forcefully designated as the culpable incendiary in Europe, one which must definitively disappear from Europe."[51] Presumably the explosions of 2 October had already been organized in September. Since Heydrich could have meant only the Führer as the authority "at the highest level," this statement implies that the decision to exterminate the Jews was already known to Heydrich in September 1941, if not earlier.

On 30 January 1942 at the Berlin Sportpalast, Hitler wrapped his prophecy of "complete annihilation" in Old Testament language, declaring that henceforth the philosophy of "an eye for an eye, a tooth for a tooth" would be applied to "the most evil world-enemy of all times."[52] It is significant that Hitler's rambling table talks from the end of January 1942 were now increasingly fixated on the responsibility of the Jews for the world war and their role as a "perpetual ferment." The need for a "radical solution" and for comprehensive measures at a European level were asserted as if the process were not yet in full swing but somehow still imminent. Yet we know from various sources, including Goebbels's diaries, that Hitler was indeed the driving force of the genocide and followed it closely. On 6 March 1942, Goebbels noted the Führer's conviction that "the greater the number of Jews liquidated, the more consolidated will be the situation in Europe after this war."[53] Two weeks later, the propaganda minister wrote with obvious satisfaction that "the Führer is as uncompromising as ever" about ridding Europe of the Jews, "if necessary by applying the most brutal methods."[54] On 27 March 1942, he described the deportation of Jews from the General Government to the east as "a pretty barbarous business."[55] Goebbels estimated that about 60 percent of these Jews had already been liquidated and another 40 percent were being taken for forced labor. "The former Gauleiter of Vienna (Globocnik), who is in charge of the operation, is carrying it out with a good deal of circumspection, and his methods do not seem to be attracting much publicity. The Führer is the moving spirit of this radical solution both in word and deed."[56]

For Hitler, the struggle against the Jews was indeed far more than a mere instrument of propaganda or a political means to achieve other ends. In his vocabulary, the Jews were constantly likened to vermin, to "propagators of infection," to the germs of a deadly plague, to bacteria or malignant disease—or, as he had called them back in 1919, a "racial tuberculosis of the peoples [*Rassentuberkulose der Völker*]." At dinner on the evening of 22 February 1942, Hitler exclaimed, "How many diseases must owe their origins to the Jewish virus! Only when we have eliminated the Jews will we regain our health." This obsessive linkage between Jews and deadly disease was one that he was constantly seeking to impress upon visiting foreign statesmen, allies, and collaborators. On 21 July 1941, he told the Croatian foreign minister that because of the Jews, Russia had become "a plague centre [*Pestherd*] for humanity."[57] During his meeting with the Hungarian ruler, Admiral Horthy, at Klessheim Castle on 17 April 1943, he warned his unreliable ally that nations "which did not rid themselves of the Jews perished." Referring to the Jews of Poland, Hitler denied that the mass killings were cruel: "If they could not work, they had to succumb. They had to be treated like tuberculosis bacilli with which a healthy body may become infected."[58]

Heinrich Himmler, the architect and organizer of the "Final Solution" as an administrative task, certainly shared this view. In his speech before senior SS officers in Poznan on 4 October 1943, Himmler spoke openly of the "Final Solution" as a hygienic measure (*eine Reinlichkeitsangelegenheit*): "We have exterminated a bacterium because we do not want in the end to be infected by the bacterium and die of it.... Wherever it may form, we will cauterise it."[59] Himmler's concern for Jewish "contagion" extended to women and children: "I did not consider that I should be justified in getting rid of the men—in having them put to death, in other words—only to allow their children to grow up to avenge themselves on our sons and grandsons. We have to make up our minds, hard though it may be, that this race must be wiped off the face of the earth."[60]

The pedantic and methodical Himmler also made much of the imagined "security threat" in justifying the Holocaust to the assembled audience of eminent SS and police officials, "for we know how difficult we should have made it for ourselves if, with the bombing raids, the burdens and depriva-

tions of war, we still had the Jews today in every town as secret saboteurs, agitators and trouble-makers. We would
probably have reached the 1916–17 stage when the Jews were
still part of the body of the German nation."[61]

The Reichsführer SS and chief of the German police also
addressed the "ethical" dilemmas and "idealism" required for
carrying out such a gigantic task. His speech was full of
memorable clichés about "honor," "loyalty," and "decency" in
the face of mountains of corpses. "To have stuck it out and at
the same time—apart from exceptions caused by human
weakness—to have remained decent men [*anständig geblieben
zu sein*], that is what has made us hard. This is a page of glory
in our history, which has never been written and never is to be
written."[62] Himmler did not hide the fact that the "Final Solution" was a "grave matter." He was even frank enough to
speak about it publicly as "the extermination [*Ausrottung*] of
the Jewish race" and to admit that this was one of "the most
frightening orders an organisation could ever receive."[63] In
his quietly sinister way, he managed to convey to his men the
sense that they were engaged not so much in murder as in a
sacred mission through which the SS elite would forge a new
race of blond, blue-eyed, Germanic heroes. Precisely because
they were a *Herrenvolk*, however, the Germans had to be pure
and "decent," incapable of theft or graft. Mass murder was
permissible and even admirable in an "idealistic" cause like
National Socialism, but misdemeanors that infringed Himmler's petit-bourgeois moral code were not tolerable. This did
not prevent him from proposing deals to the West at the end
of the war that involved trading or selling Jews for military,
monetary, or political advantage. In November 1944, on his
own initiative, Himmler ordered a halt to the gassing of
Jews, in the vain hope that he could thereby achieve a secret
arrangement with the Western Allies to join forces against the
Soviet Union.[64]

On the other hand, Hitler remained totally uncompromising to the bitter end, convinced that he had rendered a great

service to humanity by opening the eyes of the whole world to the "Jewish peril." On 13 February 1945, he boasted that National Socialism had truly "lanced the Jewish abscess," predicting that "the world of the future will be eternally grateful to us."[65] Hitler's so-called political testament was dictated on the morning of 29 April 1945 (the day before his suicide), as Soviet artillery fire bombarded the Reich Chancellery in Berlin. The document recorded his "love and loyalty" to the German people, who had given him the strength to make decisions of unprecedented difficulty. Not for the first time, he affirmed that he had never sought war against England and America. He held the Jews exclusively responsible "for this murderous struggle" and especially for the many victims of massive aerial bombing, prophesying that "out of the ruins of our towns and monuments" the hatred against "international Jewry and its helpers" would grow inexorably.[66] He had fairly warned the Jews ("these international conspirators in money and finance") that they would have to pay the price for initiating the world war. This time, however, it was not only to be the "millions of Europe's Aryan people" who would starve or "be burned and bombed to death in the cities." The Jewish warmongers would also "atone for their crime, even if by more *humane* means."[67] Hitler's last testament was both a justification for mass murder and the first act of Holocaust denial. His war against the Jews had by his own reckoning been an act of self-defense "against the poisoners of all the peoples of the world." He always sought nothing but peace. It was the "international financiers" who had forced him into war. Gassing and shooting the Jews had been his "humane" response to the Allied bombing raids on Germany, which according to the Nazi worldview were an act of "Jewish" aggression against "Aryan" humanity. This was the strange, shadowy world that the Führer inhabited. The Holocaust was indeed a logical culmination of Hitler's messianic megalomania and the perverted religiosity that had animated his politics. In its self-enclosed "finality," it resonated with sinister echoes of the last judgment, the final destruction of the Jews heralding the dawn of a new millennium, the redemption of the end of days. Hitler's apocalyptic perspective cannibalized and radicalized a long tradition of Christian and anti-Christian Judeophobia in the West, even as it destroyed the moral foundations of the European civilization that it so falsely claimed to defend. As Lucy Dawidowicz eloquently pointed out a quarter of a century ago, the Holocaust was not just another anti-Semitic undertaking: "It was part of a salvational ideology that envisaged the attainment of Heaven by bringing Hell on earth."[68]

5

BETWEEN
THE CROSS
AND
THE SWASTIKA

It is a Christian action to expel the Jews, because it is for the good of the people, which is thus getting rid of its pests.

> FATHER JOZEF TISO, *President of Slovakia,* August 1942

I must make heard the indignant protest of the Christian conscience and I proclaim that all men, Aryan or non-Aryan, are brothers, because they are created by the same God. . . . The current anti-Semitic measures are in contempt of human dignity, a violation of the most sacred rights of the individual and the family.

> BISHOP PIERRE-MARIE THÉAS (MONTAUBAN),
> protesting the deportation of French Jews, September 1942

Christianity in Germany bears a greater responsibility before God than the National Socialists, the SS and the Gestapo. We ought to have recognised the Lord Jesus in the brother who suffered and was persecuted despite his being a communist or a Jew.

> PASTOR MARTIN NIEMÖLLER, March 1946

The resurgence of Germany ("*Deutschland Erwache*") and the destruction of the Jews ("*Judah Verrecke*") had been organically related processes in Hitler's mind ever since the "catastrophe" of November 1918. They had been framed in eschatological terms as a kind of cosmic war of the forces of light against the fiendish powers of darkness. "There is no making pacts with Jews," Hitler had declared in *Mein Kampf,* "there can only be the hard either-or."[1] Pointedly, he warned his audience in the Munich beer cellars on 27 February 1925, "Either the enemy will walk over our corpses, or we will walk over his."[2] In this life-and-death fight against the satanic forces of evil, Hitler liked to pose as the chosen redeemer of the Germanic *Volk* (and of the entire non-Jewish world), conducting a millenarian struggle for salvation. This militant style of salvationist politics borrowed frequently from Christian language and imagery while adapting them to widely prevalent obsessions about impending German national doom or "Aryan" racial extinction. The extremity of the German plight was used to justify in advance the inversion of all humanitarian values. "We want to prevent our Germany from being crucified too! Let us be inhuman! But if we save Germany, we have eliminated the greatest injustice in the world. Let us be unethical! But if we save our *Volk,* we have broken a path for morality again!"[3]

When Hitler spoke of rescuing Germany, the "Aryan" nations, and European civilization from crucifixion by a "diabolical Jewish world-enemy," he did not flinch from comparing himself to the Christian savior, blasphemous though such an allusion must appear in retrospect. In his early speeches in Catholic Bavaria, he regularly evoked New Testament passages recalling that Christ "took to the whip to drive from the temple of the Lord this [Jewish] adversary of all humanity."[4] Jesus, too, he reminded his predominantly Catholic audiences, had lived in a "materialistic world contaminated by Jews," where the state power was corrupt and incompetent.[5] In Hitler's imaginary self-projection, Christ seemed more like Siegfried, a Germanic warrior-hero who had created a great world movement by preaching a popular anti-Jewish faith fused with intense patriotic idealism. Jesus's crown of thorns was his "struggle against the Jews," now made to serve as a model for Hitler's own war against the materialistic "Jewish spirit." It was as a Christian, the Nazi leader insisted, that he had a duty "to see that society did not suffer the same collapse as the Greco-Roman civilisation of Antiquity which had been driven to its ruin by this same Jewish people."[6] On 12 April 1922, he emphatically declared in Munich: "I would be no Christian ... if I did not, as did our Lord 2000 years ago, turn against those by whom today this poor people is plundered and exploited."[7] Draping himself in the colors of a fundamentalist anti-Semitic Christianity, he confessed to his Bavarian audience, "In boundless love, as a Christian and a human being, I read the passage which tells us how the Lord at last rose in his might and seized the scourge to drive out of the Temple the brood of vipers and adders. How terrific was his fight against the Jewish poison. I realise more profoundly than ever before the fact that it was for this that He had to shed His blood upon the cross."[8]

In another fiery speech in Munich, in December 1926, Hitler even claimed Jesus as a model and "pioneer" for the National Socialist cause. "The birth of The Man, which is celebrated at Christmas, has the greatest significance for National Socialists. Christ has been the greatest pioneer in the struggle against the Jewish world enemy. Christ was the greatest fighting nature which ever lived on the Earth. . . . The struggle against the power of capital was his life's work and his teaching, for which he was nailed to the Cross by his arch-

enemy the Jew. The task which Christ began but did not finish I will complete."[9] When Count Lerchenfeld, a former
prime minister of Bavaria, had stated in a local Landtag (diet)
session that his feeling "as a man and a Christian" prevented
him from being an anti-Semite, Hitler's reply was an unequivocal and total repudiation of any pacific, humanitarian
standpoint: "I say my feeling as a Christian points me to my
Lord and Saviour as a fighter. It points me to the man who
once in loneliness, surrounded by only a few followers, recognised those Jews for what they were and summoned men to
fight against them and who, God's truth! was greatest not as a
sufferer, but as a fighter."[10]

Hitler's vision of a militantly anti-Jewish Jesus developed
in large measure out of the fin-de-siècle Austrian Catholicism he had imbibed in his childhood and adolescent years.
As a young man in Vienna, he had admired the political vir-
tuosity of Karl Lueger's Christian-Social movement, in which
an anti-Jewish and anticapitalist populism, fostered by the
clergy, had played a central role. The devotion of the lower
clergy to the poor and their sense of mission had made
them—in Hitler's words—"stand out of the general morass
like little islands."[11] Indeed, the Catholic Church in his native
Austria had, as he liked to recall, served as an important
vehicle for the social mobility of many able individuals from
the ranks of the people.[12] Other features of his boyhood religion, like the "mysterious artificial dimness of the Catholic
churches," the burning candles, and the incense also made
strong impressions upon the young Hitler.

Learning from the experiences of his prewar apprentice
years in Vienna, he concluded that any open confrontation
with the Catholic Church must be avoided. The earlier failure of Bismarck's *Kulturkampf* against German Catholics in
the 1870s and of Schönerer's crusade against Rome in 1900
were object lessons. Hence, from the early days of the Nazi
Kampfzeit (time of struggle) he had avoided any involvement
in the religious disputes that could adversely affect his own

image or the unity within his movement. Those like the Thuringian Nazi leader Arthur Dinter who attempted to introduce a Protestant religious sectarianism into the NSDAP were either expelled or accused of national betrayal and of "consciously or unconsciously fighting for Jewish interests."[13] This ultimate disqualifying charge was even leveled at Hitler's former comrade in arms General Erich von Ludendorff, the vehemently anti-Catholic hero of the German *völkisch* right. Both Ludendorff and his second wife, Mathilde von Kemnitz, who had founded the Tannenbergbund in 1926, became obsessed with Jesuitism and the Roman church as implacable enemies of Germandom, no less deadly than "Judah" or Freemasonry. Hitler denounced this fanatical anti-Romanism and the internecine war between the Christian denominations in Germany as a disastrous diversion from the "Jewish peril."[14]

Hitler's concern not to alienate traditionalist opinion was eminently political and made sense in a rural Catholic region like Bavaria, which had been the cradle of the Nazi movement between 1919 and 1925.[15] Moreover, Hitler recognized the affinity between local anti-Jewish religious traditions typified by such popular festivals as the Oberammergau Passion Play (which highlighted the Jews' primary role in Christ's crucifixion) and his own violent anti-Semitism. The potency of this inflammatory strand of folk prejudice, accentuated by the linkage in the popular mind between Jews and Communism in post-1919 Munich, explains why Hitler sought to appropriate the Christian anti-Jewish tradition for his own demagogic ends. It is succinctly summed up in that notorious passage in *Mein Kampf* where he rails, "In defending myself against the Jews I am acting for the Lord [*vollziehe ich das Werk des Herrn*]."[16] The continuity is equally evident whenever Hitler's speeches passionately evoked Jesus as "the scourge of the Jews" or praised the "utterance(s) of the great Nazarene," who had always despised the golden mean, whether in politics or in life.[17] Small wonder, then, that the Nazis were eager in the early years to tap into the centuries-old tradition of Christian anti-Semitism for electoral purposes and present their doctrines as being compatible with "positive" Christianity. To understand what Hitler meant by this propagandist phrase, it is important to remember that his ideas in the 1920s were strongly influenced by the "spiritual" godfather of Nazism, the Bavarian Catholic journalist Dietrich Eckart, whom he admired as "an outstanding writer and thinker" and to whom *Mein Kampf* was dedicated.[18] Twenty years older than Hitler, Eckhart had introduced his raw, energetic protégé to Munich society, improved his social graces and his German, reshaping his racist anti-Semitism and grooming him for the role of messianic savior of Germany. Eckart had invented the Nazi battle cry "Deutschland Erwache!" (Germany awake!), the title of one of his poems. In 1919, he began publication of the ultranationalist weekly *Auf Gut Deutsch*, which attacked the Treaty of Versailles, Jewish war profiteers, Bolshevism, and social democracy.

Eckart's eclectic combination of *völkisch* racism with Catholic mysticism and his Manichaean view of the world as a battle between the forces of light and darkness (embodied by Aryan and Jew) appealed strongly to the early Hitler. He looked up to Eckart as a prophet, teacher, and father figure whose services to National Socialism were "inestimable," and he shared his view that "the Jewish Question is the chief problem of humanity, in which, indeed, every one of its other problems is contained."[19] Equally, he shared Eckart's conviction that Christ's revelation had been radically distorted by the apostle Paul and overlaid with a cold "Jewish" materialism, from which all social evils had subsequently proceeded.

In post-1918 Germany, the decadent condition of which Eckart compared to that of the late Roman Empire (where "Judaism" under the "cover" of Christianity had first engineered a moral collapse), the situation was perilous in the extreme. The prime causes of "decomposition" were capitalism, Bolshevism, and Freemasonry—three deadly modern agents of *Verjudung* (judaization).[20] The only salvation for the German *Volk* lay in a fusion of nationalism, socialism, and "positive Christianity," though this trinity would have to be stripped of any Jewish component and reinterpreted in a fundamentally "antimaterialist" spirit. Eckart died in 1924, but his ambitious pupil later implemented his millenarian program of redemptive anti-Semitism to devastating effect.[21]

By brandishing the slogan of "positive Christianity" and projecting their leader as a deeply religious figure (Hitler's frequent references to "Divine Providence" made this easier), Nazi Party image makers could suggest that their movement defended traditionalist values, especially against "godless Marxism." The fervent nationalism that had seized hold of so many German Christians in 1914, and was especially common in Protestant circles, further played into Nazi hands.[22] Among evangelical Protestants, who in the Weimar Republic remained vulnerable to nationalist appeals, there was a significant minority that became enthusiastic supporters of Nazism. They established their own "Reich Church" under Ludwig Müller, a militarist pastor already known for his hard-line nationalistic sermons and *völkisch* anti-Semitism in the 1920s. His Association of German Christians professed "heroic piety" and a virile racism that sought to harmonize belief in Christ with the "blood and soil" doctrines of Nazi ideology.[23] The German Christians were especially intent on banning marriages between Jews and Germans. But despite Müller's dogged loyalty to the regime, Hitler remained unimpressed by his efforts.

Among Protestants, only the breakaway *Bekenntnis-Kirche* (Confessing Church)—the strongholds of which were in northern and central Germany—considered Christianity to be manifestly incompatible with the Nazi worldview. These opponents of Nazism were especially exercised by the introduction of an "Aryan" paragraph into doctrines of church life (which removed converts of Jewish origins) and by the demand of German Christians to eradicate the Old Testament from church teachings.[24] Nevertheless, even in the Protestant opposition a moderate anti-Semitism was common enough. The guiding spirit of the Confessing Church, Martin Niemöller, had like many German Protestants originally welcomed Hitler's rise to power as the beginning of a national revival. He fully shared the anti-Communism of the Nazis and their detestation of the Weimar Republic, which he himself had once branded as "fourteen years of darkness." Nor was he immune to traditional German Protestant hostility to Jews and Judaism, with its impressive continuity from Martin Luther through the preacher Adolf Stoecker during the Second Reich to the Nazi theologians.[25] The Confessing Church only once raised its voice (in a secret memorandum of 1936 to Hitler) to protest the campaign of hatred against the Jews, as well as the concentration camps and the pervasiveness of the Gestapo.

The Roman Catholic Church in Germany was to prove more resistant to the incursions and blandishments of Nazi ideology.[26] In contrast to the Protestants, they did not have a Trojan horse in their ranks comparable to the Nazified German Christians. Moreover, they could look to the Vatican for institutional support and powerful moral encouragement. True, in the 1930s the Vatican under Pius XI did feel some affinity (like many Catholics in Europe and beyond) for anti-Communist authoritarian regimes that espoused corporatist, military, or clerico-fascist dictatorship. Moreover, in July 1933, in response to Hitler's own urgent requests, the Holy See took a more fateful step, signing a concordat with the Third Reich, giving a degree of much-desired international legitimacy to the Nazi regime and restricting the church to its religious, educative, and caritative roles. From the Nazi point of view, the concordat neutralized the Catholic Center Party (which consented to its own dissolution after agreeing to give Hitler special "emergency powers" in 1933), and thus removed a potential source of opposition. The Vatican, for its part, believed that the concordat could help secure the religious freedoms and legal status of the large Catholic minority in the Third Reich.[27]

In his first policy statement in the Reichstag, Hitler had set out to be as reassuring as possible, proclaiming that the new Reich government saw "in both Christian denominations the most important factor for the maintenance of our society."[28] In April 1933, in his first conversation as Reich Chancellor with the Catholic bishop Wilhelm Berning from Osnabrück, Hitler reaffirmed this intention and insisted that his anti-Jewish policy was based on principles that had been pursued for fifteen hundred years by the Catholic Church. However, he deplored the fact that in the modern liberal era the church no longer appeared to grasp the reality of the Jewish danger as clearly it had in the past.[29] Hitler still seemed hopeful that he could win over the Catholic Church, and the fact that Berning said not a single word of criticism in response to Hitler's claims that Nazi anti-Semitism was based on Catholic principle and practice, could only have encouraged him.

Not only had the concordat inhibited church opposition to the regime, but numerous Catholics now began to flock to the Nazi Party, attracted like their Protestant counterparts to the call for a national renaissance. Nevertheless, there were limits to this *Gleichschaltung,* and there was some unease in the German Catholic hierarchy. Shortly before Christmas 1933, Cardinal Michael von Faulhaber, the archbishop of Munich, preached a series of bold sermons to overflowing crowds at Saint Michael's Church in which he defended the Hebrew Bible and the Jewish origins of Christianity against vilification by *völkisch* racists. The sermons, published under the title *Judentum, Christentum, Germanentum* (1934), eloquently condemned unbridled nationalism and racial intolerance in theological terms.[30] At the same time, Faulhaber insisted that the indispensability of the Old Testament to Christianity had no bearing on "antagonism to the Jews of today," which he did not seek to oppose. Indeed, he denied suggestions made abroad that his public addresses had constituted a defense of German Jews or implied any criticism of Nazi policy.[31] Cardinal Faulhaber's ambivalence continued in the coming years, mirroring that of the German Catholic hierarchy as a whole and of the Vatican itself. On 4 November 1936, he visited Hitler at Berchtesgaden for a three-hour discussion. The Reich Chancellor demanded, among other things, that the Catholic Church openly support the Nuremberg Race Laws. (There had been no clear official response.) Against the background of the Spanish civil war, Hitler shrewdly warned the cardinal that if National Socialism did not triumph over Bolshevism, then there would be no future for Christianity and the Roman church in Europe.[32]

Faulhaber evidently came away impressed by Hitler's diplomatic finesse, believing that he would continue to respect the rights of the Catholic Church in Germany. This proved to be a fatal illusion, one that the Vatican itself corrected in the 1937 papal encyclical *Mit brennender Sorge* (With deep anxiety), issued in German by Pope Pius XI.[33] This was the only serious and unequivocal public criticism of National Socialism that the Vatican ventured. The encyclical was essentially authored by Archbishop Faulhaber himself (helped by his German Catholic colleagues) with the active assistance of Eugenio Pacelli, the cardinal secretary of state in Rome (and the future Pope Pius XII). The encyclical did contain a sharp condemnation of Nazi racism as a form of atheistic "neo-paganism" and also a denunciation of totalitarian doctrines, but no mention was made of either anti-Semitism or the persecution of German Jews. A year later, neither the German Catholic hierarchy nor the Vatican officially protested the devastating Kristallnacht pogrom, though it seems that Cardinal Faulhaber did privately aid the chief rabbi of Munich in trying to salvage some religious articles from his burning synagogue.

But the ambivalence toward National Socialism did not end there. Like the Protestant churches, the leading German

Catholic bishops appeared to be generally supportive of German foreign policy at the time of the *Anschluss* and of the Czech crisis of 1938. Furthermore, both Cardinal Faulhaber and Cardinal Adolf Bertram of Breslau found it appropriate to congratulate Hitler on "miraculously" surviving Johannn Georg Elser's assassination attempt on 8 November 1939, with a "Te Deum" being sung in Munich's cathedral to give thanks to divine providence at the Führer's escape. Cardinal Bertram had already distinguished himself earlier in 1939 with a congratulatory telegram on the occasion of Hitler's birthday, his fiftieth, a gesture that he repeated in the following years.[34]

The German Catholic hierarchy fell silent during the war in face of the horrifying atrocities against Poles and Jews, with only a few honorable exceptions. This lack of response was not due to ignorance of what was happening in their midst or in the German-occupied territories. Bishop Berning noted on 5 February 1942 that "the plan for a total elimination of the Jews clearly exists" (*"Es besteht wohl der Plan, die Juden ganz auszurotten"*).[35] He plainly wondered whether he and his fellow bishops should launch a public protest from their pulpits. Conrad Gröber, archbishop of Fribourg, informed the pope on 14 June 1942 about the massacres of Jews being perpetrated by the Einsatzgruppen in Russia and concluded ominously: "The Nazi conception of the world is characterised by the most radical antisemitism, going as far as the annihilation [*Vernichtung*] of Jewry, not only in its spirit but also in its members."[36] But despite the efforts of a small minority, including the valiant Margerete Sommer (head of a Catholic relief organization attached to the Berlin curia), who vainly insisted on a public denunciation of the Nazi murders, silence was maintained.

At a conference of Bavarian bishops on 30–31 March 1943, Cardinal Faulhaber reminded his audience that "nothing could render a better service to the greatest adversaries of the Church than to have recourse now to heavy artillery. At a

moment when we are in difficulty that would allow once
again the stab in the back to be revived. My impression is that
this is precisely what they are waiting for."[37] Faulhaber believed that the German bishops would be accused of treason,
of breaking national solidarity and serving enemy propaganda, with irreparable consequences for German Catholicism. When the mass deportations of German Jews had begun
in October 1941, the episcopate had limited its intervention
with the government to Catholic "non-Aryans." It was significant that in late 1941, when the German bishops had brought
themselves to protest proposed legislation that would force
partners in mixed marriages to divorce, Cardinal Bertram had
felt obliged to emphasize that he was by no means deficient in
love for the German *Volk* and for its dignity, "or [guilty] of un-
derestimation of the harmful Jewish influence upon German
culture and national interests."[38]

Even the most outspoken of all the high-ranking German
prelates, the aristocratic Clemens August Graf von Galen,
cardinal archbishop of Münster, was very careful to emphasize his patriotism. Galen consistently exhorted the faithful to
defend the Fatherland and "to fight against the external
enemy," though he did preach against vindictiveness, the
killing of hostages, and the murder of unarmed prisoners of
war.[39] In the summer of 1941, Galen began a series of blister-
ing sermons against the government's euthanasia program
(the so-called mercy killings), which he bluntly called "plain
murder"—probably the most effective, single episcopal protest against the Nazi regime in the twelve years of its rule.[40]
The strong public echo his words aroused sufficiently rattled
the Nazi leadership (which to that point had put to death
more than seventy thousand predominantly ethnic Germans
suffering from a variety of congenital mental or physical de-
fects) that it felt obliged to officially suspend the program of
mass gassing. Henceforth, euthanasia was conducted in such a
way that the killings would be easier to conceal. Hitler, who
still wanted to avoid a public confrontation with the Catholic

Church, swore to exact retribution from Galen but only after the end of the war—a vain threat, as it turned out.

Neither Galen nor the ecclesiastical establishments in Germany (Catholic or Protestant) made any comparable pronouncements or interventions in favor of unconverted Jews or Gypsies.[41] Nor, when German bishops eventually received reports about the mass murder of Jews in the death camps (from officers serving in the east, from civil servants, or from other sources) did their subsequent vague pronouncements specifically mention Jews. The harsh truth is that few Protestants or Catholics in Germany and Austria were ready to expose the menacing horror of bloodthirsty Nazi anti-Semitism, not least because the boundaries had long been blurred by the churches' "teaching of contempt" toward Judaism. When the genocide began, they appeared to be paralyzed. Even more striking was their failure to grasp how dangerous racist anti-Semitism was to the future of Christianity.

For at the heart of Nazism, despite its cunning pretense of "positive Christianity," there was a deep-seated rejection of the entire civilization that had been built on Judeo-Christian ethics. Indeed, the leading Nazis—Hitler, Himmler, Rosenberg, Goebbels, and Bormann—were all fanatically anti-Christian, though this was partly hidden from the German public. Had ordinary Germans been privy to Hitler's table talk, some of them might have been deeply shocked. On 17 February 1942, for example, shortly after the first gassings of Jews, the Führer proclaimed, in the presence of Himmler: "The notions represented by Jewish Christianity were strictly unthinkable to Roman brains. . . . The Jew who fraudulently introduced Christianity into the ancient world—in order to ruin it—reopened the same breach in modern times, this time taking as his pretext the social question. It's the same sleight of hand as before. Just as Saul has changed into St Paul, Mordechai became Karl Marx."[42]

The conviction that Judaism, Christianity, and Bolshevism represented one single pathological phenomenon of decadence became a veritable leitmotif for Hitler around the time that the "Final Solution" had been conceived of as an operational plan. On the night of 11–12 July 1941, shortly after the invasion of Soviet Russia, Hitler asserted that the coming of Christianity had been "the heaviest blow that ever struck humanity."[43] It had been responsible for the extinction of the Roman Empire and the destruction of fifteen hundred years of civilization at a single stroke. In comparison with the tolerance of the Greco-Roman world, Christianity was "the first creed in the world to exterminate its adversaries in the name of love."[44] Worse still, Bolshevism was "Christianity's illegitimate child," and both were "inventions of the Jew."[45] Christianity had introduced the deliberate lie of religion into the world, but Bolshevism was based on a similar kind of lying "when it claims to bring liberty to men, whereas in reality it seeks only to enslave them."[46]

It is indeed striking that as he launched the Holocaust Hitler increasingly sought to emphasize the parallels between Christianity and Bolshevism as subversive doctrines destructive of all human culture. In both cases, he insisted that they derived their "leveling" inspiration from the same tainted Jewish "ferment of decomposition." On 21 October 1941, he gave another variant on this theme: "Whilst Roman society proved hostile to the new doctrine, Christianity in its pure state stirred the population to revolt. Rome was Bolshevised, and Bolshevism produced exactly the same results in Rome as later in Russia."[47] Under the influence of the Germanic spirit, Christianity had for a time lost its "openly Bolshevistic character" during the Middle Ages and become almost tolerable. But with the contemporary collapse of culture, "the Jew restores to pride of place Christianity in its Bolshevistic form."[48] Under Jewish-Marxist rule in Russia, for example, hundreds of thousands of men had been deported and their women delivered "to males imported from other regions." In Hitler's fevered imagination, deliberate race mixing had become one of the primary features of the Judeo-Christian-

Bolshevik *Unkultur,* which National Socialism was committed to destroying. Hitler also blamed the vandalizing of the arts and civilization in ancient Greece and Rome on Judeo-Christian influence, drawing a parallel with Soviet Communism in the present as a way to justify the Holocaust.

Nor did Hitler forget to repeat his obsession with the "crypto-Marxist" instigator of revolt, Saint Paul. Following Dietrich Eckart, Hitler saw in Paul "the first man to take account of the possible advantages of using a religion as a means of propaganda." Paul had found an ideal terrain in the decadent Roman Empire for his "egalitarian theories," which contained "what was needed to win over a mass composed of innumerable uprooted people."[49] Paul's proto-Bolshevism had marked the end of the reign of "the clear Greco-Latin genius."[50] The Jews, using the disguise of Pauline Christianity, had deliberately invented the fiction of a transcendent "Beyond," in place of aesthetic harmony in the cosmos and the natural "hierarchy amongst nations." Under the mask of monotheistic religion, the Jews "introduced intolerance in a sphere in which tolerance formerly prevailed."[51] Above all, Judeo-Christianity had deliberately subverted the natural order: "It constantly provokes the weak against the strong, bestiality against intelligence, quantity against quality. It took fourteen centuries for Christianity to reach the peak of savagery and stupidity. We would therefore be wrong to sin by excess of confidence and proclaim our definite victory over Bolshevism. The more we render the Jew incapable of harming us, the more we shall protect ourselves from this danger. The Jew plays in nature the role of a catalysing element. A people that is rid of its Jews returns spontaneously to the natural order."[52]

At first sight, these thoughts seem no more than the infinitely crude and malevolent rant of an unhinged mind. While the Einsatzgruppen were busy massacring countless Jews and "Bolsheviks" on the Russian steppes, why engage in hysterical diatribes against Saint Paul? Why insist that Christianity and its offshoots in the Reformation (and more dubiously in modern revolutions) meant the death of all empires and of human civilization itself? And yet, we have arrived here at one of the deepest reasons why Hitler ordered the Holocaust. For at the root of Hitler's anti-Semitism was an apocalyptic vision of the future of civilization and of the "Aryan" destiny that necessitated the complete eradication of a rival Jewish messianism. It was the Judeo-Christian ethic that had alienated humanity from the wholeness of the natural order in pursuit of the "lie" of a transcendent God. Judeo-Christianity in its secularized form had, he believed, given birth to contemporary teachings of pacifism, equality before God and the law, human brotherhood, and compassion for the weak, which the Nazis were determined to uproot. They no longer made any secret of their contempt for Christian ideals of charity, meekness, and humility, inimical as they were to the Germanic warrior ethos.[53]

Since 1937, it had seemed to Hitler that the churches were allies of Judaism rather than of National Socialism. They persisted, for example, in treating the Old Testament as a major source of Christian revelation, and they had rejected the cult of the "Aryan" Jesus. In Protestant circles, the Confessing Church had openly challenged the Nazi-sponsored German Christians. Nor can there be any doubt that the Nazis were infuriated by Pius XI's 1937 encyclical protesting the regime's many violations of the concordat and sharply criticizing certain manifestations of National Socialist neo-paganism. True, German Catholic and Protestant leaders did not express any public sympathy for persecuted Jews, confining themselves strictly to a defense of the biblical Hebrew heritage of Christianity. But even church passivity on the "Jewish question" was interpreted by Hitler, Himmler, Goebbels, Robert Ley, and others as proof that Christianity was irredeemably tainted by "Jewish" influences. In SD reports after 1937, the churches figure prominently alongside Jews and Communists as "ideological enemies" of the regime.[54]

The real chasm between Nazism and Christianity was perhaps best summed up by Martin Bormann, the head of the Party Chancellery and private secretary of the Führer. On the night of 29 November 1944, he ominously remarked: "In the same way any doctrine which is anti-Communist, any doctrine which is anti-Christian must *ipso facto,* be anti-Jewish as well. The National Socialist doctrine is therefore anti-Jewish *in excelsis,* for it is both anti-Communist and anti-Christian."[55]

For the National Socialists, with the outbreak of war it was already clear that there would eventually have to be a "Final Solution" of the "religious question," though for tactical reasons they preferred to postpone any major confrontation with the churches in wartime. But from an ideological standpoint—especially from the summer of 1941—Judeo-Christianity was seen as the embodiment of universalist, rationalist, and humanitarian values antithetical to the Nazi creed. Hence the annihilation of the Jews had a profoundly symbolic as well as an ideological and political meaning: it simultaneously brought the Christian anti-Semitic tradition to a twisted and horrific climax while negating every positive value that Christianity had ever contained.

The danger that National Socialism represented to Christianity in general was not unfamiliar to the new pope, Pius XII, who had been elected on 2 March 1939. Having spent twelve years as papal nuncio in Munich and Berlin before 1929, his personal knowledge of German Catholicism as well as his love of the German language and culture was unrivaled in the Roman hierarchy. Well informed about domestic conditions in the Third Reich, Pacelli had been the architect of the concordat in 1933 but had also played a role in formulating the 1937 papal encyclical.[56] As pope, however, he sought to achieve a détente with Hitler in order to preserve the vital interests of the church in Germany.

At a meeting in the Vatican in early March 1939 with the German cardinals—Faulhaber from Munich, Bertram from

Breslau, Schulte from Cologne, and Innitzer from Vienna—
he emphasized that he considered the "German question" to
be the most important one and that "he reserved its treatment" to himself alone.[57] He further told the cardinals (also
on 9 March 1939) that he had no intention of breaking
with the Nazi regime, having earlier successfully persuaded
Pius XI against precisely such a drastic step. Moreover, he
forbade the Vatican newspaper, *L'Osservatore Romano,* from en-
gaging in any further criticism of events in Germany. Such
polemics had rarely mentioned the Jews, focusing rather on
Nazi harassment of the church or disapproval of the "neopagan" aberrations of biological racism. Objections to German anti-Semitism before the war generally related solely to
its violence and brutality, not to the intrinsic right of the state
to discriminate against Jews.[58] The "Jewish question" did not
have any more priority for Pius XII and his closest collaborators than it did for the German cardinals. Hence it is no surprise that Pius XII's letters to them contain so few comments
about the outrages committed against Jews. Yet there was no
lack of information on the subject nor of appeals to the pope
for his intervention. Konrad von Preysing, the bishop of
Berlin (the most perceptive and anti-Nazi of the front-rank
German Catholics), wrote to Pius XII on 17 January 1941:
"Your Holiness is certainly informed about the situation of
the Jews in Germany and the neighbouring countries. I wish
to mention that I have been asked both from the Catholic and
Protestant side if the Holy See could not do something on
this subject, publish an appeal in favour of these unfortu-
nates."[59]

As with other appeals of this kind, the Pope felt unable or
unwilling to respond. But a year later, a great deal more information was becoming available. In the Vatican as in other
European capitals, knowledge was fast growing about the
"horrible deportations" of Jews to the east. On 30 January
1942, Vatican Secretary of State Cardinal Maglione had commented to the British ambassador at the Vatican, Sir Francis

d'Arcy Osborne, about a Hitler speech in which the Nazi leader had promised: "The Jews will be liquidated for at least a thousand years!"[60] Much more concrete information soon began to pour in to Rome from many sources. In March 1942, the Vatican received news from Giuseppe Burzio, its representative in Bratislava, that the deportation of eighty thousand Slovak Jews to Poland meant "certain death" for a large number of them.[61] On 18 March 1942, Gerhart Riegner of the World Jewish Congress and Richard Lichtheim of the Jewish Agency sent a remarkably detailed report on the fate of the Jews in Poland and the rest of Europe which reached the Vatican through the Swiss nuncio in Bern, Filippo Bernardini. It spoke of more than a million Jews "exterminated by the Germans," pointing out that the old, the sick, women, and children were being systematically deported, a measure that clearly could not have been implemented for the purposes of forced labor.[62] Then, toward the end of June 1942, the London *Daily Telegraph* began to publish a series of reports on the exterminations in Poland. These reports were summarized for the pope by Osborne, who continued to supply His Holiness with similar material from BBC broadcasts on a regular basis. On 30 June 1942, for example, Osborne passed on to the pope the following item: "The Germans have killed over a million Jews in all, of whom 700,000 in Poland. Several million more have been deported or confined in concentration camps." On 9 July, he reported the condemnation by Cardinal Hinsley, the highest ranking Catholic in Great Britain, of the "utter bestiality of German methods."[63]

From the autumn of 1942, Osborne and the Vatican ambassadors representing Brazil, Poland, Belgium, and the United States began to pressure Pius XII to speak out on behalf of the mercilessly oppressed Poles and Jews. The Roman curia was upset at these moves, claiming that a public protest would only make the victims' suffering even worse and oblige the Vatican to condemn other atrocities besides those of the Germans. Moreover, so Maglione argued, the massacres were

still not verifiable as hard fact, and the pope had already deplored such actions in general terms. Furthermore, he made it
clear that it was out of the question for the pope to condemn
by name either Hitler or Nazi Germany.[64]

These arguments did not overly impress President Roosevelt's personal representative to the pope, Myron Taylor.
On 22 September 1942, in an interview with a top Vatican official, Domenico Tardini, Taylor spoke "of the opportunity
and the necessity, of a word from the Pope against such huge
atrocities by the Germans." Tardini privately agreed, even as
he wearily repeated the standard refrain that Pius XII "has already spoken several times to condemn crimes by whomso-
ever they are committed."[65] Such answers did not reassure the
American or British representatives. Osborne, writing to British Foreign Secretary Anthony Eden on 3 October 1942,
noted with some irony and regret that the "occasional decla-
rations in general terms do not have the lasting force and va-
lidity that, in the timeless atmosphere of the Vatican, they
might perhaps be expected to retain.... A policy of silence in
regard to such offences against the conscience of the world
must necessarily involve a renunciation of moral leadership."[66]

On 13 December 1942, Osborne angrily confided to his
diary, "The more I think of it, the more I am revolted by
Hitler's massacre of the Jewish race on the one hand, and, on
the other, the Vatican's apparently exclusive preoccupation
with the effects of the war on Italy and the possibilities of the
bombardment of Rome. The whole outfit seems to have become Italian."[67] The next day, he urged the Vatican to recon-
sider its duties "in respect of the unprecedented crime against
humanity of Hitler's campaign of extermination of the Jews,
in which I said that Italy was an accomplice as the partner and
ally of Germany."[68] On 18 December, he pressed Tardini
hard to get the pope to say something clear in his upcoming
Christmas Eve broadcast. The evasive reply suggested to Osborne "that His Holiness is clinging at all costs to what he

considers to be a policy of neutrality, even in the face of the worst outrages against God and man, because he hopes to be able to play a part in restoring peace."[69]

On 17 December 1942, the Allies themselves had issued a public declaration condemning the German massacres of the Jews, which Osborne promptly brought to the pope, hoping for an endorsement. The reply from Maglione was again negative, though he deplored the cruelties inflicted on innocent people. The Holy See, he explained, could only condemn atrocities in general, not particular crimes. Moreover, it was not in a position to verify Allied reports on the number of Jews who had been murdered and to know how reliable such estimates really were.[70] This was a remarkably unsatisfactory statement, given the volume of increasingly detailed information that had reached Rome from a wide variety of sources during the past six months.

In the case of Slovakia, important knowledge had been made available fairly early by the Vatican's energetic representative, Giuseppe Burzio, and the Vatican had then indeed acted. Anti-Jewish laws had been introduced almost immediately after Slovak "independence" had been declared on 14 March 1939. The fascist Slovak state was ruled by a cleric, Father Jozef Tiso, leader of the Hlinková Garda (Hlinka Guard), but there was a pro-Nazi group in the cabinet led by Prime Minister Vojtech Tuka and Alexander Mach, the interior minister. After September 1941, the Slovak government proceeded on its own initiative with the expropriation of Jewish property and then with deportations in March 1942. Initially, at least, the government enjoyed the tacit support of the Catholic bishops in Slovakia, who seemed to be concerned only with making sure that Jewish converts be granted appropriate facilities for observing their new faith.[71]

The Vatican had protested against the planned deportations of Jews on 14 March 1942, expressing some astonishment that a nation supposedly committed to Catholic principles could act in this manner. The papal chargé d'affaires (who had tried unsuccessfully to persuade the Slovak bishops to take a unified position against the codex of September 1941) now warned Tiso of serious consequences if he ignored the Vatican protest. On 23 May 1942, the Slovak government sent a chilling communication to the Vatican proudly defending its anti-Semitic policy: the mass deportation was "part of a much larger general plan" put into operation in agreement with the German government. "Half a million Jews would be transported to Eastern Europe. Slovakia will be the first State whose inhabitants of Jewish origin would be accepted by Germany."[72] The very detailed elaboration of government policy that followed (transmitted by the Slovak representative to the Holy See, Karol Sidor) spoke of the imminent deportations of Jews from France, Holland, Belgium, Bohemia, Moravia, and the German Reich. The Slovak report announced that they would be settled in areas near Lublin, where they would be "under the protection of the Reich [*sotto la protezione del Reich/Schutzbefohlene*]." This communication observed that Hungary, too, would be requested to deliver its eight hundred thousand Jews. While washing its hands of its own Jewish citizens, the Slovak government told the Vatican that the Germans had promised "that the Jews will be treated humanely."

Vatican Secretary of State Maglione seemed taken aback at the brutality of Slovak government policy and the continuing deportations, especially since Slovakia was a self-proclaimed Catholic nation and Tiso was an ordained priest, whose involvement in such massive crimes could after all compromise the honor of the Vatican and the church. On 13 July 1942, Maglione's top assistant, Tardini, pointedly noted: "It is a real misfortune that the President of Slovakia is a priest [*un sacerdote*]. That the Holy See cannot bring Hitler to heel, everyone knows. But who will understand that we cannot even control a priest."[73]

The Vatican record in Croatia was particularly open to condemnation and much worse than in Slovakia because of the monstrous crimes committed by a piously Catholic regime, headed by Ante Pavelić, the leader of the Ustashe movement, which had come to power on 10 April 1941. Ustashe violence directed against the "schismatics" (i.e., the Orthodox Serbs), resembled a "religious crusade." The Vatican deplored preaching the gospel out of the barrel of a gun, but it also knew how proud the new regime was of its thirteen-hundred-year-old links with the Holy See. The Croatian state had wasted no time in passing racial laws against the Jews—accomplishing in a matter of weeks what it had taken the Nazi regime years to achieve in Germany.[74] As early as May 1941, Jews were being rounded up and sent to concentration camps. The Croatian archbishop, Cardinal Aloysius Stepinac of Zagreb, watched these events with anxiety and perhaps ambivalence. He approved of certain Ustashe actions, for example those against abortion and indecent advertisements, and he welcomed the intense public Catholicism of the new regime. At the same time he felt bound to protest the forced conversions of Serbs and the "brutal treatment of non-Aryans during the deportations and at the camps."[75] Yet while he appealed to Pavelić for measures against Serbs and Jews to be "carried out in a more humane and considerate way," he did not challenge the racist policy as such. In this respect, Stepinac was acting consistently with the line adopted by Vatican officials during the Holocaust.

By October 1942, the Vatican had received reliable information on the massacres of Jews collected by Father Pirro Scavizzi (an Italian hospital-train chaplain), who reported to the pope that two million deaths had occurred up to that point. From this and many other sources (Allied, Polish, Jewish, and others) including its own nuncios, the Vatican knew by the late autumn of 1942 that the systematic killing of Jews was taking place all over Nazi-occupied Europe.

Eventually, in his Christmas message of 1942, Pius XII did say something. In one single sentence he mentioned that "hundreds of thousands of people, through no fault of their own and solely because of their nation or race [*stirpe*], have been condemned to death or progressive extinction."[76] As the British historian Owen Chadwick has observed, "the Pope was very careful to guard against exaggeration." Rather like the high officials of the British Foreign Office, "he thought that the Poles and Jews exaggerated for the sake of helping the war effort."[77] Hence the numbers mentioned in his broadcast were far lower than the estimates in the reports which the Vatican had earlier received. Nor was there any mention of Nazis, Jews, Poles, or other particular victims.

The pope's general appeal to the world's conscience, while angering some and pleasing others, was well understood by at least one of the German bishops. On 6 March 1943, Konrad von Preysing evoked the message when writing to Pius XII, asking him to try to save the Jews still in the Reich capital, who were facing imminent deportation, which would lead to certain death. "Even more bitterly, the new wave of deportations of the Jews which just began in the days before 1 March, particularly affects us here in Berlin. Several thousands are involved: Your Holiness has alluded to their probable fate in your Christmas Radio Broadcast. Among the deportees are also many Catholics. Is it not possible that Your Holiness tries once again to intervene for the many unfortunate innocents [*die vielen Unglücklichen Unschuldigen*]? It is the last hope for many and the profound wish of all right-thinking people."[78]

Pius XII's lengthy reply (dated 30 April 1943) covered many themes that had preoccupied him all through his wartime correspondence with the German bishops. He expressed his pain at the fierce Allied aerial bombardments of German cities and reported on Vatican efforts to secure information about German soldiers captured or missing in Russia. Pius XII did not directly respond to Preysing's appeal to speak out about the Jews. But he did articulate his satisfaction at the fact that it was specifically Berlin Catholics who had shown such fraternal love toward "the so-called non-Aryans" (*Nichtariern*) in their distress. He also wrote of the "charitable action" of the Holy See on behalf of both "Catholic Non-Aryans" and those "of Jewish confession [*Glaubensjuden*]," emphasizing that the Vatican had spent considerable sums "for the transportation of emigrants overseas" (much of this money had come from American Jewish sources, which was not mentioned).[79]

The pope also noted that while the Holy See expected neither heavenly nor earthly rewards for its humanitarian gestures, it had received "the warmest recognition for its relief work" from Jewish organizations. Pius XII even found a word of "fatherly recognition" for Father Bernhard Lichtenberg, a Catholic bishop who had been imprisoned by the Nazis for his courageous sermons (in solidarity with the deported Jews) and who was to die on his way to Dachau shortly afterward. No less significantly, Pius XII told Preysing that he gave to his pastors at the local level "the duty of determining if and to what degree the danger of reprisals and diverse forms of repression ... seem to advise caution, to avoid the greater evil [*ad maiora mala vitanda*] despite alleged reasons to the contrary."[80] The pope felt that under wartime conditions he had to exercise great care in order not "to impose useless sacrifices on German Catholics, who are already so oppressed for the sake of their faith."[81]

Perhaps in a delayed response to Preysing's appeal, Pius XII did allusively refer to the subject in an allocution to the cardinals on 2 June 1943. This was the second and last time that he would touch in public on what we now call "the Holocaust." "Do not be astonished," he said, "if we lend our ear with particularly profound sympathy to the voices of those who turn to us imploringly, their hearts full of fear. They are those who, because of their nationality or their descent, are pursued by mounting misfortune and increasing suffering. Sometimes, through no fault of theirs, they are subjected to measures which threaten them with extermination."[82] This short section was suppressed by the Axis powers in their reports on the pope's speech, but Vatican radio did broadcast it to Germany, adding that those who make "a distinction between Jews and other men" were unfaithful to God and the divine commandments.

Only on 2 June 1945, before the Sacred College of Cardinals, did the pope feel free to fully unburden himself and call things by their proper names. The pope now claimed to have foreseen the disaster of National Socialism "when it was still in the distant future, and few, We believe, have followed with greater anxiety the process leading to the inevitable crash."[83] He pointed out that "the Church did everything possible to set up a formidable barrier to the spread of ideas at once subversive and violent." In no way had the concordat implied "any formal approval to the teachings or tendencies of National Socialism."[84] He recalled how the 1937 encyclical had boldly exposed Nazism as "an arrogant apostasy from Jesus Christ, the denial of His Doctrine and of His work of redemption, the cult of violence, the idolatry of race and blood, the overthrow of human liberty and dignity."[85] This sharp drawing of the lines in 1937 had opened the eyes of many, though regrettably not of all, Catholics. There were some, he admitted, who had been "too blinded by their prejudices or tempted by political advantage" to oppose National Socialist ideology with sufficient vigor.

But the pope's own record after the German military occupation of Rome in September 1943 also left something to be desired. More than one thousand Roman Jews (out of a population of eight thousand) were deported to Auschwitz-Birkenau from under the windows of the Vatican, so to speak. True, there were also Roman Jews who were hidden in monasteries, convents, and even in the Vatican itself. But it is not clear how much Pius XII had to do with the rescue actions or whether he directly approved them.[86]

On 16 October 1943, the SS and German military police surrounded the Roman ghetto, rounding up and transporting Jews to the Italian Military College—less than half a mile from the Vatican. The same morning, the pope ordered

Maglione to summon the German ambassador, Ernst von Weizsäcker. The cardinal told Weizsäcker how "painful beyond words it is for the Holy Father that here in Rome itself, under the eyes of the Common Father [*sotto gli occhi del Padre Commune*], so many people should be made to suffer uniquely because they belong to a certain race [*appartengono ad una stirpa determinata*]." Maglione appealed to the ambassador's "tender and good heart—to try to save these many innocent people" invoking his sentiments of humanity and "Christian charity."[87] He also suggested that "the Holy See did not want to be put in a position that forced it to protest [*non deve essere messa nella necessità di protestare*]," if the German deportations continued. In such a case, "it would have to trust for the consequences in the Divine Providence." Most remarkable of all was Maglione's admission that "the Holy See had been prudent enough not to give to the German people any impression of having done or wanting to do anything against Germany during this terrible war [*per non dare al popolo germanico l'impressione di aver fatto o voler fare contro la Germania la minima cosa durante una guerra terribile*]."[88] Neither Pius XII, Maglione, nor any other high Vatican officials wanted a rupture with Nazi Germany.

Pius XII's refusal to make a public denunciation of the Roman *razzia* (roundup) was no different from the position he had adopted when vast numbers of Jews had been deported from across Europe in 1942 or murdered in Russia, the Ukraine, and Poland. Had such a protest been made, it is quite possible that more Catholics might have helped to rescue Jews in occupied countries or that more Jews might have fled in time from their Nazi hunters. Nor did the Vatican oppose discriminatory laws against Jews or the social segregation that resulted, even as the Holocaust was raging in the heart of Europe. In the autumn of 1941, a report by the French ambassador to the Holy See, Leon Bérard, confirmed to Marshal Henri Pétain that the Vatican had no objection to Vichy's draconian anti-Jewish statutes, provided that the French government acted with "justice and charity."[89] The pattern in Croatia, Slovakia, Hungary, Romania, and other countries that passed anti-Semitic legislation was almost always the same. Vatican objections were rarely directed against the principle of discrimination per se, though it did object to violence, murder, and racist assumptions about baptized Jews that conflicted with Catholic doctrine or church prerogatives. As late as August 1943, the Jesuit Father Pietro Tacchi Venturi observed that according to the principles and traditions of the Catholic Church the Italian anti-Jewish laws had "dispositions that should be abrogated but contain others worthy of confirmation."[90]

Such hesitations and ambivalence cannot be divorced from the deep suspicion in which the church still held the Jews, a distrust that the unfolding Holocaust was unable to significantly dent. They were still identified theologically as a "deicide" people in most Catholic minds; they were seen as being linked with the forces of liberation, Freemasonry, rationalism, and secularism in the democratic west and with a dictatorial and ruthless Bolshevism in the east. The Jews embodied in Catholic tradition a secular "modernity" that was considered inimical to the ideals of Christian society and its vision of redemption. The churches, both Catholic and Protestant, were unable—with a few honorable exceptions—to shake off the age-old "teaching of contempt" toward the Jews, though they neither conceived, collaborated in, nor approved of the Holocaust. To quote Emil Fackenheim, the "Final Solution" was the result of "a bi-millennial disease within Christianity *itself,* transmuted when Nazism turned against the Christian substance."[91]

6

COLLABORATION

ACROSS EUROPE

It takes a lot of imagination to find something new. In fact, after the expropriation of real estate, after the deportations and assassinations—all the rest becomes grotesque.... Sometimes there is something diabolic in anti-Semitism, but now, when we don't swim in blood, we are splashing through muddy, petty theft.

Journal of Mihail Sebastian, Bucharest, 12 November 1941

Hitler, keep your dirty hands
off our dirty Jews!

Wartime graffiti in Amsterdam

The immediate factors favourable to Jewish rescue during the Holocaust must be placed in the context of the customs and traditions of individual countries. The most pertinent tradition, of course, is the existence or absence of anti-Semitism. For many reasons, modern Italy lacked an anti-Semitic tradition.

SUSAN ZUCCOTTI, *The Italians and the Holocaust* (1987)

The Nazi Holocaust had begun on Soviet soil and was directed initially at the three and a half million Jews living there, including the recently annexed Baltic states. One of its most striking features there was its openly public character, so different from the secretive way gassings were later conducted in the death camps of Poland. As the Wehrmacht struck more deeply into the Soviet Union, the Jewish death toll mounted rapidly.[1] According to Raul Hilberg, by the end of 1943 the Germans had succeeded in killing close to two million Jews within the Soviet Union, mostly by shooting them in pits close to their homes. Only in the Soviet Union did the Germans and their helpers repeatedly shoot down hundreds of thousands of unarmed Jewish men, women, and children in broad daylight. Despite this high visibility, the Soviet regime was not interested in publicizing more than the barest details, as it was determined to cover up the evidence of extensive collaboration with the Nazi invaders by "peaceful Soviet citizens."

The example of the Ukrainians is particularly pertinent since their "collaboration" with the Germans assumed such a wide-ranging character. In the Ukraine, local police zealously rounded up Jews and herded them into ghettos, isolating them from their neighbors and weakening their physical and psychological resistance. When the mass shootings began in the late summer of 1941, it was they who took Jews to the killing sites, seeing to it that they would not escape. Although the Germans always directed and coordinated the killing of Jews through their regional SS and police leaders, the security police, and units of the mobile order police, recent research has confirmed the vital auxiliary role of the indigenous local police collaborators (*Schutzmannschaft*).[2] Together with the German gendarmerie, Ukrainian police were not only responsible for the roundups but on occasion participated directly in the pit shootings.

In the Ukraine and western Byelorussia, the *Schutzmannschaft* specialized above all in search-and-kill operations, looking for Jews still hidden in the ghettos or who had fled to the neighboring forests.[3] The local police were especially dangerous since they were often the only people able to clearly identify their former Jewish neighbors. In the areas under German civil administration, more than twenty-five thousand men volunteered in the first few months of the occupation for service in the *Schutzmannschaft*. In the rural districts of the Ukraine and Byelorussia at the time of the 1942 ghetto "liquidations," these local policemen often outnumbered the German gendarmes by a ratio of more than five to one. Thus not only were the German order police the "willing executioners" in the face-to-face killing process described by Daniel Goldhagen. Indeed, some of the more zealous perpetrators, who sought to win promotion through their prowess as murderers, were later described by eyewitnesses as even more callous toward Jewish women and children than were the Germans themselves.

The local perpetrators included a mixture of nationalist activists, brutal anti-Semites, rank opportunists, former criminals, and simple peasants looking for a more secure source of income. Their motives were equally mixed. Some were primarily influenced by sheer personal greed, others driven by alcoholism, careerism, or peer-group pressure, and others by a vicious anti-Semitism and a burning hatred of the Soviet regime.[4] Ukrainians had not, for example, forgotten Stalin's deliberately induced "terror famine" in their land, which had led to four million deaths in the early 1930s during the forced collectivization of agriculture. Although the Stalinists no more than the Nazis could realistically aim at wiping out all thirty-six million Ukrainians, both sought to break the back of their tenacious nationalism.[5] As had happened elsewhere in eastern Europe, Ukrainian nationalists in the 1930s frequently identified Jews with the hegemonic oppressor—in this case, the Russians. As in Germany, this "Judeo-Bolshevik" amalgam fatally intensified the anti-Semitism woven deep into the fabric of Ukrainian popular consciousness since the seventeenth century—an ethnic and socioeconomic hatred that periodically erupted into bloody pogroms in 1881, 1905, and again during the Russian civil war.[6]

Collaboration with the Nazi invaders, welcomed by many Ukrainians as a "liberating" force from Soviet Communism and the Jews, was all too common in the early stages of the German occupation. Such cooperation would have assumed much greater proportions were it not for the unbounded racial hubris and folly of the German conquerors, who treated millions of their Ukrainian subjects as if they really were Slavic *Untermenschen*—exploiting and killing them in large numbers.[7] Yet in the initial euphoria of the German invasion, there had been no shortage of Ukrainians who seized Jewish possessions and occupied their homes.

In Lithuania, too, the Germans and their local collaborators had begun to murder Jews systematically, almost immediately after the invasion. Reinhard Heydrich's instructions to the Einsatzgruppen had been to encourage the local population "to act spontaneously" against the Jews. In the event, Lithuanians needed no prompting, such was the zeal and frenzy with which they carried out pogroms. The first killings of 1,500 Jews in Kovno on the night of 25–26 June 1941 were perpetrated by Lithuanians with a bestial savagery that surprised the Germans themselves.[8] It was the ultranationalist, anti-Soviet Lithuanian "partisans" who volunteered most eagerly to kill many thousands of Jews in Kovno, Vilna, and the numerous *shtetlach* in the Lithuanian provinces. In these *Aktionen*, they outstripped the Germans both in the scale and intensity of their involvement and in the number of victims they wiped out. Perhaps as much as two thirds of Lithuanian Jewry were extinguished by local units.

Altogether, more than 90 percent of Lithuanian Jewry was killed in the Holocaust, the highest single death rate for any major Jewish community in Europe. The great majority were murdered very swiftly indeed, in the five months between the end of June and December 1941. None of these horrors would have been possible without what Dina Porat has described as "a fatal combination of Lithuanian motivation and German organisation and thoroughness."[9] She points out that though the Germans provided the framework and "legitimacy" for the killings, Lithuanian national aspirations and hatred for Communism were the fuel driving the murder machine. Feelings that had been bottled up during the oppressive Soviet rule of Lithuania (1940–1941), when its indigenous citizenry saw their independence erased, exploded into a crazed anti-Semitic fury once the Germans arrived. Though they had no pogrom tradition analogous to those of Poland, the Ukraine, Romania, or Russia, Lithuanians proved to be highly proficient in face-to-face killing. Once local police battalions (numbering about 8,500 people) were close to completing their macabre work, some of them were sent to Byelorussia and Poland to continue their murderous activities in small towns, camps, and ghettos. Their members could also be found as guards in death camps such as Treblinka or Majdanek and as auxiliaries assisting General Stroop's forces in crushing the Warsaw ghetto uprising. As hangmen and sadists, their reputation was second to none.

Croatia stands out as another place where human bestiality became closely allied to fanatical nationalism. The ruling clique under Pavelić required no encouragement from the Germans to kill Jews and even less to murder almost half a million Serbs. Here, too, the German Army was momentarily taken aback (despite its own appalling record in Serbia) by the bloody fury of the Ustashe fascists who had come to power in April 1941.[10] For the Croats, the prime enemy remained the Christian Orthodox Serbs, who were designated to be exiled, killed, or returned to Catholicism—allegedly the "true faith of their fathers." The "new Croatia" did indeed forcibly convert hundreds of thousands of Greek Orthodox Serbs at gunpoint, amply confirming Jonathan Steinberg's description of it as "the only Axis satellite to have murdered more non-Jewish than Jewish civilians."[11] Genocide was official, state-directed policy in wartime Croatia, and it did not spare thirty-eight thousand Jews and twenty-seven thousand Gypsies.[12] Within three weeks of coming to power, the new regime had passed anti-Jewish race laws that prohibited intermarriage, removed Jews from the civil service and professions, forced them to register their property, marked their stores, and "Aryanized" their capital. Following the example of the Nuremberg Race Laws, Jews were forbidden to employ "Aryan" female servants. Soon, the bulk of Croatian Jews was sent to the notorious Ustashe concentration camps, while seven thousand of them were deported by the Croats at German request.[13] In the summer of 1943, Archbishop Stepinac deplored the "inhumane and brutal treatment of non-Aryans during the deportations and at the camps, and even worse, that neither children, old people nor the sick are spared."[14] Pavelić did not even respect the human rights of Jewish converts to Catholicism, much to the dismay of Stepinac and an accredited apostolic visitor, Msgr. Marcone.[15]

Romania was another example of primitive, Balkan-style ferocity, where once again, to quote Hannah Arendt, "even the SS were taken aback, and occasionally frightened by the horrors of old-fashioned, spontaneous pogroms on a gigantic scale."[16] In the nineteenth century, Romania had rivaled tsarist Russia in its persecution of Jews and intransigent insistence on regarding them as aliens. Under enormous pressure from the Western Allies, it had grudgingly granted citizenship to its Jewish minority after the First World War, a step the Romanian government canceled in December 1937. At that time, Romania had a very large Jewish population of 750,000. By 1940, several hundred thousand Jews had lost their civil rights, possessions, and jobs. Neither the Romanian government nor the fanatical ultranationalists in the fascist Iron Guard movement needed any prodding from Nazi Germany. Romanian nationalism had become almost synonymous with anti-Semitism and slogans connecting the Jews with Communism, capitalism, and plutocracy fell on fertile soil.[17] The Iron Guard won 15.5 percent of the vote in the 1937 elections, and the more moderate forces in Romania felt obliged to engage in racist and xenophobic rhetoric simply to keep it in check.[18] In August 1940, the head of the new Iron Guard dictatorship, Ion Antonescu, declared almost all Romanian Jews stateless (only about ten thousand Jews were exempt), initiating some of the harshest anti-Jewish legislation hitherto seen in Europe. This step prompted Hitler to remark that "Antonescu proceeds in these matters in far more radical fashion than we have done up to the present."[19]

In January 1941, the Iron Guard carried out a savage pogrom in Bucharest in which 170 Jews were murdered. The following month, Romania entered the war, and its legions were soon involved in horrific massacres of Jews in the east, especially in the Crimea and southern Ukraine. In Odessa alone, Romanian troops butchered about thirty thousand Jews with unsurpassed cruelty. Even after the Iron Guard left the government, the slaughter continued unabated in the summer of 1941. Romanian troops were further used to send thousands of Jews on forced marches into designated killing areas, to drown them in the Dniester, or push them into the German zone of the Ukraine. The deportations of nearly 150,000 Jews to the newly annexed province of Transnistria were especially horrific. The Jews were herded into freight cars and often died of suffocation as the trains traveled through the countryside for days on end. The ghettos and concentration camps in Transnistria were as horrible as anything in the German Reich. Not surprisingly, three quarters of the Jews in Transnistria perished.

Although Antonescu's government acted with complete ruthlessness against the nonassimilated and non–Romanian speaking Jews of Bessarabia and Bukovina (seized from the Soviet Union in 1941), it was much less inclined to cooperate with German demands to deport to the east the acculturated Jews of the Romanian heartland.[20] Antonescu made no secret of his opposition to any encroachment on his national sovereignty. Probably he also felt that Romania had already achieved its territorial ambitions by the autumn of 1942 and was better off disengaging itself from Nazi Germany. His regime had already killed about one quarter of a million of its own Jews, mostly without German assistance. But as the tide of war turned against Germany, Antonescu preferred to hedge his bets, maintaining his channels to the West and gradually distancing himself from Hitler's "Final Solution."

From the end of 1942, a flourishing trade in exemption certificates for Jews developed, as Romanian officials discovered that the sale of Jews abroad for hard currency could be profitable. Romania became an enthusiastic convert to the idea of Jewish emigration and an outlet for Jews seeking to reach Palestine. The one country in Europe (outside of Germany) that had practiced mass extermination of Jews entirely on its own initiative also proved to be the most mercenary, and this corruptibility led to a new "moderation" on the "Jewish question." Antonescu first tried and ultimately failed to persuade the Nazis to permit the departure of Jews to the Middle East. Then, ignoring German pressure, he decisively obstructed the deportation of Jews from the Regat region. Despite Antonescu's record of murderous anti-Semitism, about three hundred thousand Romanian Jews (more than half the Jewish population) survived the Holocaust.

Hungary was an exceptionally tragic case, for had the Germans not invaded the country in March 1944, far more Jews would have been spared than in Romania. Instead, in a dizzying, accelerated process of destruction that took fewer than four months, more than 60 percent of Hungary's 725,000 Jews were packed off to the gas chambers of Auschwitz-Birkenau. By 8 July 1944, almost 440,000 Jews had been deported, and toward the end of the year, except for the Jews of Budapest, the country was virtually *Judenrein.* The speed seemed all the more shocking given the late stage of the war, the certainty that Nazi Germany would be defeated, the widespread knowledge of the Holocaust, and repeated Allied warnings to the Hungarian government. The two hundred Germans in Adolf Eichmann's Sondereinsatzkommando (Special Operations Unit), aided by another six hundred Gestapo men, could hardly have deported Hungarian Jewry to the death chambers on their own. The collaboration of the Hungarian Army, the gendarmerie (who played the key role), politicians, civil servants, fascist Arrow Cross militia, and transport workers was essential. The process was made much easier by the spinelessness of the Hungarian regent, Admiral Horthy, and the hostility of ordinary Hungarians who seemed to sympathize more with the persecutors of the Jews than with the victims.[21] There were no fewer than thirty-five thousand Hungarian denunciations and betrayals of Jews in the first weeks of the German invasion. Moreover, the Christian churches and the Primate of Hungary, Cardinal Justinian Seredi, displayed remarkably little resistance (except on the issue of converts) to the anti-Jewish measures that ultimately led to the deportations.[22]

Jewish resistance, while difficult in Hungary's open plains, was also minimal. One of the reasons why so few Hungarian Jews resorted to arms lay in the depth of their integration in Hungarian society, ever since their emancipation in 1867. Before 1914, they had been important allies for the Magyars in the multiethnic Hungarian state that was still part of the Habsburg Empire and faced with constant demographic and political challenges from Romanians, Germans, Slovaks,

Serbs, and Croats.[23] During the First World War, however, the short-lived Soviet Republic established by Béla Kun and his associates (two thirds of whom were Communists of Jewish origin) changed perceptions decisively for the worse, even though the revolutionaries were as hostile to Judaism as they were to the Christian churches. This was especially true for the conservative, landowning elites who had traditionally looked to Jews as their natural business partners.

In 1920, Hungary had been the first modern state in post-war Europe to institute a *numerus clausus* in order to reduce Jewish admissions to the universities to 6 percent. In 1938, the first anti-Jewish law limited Jewish representation in commercial, financial, and industrial concerns, as well as in journalism and the professions, to 20 percent. A second anti-Jewish law of wider scope followed in May 1939, restricting Jewish participation in professional and economic life to 6 and 12 percent respectively. The third anti-Jewish law of July 1941 was much more openly racist, forbidding mixed marriages between Christians and Jews and narrowing exemptions.[24] This barrage of legislation reflected in its own way the exceptional importance of the role that Jews had played in Hungary's economic and cultural life for many decades.

As in Romania, during the 1930s successive Hungarian governments tried to outflank the far right by adopting more moderate anti-Semitic legal measures. But this tactic did not stop the Nazi-style Arrow Cross from winning 45 out of 260 parliamentary seats in the May 1939 elections. The Arrow Cross immediately demanded far sterner measures against the Jews, which were partly satisfied by the new legislation of July 1941. Then, in June 1942, Prime Minister Miklós Kállay, a cosmopolitan Catholic aristocrat, introduced a bill to expropriate Jewish-controlled estates. A few weeks later, the Jewish religion was deprived of equal treatment with other denominations, which it had enjoyed since 1895. But Kállay firmly rejected German demands to expropriate all Jewish wealth, to impose the yellow star, or to deport the Jews to the east.[25] When Hitler summoned Admiral Horthy to Klessheim Castle on 17–18 April 1943, it was evident that both he and Ribbentrop were profoundly irked by the fact that Jews still held positions of economic and political influence in Hungary. This was almost certainly a factor in the German invasion of Hungary nearly one year later.

After the March 1944 invasion, the new Hungarian prime minister, Döme Sztójay, was ready to give the Germans what they wanted. Adolf Eichmann soon found three Hungarians on whom he could rely completely for the concentration of Jews in the provinces with "lightning speed" and then for the transportation to Auschwitz-Birkenau of nearly half a million Jews: Lieutenant Colonel Ferenczy, who had direct charge of the deportations; László Baky, in the Interior Ministry, who controlled the gendarmerie; and László Endre, State Secretary in Charge of Political Jewish Affairs, a particularly rabid anti-Semite.[26] Collaboration now proceeded on a very broad scale. Deportations in every locality required the intervention of the mayor, the police chief, and gendarmes as well as civil servants, who, along with other Hungarians, often enriched themselves by plundering the belongings and property of the departing Jews. The lack of resistance by most Hungarian Gentiles to this forcible uprooting of so many Jews (some of whom had lived continuously in certain communities for centuries) within a matter of days was all the more stunning, given the extent of assimilation on which Hungarian Jewry had long prided itself. Eventually, Admiral Horthy did buckle to pressure from the Western Allies, Pope Pius XII, the king of Sweden, and other dignitaries; he stopped the deportations on 7 July 1944. Undoubtedly, he feared retribution after the American bombing raids on Budapest (2 July 1944), the approach of the Red Army from the east, and the Allied advances in Normandy. He could not but take note of President Roosevelt's ultimatum that "Hungary's fate will not be like any other civilised nation … unless the deportations are stopped."[27]

But in mid-October 1944, the Germans overthrew the Horthy government, appointing the violently anti-Semitic Arrow Cross leader Ferenc Szálasi as head of state. Now began the gruesome last phase of the Hungarian Holocaust—a reign of terror in which the Danube turned red with the blood of more than twenty thousand Jews, tormented and butchered by Arrow Cross fanatics.[28] It was a period of feverish appeals by world Jewry to Allied governments, to the International Red Cross, to the Vatican, and to neutral countries. Protective passes—an idea inspired by Raoul Wallenberg, the heroic Swedish diplomat—saved at least fifteen thousand Jews in Budapest. Jewish lives were also saved by the energetic papal nuncio, Angelo Rotta, and through Swiss diplomatic protection in specially acquired safe houses.[29] A sustained Swiss press campaign did much to ignite the indignation of Western leaders at the fate of Hungarian Jews in the summer of 1944.[30]

The position of Jews in the "independent" Slovak state established with German help in 1939 was even shakier than in Hungary. The fascist militia (the Hlinka Guard) in this small, weak, backward puppet state was Catholic in outlook but also ultranationalist, pro-German, and very anti-Semitic. Most of the Catholics in the Slovak government did not fully share the "modern" racism of the Nazis and still favored the traditional Catholic distinction between baptized and unconverted Jews.[31] By the end of 1941, they were certainly interested in deporting the Jews and taking over their property but as yet unaware of the "Final Solution." However, there were powerful figures such as Alexander Mach (the interior minister) and the German-oriented prime minister, Vojtech Tuka, who wished to imitate the Nazi handling of the "Jewish question." These men were the driving force behind the deportation of nearly ninety thousand Slovak Jews, which began in early

1942. The evidence suggests, as Yehuda Bauer has argued, that it was the Slovaks, rather than the Germans, who initiated the deportations.[32] The Slovak leaders did not definitively know until May 1942 of the mass murders in Poland, though they had probably received some indications before then. By the end of July 1942, however, fifty-two thousand Jews had been transported to Poland, including women, children, the very young, and the infirm. Nazi Germany demanded five hundred Reichsmarks for every Jew received but did not make any claim on their property. The Slovak government, eager to cooperate, expected to benefit handsomely from the massive expropriation of Jewish possessions.

It was in Slovakia that a Jewish Center (Ustredna Zidov) first emerged that tried to prevent the deportations by bribing Slovak officials and negotiating with Eichmann's representative in Bratislava, Dieter Wisliceny. Though nominally part of the Tiso regime's apparatus (and including at least one collaborator with the Germans), the Jewish Center's members tried to subvert the machinery of destruction as best they could. They established intelligence networks, smuggled and aided some eight thousand Jews in reaching the comparative safety of Hungary, passed information about deportations on to the west, and engaged in other underground activities. There was also a working group that emerged apart from the center, led by a courageous Zionist, Gisi Fleischmann, and the ultra-Orthodox rabbi Michael Dov Ber Weissmandel, who conceived the plan of trying to stop the deportations by offering a major bribe to Wisliceny.[33] Toward the end of 1942, the working group suggested a sweeping idea to Wisliceny, called the Europa Plan, which was intended to halt all the deportations to Poland (and perhaps even the killings) in return for an initial down payment worth $200,000, with more cash to follow. Rabbi Weissmandel (who wrongly assumed that the first payment to Wisliceny had succeeded in halting the deportations from Slovakia in the summer of 1942) later denounced the outside Jewish world for having failed to save

European Jewry by not sending the money in time. But his accusations were based on ignorance of what had really happened in Slovakia and of the financial constraints on the Jewish side, as well as on a misreading of Nazi intentions.[34]

There were, as we have seen, countries that preceded or even rivaled the Germans in their brutal treatment of Jews. But there were also opposite cases where the "Final Solution" was partially or wholly sabotaged. A dramatic example was Bulgaria, whose fifty thousand indigenous Jews survived the war, despite considerable German pressure on its wartime ally to deliver them up for deportation.[35] The Bulgarian monarchy had enjoyed extensive territorial aggrandizement (at the expense of Greece, Yugoslavia, and Romania) thanks to its alliance with Nazi Germany. Unlike Hungary and Romania, however, it did not send even a token force to fight against the Soviet Union. Also, in contrast to Slovakia, Croatia, Romania, and Hungary, its native fascist movement was small and without political influence. Moreover, the country had a highly respected parliament, which worked harmoniously in tandem with the monarchy. Above all, Bulgarians were strikingly free from the anti-Semitism that was so pervasive in most of eastern Europe—a critical factor in their opposition to surrendering native Jews to the Nazis. The predominantly Sephardic community, which was well integrated into national life, was simply not regarded by most Bulgarians as a threat to their society.[36]

In January 1941, the Bulgarian government did pass some anti-Jewish laws, but they were far milder than those in most European countries and mitigated by many exemptions. For example, all baptized Jews (irrespective of their conversion date) were automatically exempted. Five thousand Jews—a tenth of the entire Jewish population—were given special privileges. A *numerus clausus* was imposed, but it was based on the percentage of Jews in the cities, which made it rather high. The most severe measure, mobilizing six thousand able-bodied men for work, was hardly guaranteed to enthuse the

Nazis, who bemoaned Bulgaria's failure to understand the "Jewish problem." Even when a yellow badge was briefly introduced (and then removed), it was extremely small, and most Jews did not even bother to wear it. An SD report to the Foreign Ministry in November 1942 noted that those who did wear it received much sympathy from "the misled population."

When Hitler asked King Boris III of Bulgaria to transfer the Bulgarian Jews for work in Germany's eastern territories, the monarch resisted, claiming that the Jewish workforce was required in the country to build roads and railway trucks. Not even the arrival of the zealous SS Jewish expert Theodor Dannecker in Sofia, early in 1943, succeeded in changing the situation, largely because the parliament and a wide section of the Bulgarian population was opposed to deportation. Nonetheless, Dannecker did negotiate an agreement with Aleksandr Belev, the commissar for Jewish affairs, to deport twenty thousand Jews. Politicians, clerics, intellectuals, and civil servants were on the side of the Jews, however, and as soon as the news reached the king, he instructed the prime minister to cancel the deportations.[37] The Jews were resettled from the capital to rural areas, which, much to German displeasure, dispersed rather than concentrated them. The Greek Orthodox metropolitan Stephan of Sofia declared publicly that "God had determined the Jewish fate, and men had no right to torture Jews, and to persecute them." This was considerably more explicit than anything Pope Pius XII could bring himself to say in public.

In his study of the subject, Michael Bar-Zohar gives special credit to the efforts of Dimiter Peshev, the vice president of the Bulgarian parliament, who with forty-two MPs pressured the prime minister to save the Jews. He also reveals the intense lobbying by the Bulgarian Jews themselves and the secret action of Belev's secretary, who warned a leading member of the Jewish community when the first deportations were imminent. As a result of the rescue action, local German officials became unsure of themselves. The German ambassador in Sofia wrote in June 1943 to his foreign minister that the situation was hopeless: "There is no point in pressing Bulgaria any further to hand over their Jews for deportation because the Bulgarians do not have the same concept and ideas about the Jews as prevail in Germany. The Bulgarians have been accustomed to living for centuries in harmony with their minorities of Turks, Jews, Gypsies, Armenians etc. Simply because no distinct differences in characteristics separate them, as in other countries."[38]

The Germans soon abandoned their efforts, and not a single native Bulgarian Jew was deported during the war. But the 11,363 Jews living in the newly occupied territories of Macedonia and Thrace were deported by the Germans with the help of Bulgarian police units under their command. The sovereignty of the occupied territories had not yet been determined, and possibly there was not much that King Boris or the Bulgarian state could have done. But unlike the case of Denmark (of which Bulgaria is reminiscent in other respects) there is no evidence of any action planned or undertaken to rescue the Jews of these territories.

Denmark was the one country in Nazi-occupied Europe where the entire Jewish community was saved as a result of massive popular opposition to Nazi policy.[39] Although it had been conquered in April 1940, the country was treated by the Nazis as if it were a neutral state, retaining an independent government with which the Germans did not interfere until the fall of 1943. Unlike in neighboring Norway, there were no enthusiastic collaborators organized into a serious fascist or Nazi movement. In contrast to Germany itself, the Lutheran tradition had spawned no significant religious anti-Semitism, and Protestant pastors were in the forefront of protests on behalf of the Jews. Like Bulgaria and Italy, Denmark was relatively immune to Judeophobia, but it did not go through any complex contortions and double-dealing to rescue its Jews. In Denmark, the Germans did not even introduce their ploy of softening resistance by distinguishing between the 6,400 native Jews and the 1,400 "stateless" refugees from Germany, who had been given asylum before the war.

Not only was the Jewish community in Denmark small, relatively homogeneous, and highly assimilated, it had the good fortune of being in a country where a democratic civic consciousness extended through all of society.[40] This seemed to have an influence even on some of the German occupiers themselves, including the military commander, General Hermann von Hannecken. The German plenipotentiary, Dr. Werner Best, also played a somewhat ambiguous role in Denmark after November 1942. Despite his fearsome record as a "desk murderer" and close collaborator of Heydrich, there is evidence that he helped to sabotage Himmler's orders to deport Danish Jews. No more than 477 out of more than seven thousand Jews were finally rounded up by German troops, who were forbidden by Best to break into Jewish apartments. Jewish leaders, who had been tipped off by Danish government officials about the deportation plan, which had been set for 1 October 1943, communicated the news in the synagogues during New Year services, which allowed just enough time for Jews to go into hiding. Here, too, they were fortunate that their Danish neighbors stood ready to receive them. Through October, the Jews were ferried across the narrow strip of water to neutral Sweden, where even the non-Danish Jews were given permission to work. The Danish fishing fleet helped with the transportation, and the costs were largely borne by wealthy Danish citizens. This generosity stood in stark contrast to conditions in many other countries, where Jews often had to pay extortionately large sums simply to obtain exit permits. The open resistance demonstrated by Denmark to Nazi Jewish policy during the Holocaust was in fact unique, though it was much helped by having an understanding neighbor in Sweden, one by no means immune to anti-Semitism but willing to take in Danish Jews without conditions.[41] Finland, too, which categorically refused even to discuss with Nazi officials the deportation of its two thousand Jews, proved that resistance to German demands was feasible. Ironically enough, the Nazis experienced their biggest failure on the "Jewish question" among their Scandinavian "blood brothers." With rare exceptions, their fellow Nordics proved most unhelpful, whereas all too many of the so-called *Untermenschen* of the east, reviled by the Nazis, collaborated with alacrity in the despoliation and murder of their Jewish neighbors.

Holland shared with the Scandinavian countries a fairly modest level of anti-Semitism (though German Jewish refugees before 1939 had not received especially warm welcomes), and there was widespread hostility to the anti-Jewish measures imposed under the German occupation. Support and assistance for Jews was particularly prevalent among Dutch Calvinists. Equally, Catholic Archbishop de Jonge of Utrecht forbade his constituents to assist Germans in rounding up Jews.[42] In February 1941, after widespread arrests of Jews and outbursts against them by the local Nazis, workers called for a general strike in Amsterdam, which lasted for two days. This was the first public demonstration against Nazi Jewish policies anywhere in wartime Europe. But the Nazis were able to crush most of the local Dutch resistance with comparative ease, not least because of the flat, open terrain that made guerrilla warfare unfeasible. The Germans also learned a lesson from the public protests by halting police raids in the streets and subsequently carrying out their persecution of Jews through decrees published in official newspapers. They had Dutch helpers, too. They could, for instance, rely on Anton Mussert's National Socialist Movement, which was relatively strong in the Netherlands. Though it was not notably anti-Semitic before 1939, it later proved more than willing to help ferret Jews out of their hiding places. Still more important was the assistance given by the Dutch bureaucracy, with its meticulously precise information about the Jews' addresses, jobs, and personal backgrounds.

The Dutch police, too, played a crucial and deliberate part in collaborating with the SS in the removal of the Jews. Much of the blame can be attributed to the charismatic wartime superintendent of the Amsterdam police, Sybren Tulp, a fervent admirer of Hitler. Because Amsterdam contained the majority of Holland's 140,000 Jews (especially after other Dutch Jews were forced to move there in 1942), his influence was especially disastrous.[43] Only twenty-five thousand Dutch Jews were able to hide successfully from the police, though this might be regarded as a relatively high figure for a small country without mountains or big forests. Nevertheless, 107,000 Dutch Jews were deported, and less than five thousand returned after the war.[44] This was a catastrophe unparalleled in any other western European country, with more than 80 percent of the Dutch Jews ending up in the death camps of Poland. The gullibility of the Dutch Jewish leadership was, unfortunately, a factor in this disaster.

The Dutch Jews had been organized by the Germans into a Joodse Raad (Jewish Council), which published the Nazi anti-Jewish ordinances in its newspaper, distributed yellow badges, and generally enjoyed a "privileged" status. It assisted in deportations, avoided any resistance, and even handed over the names of seven thousand council members to the Germans. The leaders of the Joodse Raad persisted for a long time in believing that only German Jewish refugees or other "foreigners" would actually be deported. Perhaps they simply refused to believe the worst, naïvely trusting in universal respect for the law and something they called "civilization." Perhaps there was little that they could do to avert the "evil decrees," but a less benign interpretation would say that, as happened elsewhere, they allowed themselves to become part of the machinery of destruction, with particularly disastrous results.[45]

In Belgium, the situation of the Jews was different in virtually every respect. Before the war, there had been about ninety thousand Jews, of whom one third were German Jewish refugees, while an even higher number came from Poland, Czechoslovakia, and elsewhere. By the end of 1942, nearly forty thousand Jews had fled (including the most prominent leaders), and there were barely five thousand native-born Belgian Jews among the fifty thousand still remaining in the country.[46] The majority of stateless or recently naturalized Jews were easily identifiable, and it was difficult to hide in such a small, highly urbanized, and industrialized country. By the end of 1942, about fifteen thousand of these Jews had been deported to Auschwitz-Birkenau. But when the Germans began to round up native Belgian Jews in 1943, there were public protests, which led to the release of some of the internees. What helped in this and other cases was the attitude of the top German military authorities: Governor General Alexander von Falkenhausen (later involved in the 1944 conspiracy against Hitler) and Brigadier General Eggert Reeder. Both had opposed the imposition of the yellow star in Belgium and successfully restricted the authority of the SS and Gestapo. It was also significant that (unlike in Holland) the Belgian police chose not to cooperate with the Nazis, and railway workers were at times deliberately lax with the deportation trains, permitting some Jews to escape. In Belgium, there were relatively few collaborators with the Germans, except among the Flemish-speaking population. Even the fascist Rexist Party headed by Léon Degrelle (which lost influence after 1939 among the French-speaking Walloons) was much less collaborationist than Mussert's National Socialist Movement in Holland. As a result of these factors, the death count—about twenty-five thousand Jews in Belgium (44 percent)—was considerably lower than in Holland.[47]

France, on the other hand, had both the largest Jewish community in western Europe and an indigenous tradition of anti-Semitism, unrivaled in its literary brilliance by that of any other nation in Europe.[48] At the same time, it had been the cradle of European Jewish emancipation—an achievement that remained intact for 150 years until the fall of France in 1940. The Jews of France were already well integrated into French society, culture, and politics under the Third Republic. In the 1930s, however, the earlier climate of tolerance had become frayed, as thousands of refugees (many of them Jewish) entered the country. In 1940, it was estimated that of the 330,000 Jews in France about 195,000 were native French. It is undoubtedly significant that about 50 percent of the foreign Jews were deported to their deaths, as opposed to roughly 10 percent of the *israélites français*. Altogether, eighty thousand persons (one quarter of all French Jews) died in the Holocaust, which was a terrible stain on modern French history but a relatively low body count in the larger European chamber of horrors.

The military debacle of June 1940 and the subsequent German occupation was the prerequisite for the institution of Marshal Pétain's "national revolution" and the Vichy regime in the southern half of the country. The French government, as a result of the armistice, retained some attributes of sovereignty and in their own zone could limit German intervention on the "Jewish question" and on many other domestic matters. Thus, for example, the yellow star, which had been decreed in the German-occupied zone after 7 June 1942, was not introduced in Vichy.[49] On the other hand, the French government did energetically persecute the Jews during the war years; indeed, it passed anti-Semitic laws on its own initiative that were as severe as anything the Germans had yet concocted. This autonomous legislation was based on a homegrown French combination of traditional Catholicism, xenophobia, exclusivist nationalism, and racist assumptions about Jewry.[50] The law of 4 October 1940 authorized prefects (as agents of the French state) to intern foreign Jews in "special camps" or to place them under police surveillance in remote villages. On 7 October 1940, the French state summarily deprived the Jews of Algeria of the French citizenship that they had possessed for seventy years.

The Vichy *statut des Juifs* spoke explicitly about race. It classified persons with only two grandparents "of the Jewish race" as being Jews if they had a Jewish spouse—a definition that was harsher than the existing German legislation. The Vichy government was especially concerned to prevent further immigration of Jewish refugees and to promote the reemigration of those already in France. It was determined that everything foreign, "non-French," and "unassimilable" had to be driven out of French culture. Already, Vichy laws had sealed off public service and certain professions from those not born of a French father. A quota on Jews in the professions soon followed. There can be no doubt that the Vichy regime was thoroughly permeated by anti-Semitism. It even established a special department for Jewish affairs, headed first by the more traditional conservative Catholic nationalist Xavier Vallat and then by the fanatically racist and anti-Semitic Louis Darquier de Pellepoix.[51] It was self-evident for Vallat that Jews were dangerous, unassimilable foreigners "whose implantation tends to form a state within a state." At the same time, he favored a more moderate "state anti-Semitism" in the tradition of the right-wing *L'Action Française* that would drastically reduce Jewish numbers and influence while avoiding the more extreme positions of the Nazis and the pro-German French collaborationists.

Between June and December 1941, a string of Vichy decrees limited Jews to 2 percent of the professions (medicine, law, and others) and 3 percent of the students in higher education. Vallat also introduced a detailed census of all Jews in the Unoccupied Zone as well as proposals (which became law on 22 July 1941) to "organize" Jewish property and enterprises. The object was "to eliminate all Jewish influence from the national economy." In November 1941, Jews were removed from a whole range of commercial and financial activities, including banking, merchant shipping, real estate, and wholesale trading, as well as publicity, news services, publishing, film, theater, and radio. They were forbidden to buy land unless they cultivated it themselves. Vichy France, by this draconian legislation, evidently hoped to assert its own sovereignty in Jewish affairs while fulfilling the anti-Semitic program that was an integral part of its ideology.[52]

By the spring of 1942 the Germans had developed more far-reaching anti-Jewish projects for France. In May 1942, Vallat was replaced by Pellepoix—a move that followed in the wake of intensified German police operations in France. Already on 27 March 1942, the first trainloads of Jews had left the Drancy concentration camp for Auschwitz-Birkenau, ostensibly in reprisal for attacks on German servicemen in France. When more railway cars were made available in June 1942, more Jews were dispatched. But the Reich could not pursue its anti-Jewish actions in France unless it had the active help of the French administration, public services, and police force, not to mention railroad officials. The Germans did not, however, have to bargain too hard to persuade Premier Pierre Laval to agree to the deportation of foreign and stateless Jews; that was already an item in Vichy's own program, though there is no evidence that mass extermination was any part of the French government's plans. The Vichy regime was, however, eager to get rid of its foreign Jews (pressing the Germans to include them in transports), even as it opposed measures against the French Jews. On 4 July 1942, René Bousquet, head of the French police, relayed to the Gestapo the agreement of Pétain and Laval to the deportations as "a beginning" for removing "all stateless Jews from the Occupied and Unoccupied zones." For the Germans, this was merely a temporary limitation. But Laval was certainly aware of the negative reactions in French public opinion to the radicalized German policy during the summer of 1942. The introduction by the Germans of the yellow star in the Occupied Zone, for example, provoked the first open resistance to anti-Jewish persecution in wartime France. It exposed the full gravity of anti-Semitism in a much more concrete way to many French people who had previously gone along with racist laws against the Jews.[53]

The Germans in mid-1942 did not have enough men (no more than three battalions of police numbering just under three thousand) to carry out their policy of roundups, internment, and deportation. Hence, the far more numerous French police force, with its efficient card-file system, listing almost 150,000 Jews in the Parisian Department of the Seine alone, was indispensable to their aims. The vast collaborative effort in which the French police engaged with the Germans proved, then, to be the critical factor in the deportations. Perhaps the most notorious example of such collaboration was the Velodrome d'Hiver roundup of 16 July 1942 by the Paris police, who packed seven thousand Jews (including more than four thousand children) like sardines into an indoor sports arena, so that there was barely space to lie down. Altogether, 12,884 Jews were netted in the two-day *Aktion,* but this was less than half the number the Germans had hoped to seize.[54]

By September 1942, more than twenty-seven thousand Jews had been deported from both zones of France. A month earlier, Laval had told an American Quaker group that "foreign Jews had always been a problem in France and that the French government was glad that a change in the German attitude towards them gave France an opportunity to get rid of them."[55] It was evident to the American chargé d'affaires in Vichy, who also spoke with Laval about the deportations at this time, "that he [Laval] had neither interest nor sympathy in the fate of any Jews, who, he callously remarked, were already too numerous in France."[56] Pétain's response seemed even more detached. He gave petitioners the impression that he only vaguely understood the full seriousness of the roundups and the deportations. Indeed, one of the blackest stains on Vichy's record was that it offered to deliver the children of foreign Jews to the Germans for deportation even before the Nazis asked for or were ready to accept them. More than one thousand children under six years old as well as 2,557 under twelve years and almost 2,500 Jewish adolescents were packed off to Auschwitz-Birkenau at the French initiative during 1942 alone. For the Vichy administration, there was never any question of taking them in hand through public charity or rescuing them. In mid-September 1942, Laval made it crystal-clear that nothing would deter him "from carrying out the policy of purging France of undesirable elements, without nationality."[57]

After women and children were put into the cattle cars by French police along with the men (some of whom were French citizens) and were never heard from again, public opinion began to turn. Voices of protest were raised in the Catholic Church (previously very supportive of Pétain and Vichy) and among the Protestants, led by Pastor Marc Boegner. Archbishop Jules-Gerard Saliège of Toulouse on 23 August 1942 drafted his famous pastoral letter, which attained a wide distribution: "That children, that women, fathers and mothers be treated like cattle, that members of a family be separated from one another and dispatched to an unknown destination, it has been reserved to our own time to see such a sad spectacle."[58] Saliège reminded the French public that Jews and foreigners "are real men and women ... part of the human species," who could not be abused without limit. Others like the bishops of Montauban and Marseille followed suit, though the protestors actually represented fewer than half of the prelates of the Unoccupied Zone. Laval tried, at first, with only partial success, to warn church officials against mixing into politics. But the initial crisis between the regime and the church had faded by the end of October 1942, and the furor in public opinion about the deportation of the Jews died down. Nevertheless, the legitimacy of the Vichy regime had suffered a blow.

On 11 November 1942, the period of full German occupa-

tion began as Hitler's armies swept down to the Mediterranean coast of France, to counter the American landings in
North Africa. With regard to the Jews, the powers of the German police were now extended across France, though their
manpower was severely overstretched in the southern zone.
But the French police continued and even increased their re-
pressive actions with mass arrests of foreign Jews in February
1943. In the northern zone, too, deportations from Drancy to
Auschwitz-Birkenau resumed in January 1943. By 6 March,
according to German calculations, approximately forty-nine
thousand Jews had already been to the East. As the pressure
intensified through 1943, some of the hunted Jews fled to
Spain and to Switzerland or more often found refuge in
French homes and religious institutions, especially in the
countryside.

Through 1943, the French police continued to accompany
convoys and escort trains carrying Jews for deportation and to
hunt down escapees. But they were noticeably less enthused
about deporting French Jews, and the Germans now felt that
they lacked the requisite initiative in the "struggle against Judaism." German pressure on Vichy to strip French Jews of
their citizenship (denaturalization) grew in the summer of
1943. Darquier de Pellepoix ardently supported this idea, but
Laval prevaricated and then retreated from this step on 7 August 1943. Pétain, too, resisted the idea of indiscriminate deportation of French Jews based on denaturalization. He had
to maintain order in France, and for the sake of his own conscience he wanted to examine each case individually. Vichy's
newfound obstructionism was connected closely to shifting
military fortunes and the increasing likelihood that Germany
would lose the war. There was the growing anti-German
mood in France to reckon with and the displeasure of the
Vatican to consider. Foreign opinion, especially in the United
States, also entered into the calculations at Vichy. Moreover,
the French public itself was becoming more restive and dis-
enchanted with the Vichy regime. German arrests of French

Jews were now regarded by growing numbers of French people as a national humiliation. As a result, even Laval was becoming less cooperative. The Nazis therefore turned to direct action, dispatching one of the most ruthless SS Jewish experts, the Austrian-born Alois Brunner, from Salonika (where he had helped to speedily deport more than fifty thousand Greek Jews to Auschwitz-Birkenau) to take over the deportations from France. Brunner and his SS team descended on the south of France in the fall of 1943, continuing their sweeps until the spring of 1944, this time without much support from the French police. They were, however, assisted by the Milice, a French paramilitary force that relentlessly pursued Jews out of a certain level of ideological conviction.

Although they no longer had the full resources of the French police to help them, the Germans still managed to send 33,500 Jews to the east in 1943–1944. Most of them were gassed immediately—mainly in Auschwitz-Birkenau—and a mere 2,500 out of the deported eighty thousand survived.[59] Nevertheless, from the Nazi standpoint, the overall results in France were disappointing: only one in four Jews had been trapped in the web of the "Final Solution." From August 1943, some Gestapo officials were convinced that Vichy was no longer dependable and even sabotaged their work. But there is little evidence that Pétain and Laval consciously sought to protect native French Jews, though it seems clear that they did become obstructive once a German victory appeared in doubt, and they were certainly concerned at their loss of face in French public opinion. What is less obvious is when they realized the true meaning of the "Final Solution." The official French (and German) line about the deportations was that Jews were being transferred to work colonies in Poland. But after June 1942, the inclusion of women and young children on the transports, as well as the sick and the aged, made this fiction seem scarcely credible. By the end of August 1942, Jewish organizations in France (like the Consistoire Central de Israélites de France) were telling Laval that

Jews were being exterminated "pitilessly and methodically," though they could not yet verify the existence of a total plan.[60] Pastor Boegner also talked with Laval in September 1942 about the mass murder but was fobbed off with stories about Jews building an agricultural colony in the east. Vichy officials nonetheless knew that many Jews would die, simply from looking at the atrocious conditions of departure from France. After 1943, French officials said as little as possible about the Jews, which in the circumstances can be regarded only as a guilty silence.

French complicity in the "Final Solution" cannot be separated from the deeply entrenched anti-Semitic tradition that had been sharpened by the trauma of defeat in 1940. Vichy's racist measures against the Jews were inhuman, its despoliation of Jewish property rapacious, and its anti-Semitic propaganda repulsive, though it never sunk into the truly venomous abyss of the pro-Nazi French collaborationist press, based in Paris.[61] Vichy did partially protect native Jews (as did Romania and Hungary before the German invasion), but its efforts were hardly vigorous or robust. It zealously volunteered to hand over foreign Jews from the Unoccupied Zone and to add Jewish children to the transports well before the Germans asked for them. These were actions of a particularly vile character. On the other hand, the Vichy leaders never deliberately planned to murder Jews en masse or encourage executions comparable to those in Germany, Austria, Croatia, Romania, the Ukraine, or Lithuania. Through its perfidious policy, Vichy sought to reduce the number of Jews in France by every possible means but its role in the "Final Solution" remained ambivalent.

While three quarters of French Jewry survived under Vichy, it must also be said that the French government proved much more severe toward the Jews than did the Italians. Laval was infuriated by Italian actions to help Jews in the eight departments of southern France that they occupied after November 1942, and he even requested German intervention, though this failed to change the situation. In February 1943, the Italians not only blocked the attempts of French police and prefects to round up and transfer all Jews (French or foreign) from their zone but formally brought them all under Italian protection. As a result, thousands of Jews made their way to the the Côte d'Azur. Nice even became a Jewish cultural and political center under Italian military rule, much to the disgust of Berlin and Paris. Only with the Italian evacuation in September 1943 and the entry of the German forces did the anti-Jewish terror in the south of France begin.

The Italian sabotage of the Holocaust was at first sight all the more astonishing given that Italy was the leading ally of Nazi Germany in Europe. Until the coup d'état by Marshal Pietro Badoglio in July 1943, it had been treated by the Germans as a sovereign, independent state. Already in *Mein Kampf* Hitler had pointed to fascist Italy (along with Great Britain) as a natural ally for Germany against French hegemonic ambitions.[62] He greatly admired Mussolini as the founder of fascism and had learned much from him about techniques of mass mobilization. It was from Mussolini that he adopted in the early 1920s the use of uniforms, colored shirts, and the extended-arm salute. Paramilitary methods, shock troops (*fascio di combattimento*), the Führerprinzip, militarism, extreme nationalism, and militant anti-Bolshevism were innovations of the Italian fascist program, adapted by the Nazis for their own needs.[63] Both fascist and Nazi ideologies exalted youth, activism, and movement for its own sake. They thundered against the decadence of a moribund bourgeois era while declaring a war to the death against Marxism. Both looked back to myths of power and imperial greatness— Hitler to the German Reich and Mussolini to ancient Rome. But it was Mussolini who was the first to pioneer a new Caesarism based on mass politics and spectacular ritualized displays of power.

To no other living statesman did Hitler feel a comparable sense of loyalty or reverence. During the Duce's visit to

Berlin at the end of September 1937, Hitler had acclaimed his Italian visitor as one of those "lonely men of the ages on whom history is not tested, but who themselves are the makers of history." Unlike other leading Nazis, Hitler never seemed to fully grasp the ideological gulf separating his own movement and outlook from Mussolini's fascism, despite many outward similarities. For example, "race" for most Italian fascists was not a biological concept but tended to be synonymous with the nation. Until the mid-1930s, Mussolini treated the Germanic version of "Nordic" racism as pretentious, pseudoscientific nonsense offensive to a sophisticated Mediterranean people. Similarly, he regarded the persecution of the Jews as an embarrassing mark of Nazi "immaturity," although in his own party he still tolerated fanatic Jew-baiters like Giovanni Preziosi and Roberto Farinacci. In periodic outbursts of anti-German resentment, he could be particularly scathing about Hitler and his quirks. In November 1934, he told the Zionist leader Nahum Goldmann: "I know Herr Hitler. He is an idiot, a rascal, a fanatical rascal, an insufferable talker. It is a torture to listen to him. You are much stronger than Herr Hitler. When there is no trace left of Hitler, the Jews will still be a great people."[64]

The Duce knew perfectly well that the forty-five thousand Jews in Italy were model patriots, thoroughly integrated into Italian society. They had blended easily enough into the Italian population, and they were little different from their neighbors, apart from their religion. Since the Risorgimento in the mid-nineteenth century, Italian Jewry had played a prominent part in economic life (especially banking, business, and insurance), and in journalism, education, the sciences, the arts, and literature. They had produced (despite the small size of the community) two prime ministers, a defense minister, and fifty generals—a record unmatched in Europe. Assimilation was a reality in Italy, not a mere ideology, myth, or self-deception, as it often proved to be elsewhere. There was no "Jewish question" in Italy, and no political anti-Semitism comparable in severity to that in France, Germany, Austria, or eastern Europe.

The Italian Jewish community did not suffer any serious harassment or persecution for sixteen years after the fascist seizure of power in 1922. Jews, like other Italians, flocked into the fascist movement without encountering any popular opposition. Mussolini himself acknowledged their patriotism, and his official stance was to encourage intermarriage and integration. This was the exact opposite of Nazi policy. Hence, the new race laws of 1938 stunned public opinion and were immediately unpopular, both with the established elites and with ordinary Italians, as well as in the Catholic Church. The legislation was widely seen by many Italians as a somewhat ridiculous kowtowing to Nazi Germany, a pathetic attempt by Mussolini to ideologically and politically align himself with Hitler, though this lack of popular enthusiasm was small consolation for Italian Jewry. Nevertheless, Italian policy continued to deviate considerably from the German pattern. There were numerous exemptions—for example war veterans, Jews decorated for their services to the state, and former members of the Fascist Party, including their parents, grandparents, wives, children, and grandchildren. The "Aryanization" policies in Italy were also far more liberal than those in Germany or Austria. Even more important, the Italians after 1939 defended foreign Jews as well as their own nationals, not only in Italy but also in southern France, Tunisia, Greece, Albania, Montenegro, and Croatia.[65]

It is a striking fact that wherever the Italian Army was in occupation during the war years, the Jews did not come to any serious harm.[66] For example, when they left France in 1943, the Italian military helped to transport Jewish refugees across the mountains; while in those parts of Yugoslavia occupied by Italy, Jews fleeing from the Croatian Ustashe and the Nazis were helped by Italian soldiers, who were appalled by the atrocities inflicted upon them. Many were taken on Italian Army trains, dressed in military uniforms, and brought to

Italy, where they were concealed. One can hardly fail to no-
tice the chasm separating the ruthless German military, with
its rigid discipline, obedience, and clockwork efficiency, from
the Italian Army, which, though stunningly ineffective as a
fighting force, showed mercy and compassion in many instances. The Wehrmacht and the German Air Force were responsible for the massive destruction of whole cities, small
towns, and villages, the uprooting of populations, and repeated cold-blooded murders of Jewish civilians in Russia,
the Ukraine, Serbia, and other areas in the east. While the
Italian military's record toward colonial populations was far
from exemplary, it often behaved with impeccable humanitarian sensitivity toward Jewish refugees who were complete
strangers. As Jonathan Steinberg has pointed out, even stereotypical Italian vices of laziness, corruption, inefficiency, and
chaotic indiscipline became virtues in the context of the
Holocaust, allowing rules to be constantly bent in the name of
common humanity. On the other hand, Prussian military
virtues of punctilious order, sense of duty, blind obedience,
and rigid perfectionism turned into fearsome tools of destruction when hooked up to the dictates of Hitler's racial
war.[67]

Mussolini after 1940 was certainly guilty of cooperating
fully with Hitler in the prosecution of war. Even before then,
he had implemented his own version of anti-Semitism
through the Italian educational system, in the press, on the
radio, and throughout cultural life. Most Italian Jews were
shattered by the shock of their sudden social exclusion, having been robbed of their citizenship and deprived of their
livelihoods in a nation that they had served loyally and well.
But inexcusable though these actions were, their impact was
partially mitigated by the scale of the exemptions, the re-
sourcefulness of the Italian Jews themselves, and the help
they received from their neighbors.[68] Even Italian government officials and some veteran fascists seemed to be infected
by this popular mood and a general unwillingness to toe the

Nazi line. The Germans were well aware of the "lack of zeal" shown by Italian officials in the implementation of anti-Jewish measures. On 13 December 1942, Goebbels noted in his diary: "The Italians are extremely lax in the treatment of Jews. They protect the Italian Jews both in Tunis and in occupied France and will not permit their being drafted for work or compelled to wear the Star of David. This shows once again that Fascism does not really dare to get down to fundamentals but is very superficial regarding problems of vital importance."[69] On 23 June 1943, after a conversation with Hitler, Goebbels recorded that the Führer apparently expressed dissatisfaction with the Italians for failing to deal radically with the Jewish question. Mussolini, he reportedly said, was no revolutionary like himself or Stalin. Despite these private criticisms, Hitler's loyalty to his ally still remained intact.

On 25 July 1943, the Duce was summoned by King Victor Emmanuel III to his villa and arrested. Not long afterward, the Italian Army surrendered to the Allies. Mussolini was nonetheless rescued by the Nazis and set up the Italian Social Republic of Salò in northern Italy. The Duce quickly issued a manifesto declaring Jews to be "enemy aliens" and had an anti-Jewish law passed that dissolved the Jewish communities and charitable institutions and also confiscated their property. German troops invaded Italy, and the SS began to subject Italian Jews to deportation, including the seizure of more than one thousand Jews from Rome in mid-October 1943. This was to be the blackest period in the history of Italian Jewry, when the most fanatical elements in Italian society surfaced to terrorize the Jews, kill partisans, and execute German orders. Some had their hiding places betrayed by Italian citizens, usually motivated by greed. Thousands of Jews were arrested and interned, many ending up in concentration camps near the Austrian border. The most notorious of these camps was established in October 1943 at La Risiera di San Sabba, near Trieste, and had a gas chamber and crematorium.[70] About five thousand Jews, as well as Italian antifascists and Slovenian partisans, were killed there. However, several thousand foreign Jews (and some native Italian Jews as well) who were interned at the Ferramonti-Tarsia concentration camp in southern Italy, occupied by the Allies in 1943, were able to survive the war.

In the spring of 1944, the Germans broke an earlier promise and began transporting Jews from Italy to Auschwitz-Birkenau. Altogether, some eight thousand Jews died as the Holocaust descended upon northern Italy with unexpected force, bringing death and destruction to about 15 percent of Italian Jewry. The casualties would certainly have been far higher without the humanity shown by many ordinary Italians, whether clerics or laypersons, resisters or nonresisters, soldiers or civilians, nominal fascists, liberals, or communists. Jews found hiding places in the cities and the countryside, in the hills and on farms, in convents and monasteries, and a few were even concealed in the Vatican. They were received and spontaneously assisted, despite the risks involved, because they were seen as human beings with an equal right to live. The history of collaboration in the Holocaust was all too often a story of indescribable cruelty, callousness, indifference, and insensitivity. But there were also islands of charity and simple human decency that stand out all the more sharply as testaments of hope in the prevailing darkness.

7

BRITAIN,

AMERICA,

AND THE

HOLOCAUST

Let my death be an energetic cry of protest against the indifference of the world which witnesses the extermination of the Jewish people without taking any steps to prevent it.

SHMUEL ZYGELBOYM, Bundist deputy to the exiled Polish National Council in London, shortly before his suicide on 12 May 1943

[The guilt] lies with the Nazis.... But can we escape blame if, having it in our power to do something to save the victims, we fail to take the necessary action, and take it swiftly? ... If the British and American Governments were determined to achieve a programme of rescue in some way commensurate with the vastness of the need, they could do it.

GEORGE BELL, BISHOP OF CHICHESTER, 18 May 1943

What have you done to us, you freedom-loving peoples, guardians of justice, defenders of the high principles of democracy and the brotherhood of man? What have you allowed to be perpetrated against a defenseless people while you stood aside and let them bleed to death? ... If instead of Jews, thousands of English, American, or Russian women, children, and the aged had been tortured every day, burnt to death, asphyxiated in gas chambers—would you have acted in the same way?

DAVID BEN-GURION, speech on Mount Scopus, Jerusalem, 10 July 1944

The Allied response to the Holocaust has been overladen with charges of "complicity," "abandonment," and culpable indifference to the unfolding Jewish tragedy. Some historians have implied that the American and British governments could have saved hundreds of thousands of Jews with a more energetic rescue policy. David Wyman, for example, believes that President Roosevelt, though well informed about the murder of the Jews, was not prepared to take any risks for them and that this indifference was "the worst failure of his presidency."[1] Political expediency largely determined his policy, but like most other Allied decision makers he had only the most superficial understanding of Jewish issues. Roosevelt most probably did not think much about what was happening to the Jews in the midst of the gigantic global confrontation in which the United States was engaged, except when specific Jewish requests were made. Then, the standard answer that the Americans (like the British) gave to such pleas was: the only way to help the Jews is to win the war as swiftly as possible. But while no serious historian would deny that there were strategic realities that limited the chances of rescue, reluctance to help Jews or open doors to them suggested to perpetrators, bystanders, and victims alike that Jews were expendable, an idea that encouraged Hitler in his belief that the world would not seriously obstruct his desire to destroy them.

The criticism directed at the United States (and to a large extent Great Britain) usually contains a triple indictment. First, the American government adopted a highly restrictive immigration policy (which was never modified between 1933 and 1945) and did so in response to racist and xenophobic pressures in American society, which it was unwilling to seriously confront.[2] Second, it refused or obstructed (knowingly in the case of the State Department) German offers of negotiation or other possibilities to remove Jews from Hitler's clutches. Finally (and again like the British), the U.S. Air Force was unwilling and not instructed to bomb the railway lines leading to Auschwitz-Birkenau or to destroy the extermination facilities within the camp itself.[3]

Of these indictments, the best documented is the general hostility in the interwar period toward an "alien" influx into American society.[4] There is no doubt that the passage of the U.S. Immigration Act of 1924, which set tight quotas by country of origin with a particular bias against eastern and southern Europe, was aimed at excluding as many Jewish, Slavic, and Italian immigrants as possible. Its underlying assumptions of "Nordic supremacy," while not driven exclusively by anti-Semitism, were analogous to Hitler's notions of racial purity. A xenophobic climate of opinion in the aftermath of the First World War had favored racist and anti-Semitic organizations such as the Ku Klux Klan, which reached the peak of its influence in the 1920s. It was also a decade that witnessed the efforts of automobile millionaire Henry Ford (much admired by the Nazis) to spread his fantastic anti-Semitic theories about a worldwide Jewish conspiracy via the *Dearborn Independent*.[5] There were evangelical fundamentalist preachers such as Gerald L. K. Smith and Gerald Winrod who peddled anti-Semitism, as did William Dudley Pelley's Silver Shirts and Fritz Kuhn's German-American Bund in the 1930s.[6] As the Great Depression deepened, the receptivity toward such bigotry broadened considerably in America, as evidenced by the impact of Catholic radio priest Father Charles Coughlin, who reached an audience of millions with his ranting against the New Deal and the Jews in the late 1930s.[7] Particularly worrying for American Jews was the developing link between powerful isolationist currents and anti-Jewish sentiments as the European war approached. In

September 1941 (three months before America's entry into World War II), the aviator hero Charles Lindbergh—a long-standing admirer of Hitler—made the connection fully explicit. In a notorious speech on behalf of the America First Committee, he warned that Jews should not push the United States into war (they did indeed tend to be strong supporters of intervention) because they would be the first victims.

Although anti-Semitism in America never crystallized into a coherent, organized political movement or seriously infiltrated the mainstream political parties, it was nonetheless pervasive enough in the 1930s and 1940s to affect American responses to the Holocaust. Opinion polls indicated that on the eve of the war 75 to 85 percent of Americans opposed relaxing the drastically prohibitive immigration quotas to help Jewish refugees. At the end of the 1930s, anti-immigration sentiment was so strong in Congress that proposed legislation to open America's doors to refugees had to be withdrawn.[8] The same fate awaited Senator Robert Wagner's bill in 1938 to admit twenty thousand Jewish children over the existing narrow quota. Then, early in 1939, the American government callously turned back German Jewish refugees on the ocean liner *Saint Louis,* who had been refused Cuban entry visas. It was yet another sign of the strength of popular sentiment against changing the immigration laws.

America's entry into the war, ostensibly to make the world safe for democracy against Nazism and fascism, weakened the potential impact of anti-Jewish sentiments. Yet opinion surveys indicate that, after the Japanese and the Germans, Jews were considered the greatest menace to American society during the war years. In 1944, one poll found 65 percent of Americans declaring that Jews had too much power (a figure about three times higher than estimates for Great Britain), and stereotypes of Jews as dishonest, greedy, materialistic, aggressive, and subversive were rather widespread.[9] Such prejudices played a role in shaping the behavior of top State Department officials like Assistant Secretary of State Breckinridge Long, Jr., who was responsible for refugees during the Roosevelt administration. Long was a paranoid anti-Semite who thought *Mein Kampf* "eloquent in opposition to Jewry and to Jews as exponents of Communism and Chaos."[10] Not surprisingly, when Henry Morgenthau's Treasury Department attempted to license the transfer of money from Jewish charities to fund a program for the relief and rescue of Jews, Long and other officials delayed it for months. They were encouraged in this prevarication by the British government, which in December 1943 cabled Washington that it was opposed to such relief programs because "of the difficulties of disposing of any considerable number of Jews should they be rescued."[11] This callous response stunned Morgenthau and Secretary of State Cordell Hull into action. An internal investigation of the State Department's handling of the question of rescue produced a document dated 13 January 1944 and starkly entitled "Report to the Secretary on the Acquiescence of this government in the murder of the Jews."[12]

This unrelenting indictment demonstrated that not only did certain State Department officials fail to use the American governmental machinery at their disposal to rescue Jews from Hitler, they sought to prevent such aid. They failed to cooperate with private organizations seeking to develop their own relief programs and even actively obstructed them. Further, they had surreptitiously tried to stop the obtaining of information by various Jewish and other organizations concerning the massacres in Europe and then issued false and misleading statements to cover up their guilt. Roosevelt was shocked by the report and realized that the facts, if known, would be political dynamite. The result was the creation in January 1944 of the War Refugee Board to assist in rescuing the Jews in Europe.[13] It was the only such Allied government agency created during the war, but it was too little and too late. No military resources whatever were diverted to it, and it succeeded in obtaining the admission of no more than one thousand refugees.

The prevailing anti-Jewish climate inhibited the willingness of most American Jews to lobby the Roosevelt administration to change U.S. policy in the face of the Holocaust. American Jewry was profoundly shaken by what it took to be a steep rise in anti-Semitism in America. As recent immigrants, many Jews still felt insecure about their own position and rights. Hence, they were reluctant to do anything to "make *rishis*"—to create a fuss for fear that their own loyalties would be questioned and the wrath of the Christian world might be stirred up.

The American Jewish community, which numbered about 4.5 to 5 million during the war years, was far from monolithic. Indeed, never had its internal ideological and political divisions seemed greater than in the 1930s. There were Orthodox and Reform, uptown and downtown Jews, "Germans" and "Russians," not to mention the Galitzianers and secularists of all shades—socialist, Communist, labor and "revisionist" Zionists. The bonds of religious and ethnic solidarity had been eroded considerably by secularization and acculturation to American life, weakening the cultural ties with the Jews of Russia, Poland, Germany, and Palestine.[14] What united most American Jews much more than links across the ocean was the desire to prove their newfound American patriotism. This imperative was spectacularly demonstrated by the fact that more than half a million young Jews served in the armed forces of the United States. Responses of American Jews to the Holocaust were very much shaped by such acculturating trends. For example, the more Americanized Jews tended to marginalize or underestimate the scale of the disaster, much like Gentile Americans. This was less true of Jews in the immigrant centers, such as the Lower East Side of Manhattan or Williamsburg in Brooklyn, for whom the European Jewry that was being destroyed was far from being an abstraction. Not surprisingly, the Yiddish-language press covered the events of the Holocaust more closely and intensely than its counterparts in the English-language news media.[15]

But the harsh truth is that rescue was not a particularly high priority for the major American Jewish organizations and barely featured on their wartime agendas. There were a few private approaches to the president and high government officials, but even these feelers were not intensively followed up. Such apathy notwithstanding, the leaders of American Jewry did find a common voice in condemning the activities of the Emergency Committee to Save the Jewish People of Europe, founded by a complete outsider, the militant Peter Bergson, a representative of the Palestinian Jewish Irgun Zvai Leumi in the United States.[16] They objected to the committee's loud, provocative style of advertisement in reminding the American public and Congress of what was actually happening in Europe; they disliked the violence of its anti-British tone, its insistent emphasis on the need for a Jewish army, and its emotionally raw, immoderate language.[17] Above all, the Jewish establishment was displeased at this unexpected invasion of their organizational territory and at being upstaged by a tiny group, linked from 1944 onward with the terrorist activity of the Irgun against British colonial rule in Palestine.

Mainstream American Zionists also disapproved of the extremism of the Bergsonites, notwithstanding their own opposition to British policy. Having observed the American government's unwillingness to open the door to Jewish refugees in the 1930s, they concentrated their energies on helping to build up the Jewish National Home in Palestine. They cooperated with David Ben-Gurion and the rest of the Yishuv leadership in protesting the British White Paper of 1939, which in effect blocked any prospect of a future Jewish majority in Palestine, and rallied around Ben-Gurion's arguments in favor of Jewish statehood as an immediate postwar goal. This aim was formally endorsed on 6 May 1942 at the Biltmore Hotel in New York.[18] At the conference, Chaim Weizmann (at that time still the leader of world Zionism) grimly predicted that a quarter of eastern European Jewry would probably perish as a result of Nazi atrocities, while some four million homeless Jewish survivors would remain suspended somewhere between heaven and hell.[19] The Gentile world would, however, be persuaded by Zionism, because Palestine offered the only practical solution to Jewish homelessness. At long last, Weizmann suggested, Jews would relieve non-Jews "of the trouble of settling our problems."[20]

In August 1942, three months after the Biltmore meeting, the best-known American Zionist (and leader of the World Jewish Congress [WJC]), Stephen Wise, was given a telegram from Dr. Gerhart Riegner (representing the WJC in Geneva) outlining the existence of a German plan to systematically destroy all the Jews of Europe at one blow.[21] The State Department had initially withheld this information from him, but he was finally authorized by Undersecretary of State Sumner Welles to release it on 24 November 1942. The devastating news had a brief galvanizing effect on Jews in the United States, with American Zionists in the forefront of efforts to lobby the Roosevelt administration to undertake a more serious rescue program. On 1 March 1943, more than twenty thousand people (mobilized primarily by the WJC), jammed into Madison Square Garden in New York to express support for the millions of European Jews threatened with extinction.[22] A week later, a similar number attended the spectacular ninety-minute pageant *We Will Never Die,* which included a searing recitation of some of the atrocities that the Nazis had perpetrated against Jewry. Its initiator, the popular author and dramatist Ben Hecht, hoped to pierce the veil of silence around the tragedy of the Jewish people with flaming rhetoric: "The corpse of a people lies on the steps of civilization. Behold it. Here it is! And no voice is heard to cry halt to the slaughter, no government speaks to bid the murder of human millions end."[23] *The New York Times* and some of the other daily papers were sympathetic to the pageant, helping to reopen the public debate over helping the Jews. One indirect result was the Bermuda Conference of April 1943, at which British and American officials (belatedly aware of the political risk of doing nothing) announced that they would try to develop plans to aid European Jewry, a vain promise, as it soon turned out.

The Anglo-American conference began on the first day (19 April 1943) of the doomed Warsaw ghetto uprising, which also happened to coincide with the first night of Passover. The coincidence of dates was a particularly cruel irony, since the conference would reveal that the Allies had abandoned European Jews to their fate, despite optimistic pronouncements to the contrary. The two delegations categorically ruled out any appeal to Hitler to release Jews in Nazi-occupied countries, any exchange of Nazi POWs and internees for Jews, or the sending of food (through the Allied blockade) to help feed the Jews of Europe.[24] After quickly and smoothly settling the problem of dealing with non-Jewish Polish and Greek refugees, the delegates had much more difficulty in agreeing about even a relatively small item like the temporary settlement of Jewish refugees in North Africa. Eventually, an Anglo-American compromise was struck, based on one fundamental and tacit assumption: the Americans would not press the British over Palestine, while the latter would act with similar discretion about Jewish immigration to the United States.[25]

After the conference, Richard Law, minister of state at the British Foreign Office, wrote to Foreign Secretary Anthony Eden, commenting on the different internal pressures concerning refugees that faced the American and British governments. In Britain, he alleged, public officials felt extreme pressure from an alliance of Jewish organizations and archbishops "but as yet no counter-pressure from the many people who feared and opposed alien immigration."[26] In America, Law observed, there was, in addition to Jewish pressure, a body of opinion "which, without being purely anti-Semitic, is jealous and fearful of an alien immigration *per se.* And in contradistinction to the position at home, that body of opinion is very highly organised indeed. The Americans, therefore, while they must do their utmost to placate Jewish opinion, dare not offend 'American opinion.' "[27] Law was probably correct in his assessment. President Roosevelt had been eager since 1939 not to give any credibility to anti-Semitic claims that he was an "instrument of the Jews," especially while he was strenuously seeking to involve America more closely in the war, against the powerful weight of isolationist and nativist opinion.[28] He also knew, as a practical political matter, that reversing congressional or popular sentiment on the immigration laws was not feasible either before or during the war.

What of later possibilities of rescue or slowing down the German genocidal machine by the bombing of Auschwitz-Birkenau? After September 1943, American and British bombers were able to reach targets all over the Reich, especially from airfields in southern Italy. On 4 April 1944, an Allied reconnaissance plane took off from an Italian base and, after a flight that took two and a half hours, managed to photograph the new industrial installations at Auschwitz-Birkenau. The photographs showing a synthetic-oil refinery were examined minutely, but no attention was paid to the gas chambers and crematoriums.[29] On 20 August 1944, 127 Flying Fortresses escorted by a hundred Mustang fighters successfully dropped their bombs on a factory fewer than five miles from Auschwitz-Birkenau. On other occasions, too, the Allies targeted the nearby industrial complex of Auschwitz III (Buna-Manowitz), passing over the death camp and railway lines leading to it, which were not viewed as military targets.[30]

Already in the summer of 1944, as hundreds of thousands of Hungarian Jews were being deported to their deaths at Auschwitz-Birkenau, Jewish leaders in Slovakia, especially Rabbi Weissmandel, pleaded that the camp be bombed.[31] Some Jewish organizations and the War Refugee Board also called, more circumspectly, for action.[32] But by no means all Jewish leaders were agreed. Some of them, including the Jewish Agency for Palestine, feared the resulting casualties among the inmates of the camps.[33] American Jewish leaders seemed far from enthusiastic. The proposal was initially opposed even by Leon Kubowitzki (head of the WJC Rescue Department), who had forwarded a formal request to John J. McCloy, assistant secretary of war. The reply from McCloy misleadingly claimed that a feasibility study had been made and that experts had concluded that "the diversion of considerable air forces now engaged in decisive operations elsewhere ... would be of such doubtful efficacy that it would not warrant the use of our resources."[34] McCloy added that such an effort might provoke even more vindictive action by the Germans. These were not trivial arguments, as is sometimes claimed. But it would have made far more sense for McCloy to say that the Germans could always revert to mass shooting if the gas chambers were rendered inoperable. One should not deduce from this negative response (or the similar British refusal) that there was a deliberate cover-up or sheer callousness at play. However, a disinclination to act upon Jewish requests, along with bureaucratic indifference and more than a tinge of anti-Semitism, did indeed exist among high-ranking American and British officials, as well as among Allied military leaders.[35]

Above all, the "Jewish question" was ultimately marginal to Roosevelt, who certainly had little understanding of its centrality to the Nazis. Once America became involved in the war, it became even less important compared to the supreme goal of an Allied victory. Like Churchill, Roosevelt was far too involved in the larger global military and diplomatic strategy to devote much time after December 1941 to specific issues of Jewish rescue. Nevertheless, he did periodically make himself available to Jewish organizations. When Stephen Wise finally asked him in December 1942 to draw world attention to the Nazi "Final Solution," he did not refuse. Nor did he try to discourage Wise from pursuing a plan for the

evacuation of Jewish refugees from Romania (which unfortunately led nowhere). More important, from the end of 1943
Roosevelt supported the Treasury and its high officials in taking the initiative on rescue actions.[36]

The creation of the War Refugee Board, in early 1944,
however belated an act, was an important and positive step.
For the first time during the war years, the issue of relief for
Jews was partially freed from the obstruction of the American
State Department and the British Foreign Office. After the
German invasion of Hungary, Roosevelt (once again over
some internal opposition) warned in a statement of 24 March
1944 that those who took part in deporting the Jews would
be punished. The fourth paragraph of his statement referred
to the "wholesale systematic murder of the Jews of Europe,"
describing it as "one of the blackest crimes of all history."[37]
Again, on 26 June 1944 (the day after a rare public plea by
Pope Pius XII), President Roosevelt demanded that Horthy
halt all deportations from Hungary.

But Roosevelt was not immune to a "liberal" version of
anti-Semitism. At Casablanca in January 1943, he had proposed to the French Governor-General of Morocco that "the
number of Jews engaged in the practice of the professions
(law, medicine etc) should be definitely limited to the percentage that the Jewish population in North Africa bears to
the whole of the North African population."[38] This Roo-
seveltian *numerus clausus* "would further eliminate the specific
and understandable complaints which the Germans bore
towards the Jews in Germany, namely, that while they represented a small part of the population, over fifty per cent of the
lawyers, doctors, school teachers, college professors, etc, in
Germany were Jews."[39] Equally simplistic notions surfaced
in Roosevelt's meeting with King Ibn Saud of Saudi Arabia in
February 1945. No doubt influenced by American oil interests, he declared himself very impressed by the Saudi
monarch's (highly partisan) view of the Middle East conflict,
which of course totally precluded any possibility of a Jewish

state. Roosevelt added that "the Germans appear to have killed three million Polish Jews, by which count there should be space in Poland for the resettlement of many homeless Jews." This assumption, shared by British officials, was based on a stunning misconception of the Jewish condition and mind-set in the aftermath of the Holocaust.[40]

For the Zionist movement, Roosevelt's sudden death in April 1945 was probably a stroke of luck, since his successor, Harry S. Truman, proved considerably more sympathetic to its aspirations. American Zionists had already drawn their own conclusions from the miserable failure of the Bermuda Conference two years earlier.[41] The unseemly farce in the Caribbean seemed like another glaring illustration of the general indifference of the Christian world (including supposedly "friendly" governments like those of Roosevelt and Churchill) to Jewish suffering and demonstrated the futility of relying on humanitarian appeals. Abba Hillel Silver, the firebrand of American Zionism, angrily summed up this sentiment on 2 May 1943, not long after Bermuda: "The enemies of Israel seek us out and single us out but our friends would like to forget our existence as a people."[42] Silver believed that if the Jews had possessed their own Palestinian state in 1933, then German, Austrian, and eastern European Jewry would have found a refuge in large numbers. This was also the argument made by another leading American Zionist, Emanuel Neumann, who added that if American Jews in 1943 did not put an end to the long history of their people's persecution by supporting a postwar Jewish commonwealth in Palestine, "we shall be contemptible in our own eyes."[43]

The Zionist leadership of the Yishuv was fully committed to fighting for the realization of a Jewish National Home and had for the past twenty years urged that everything be subordinated to this priority. The 1933 *Ha'avara* agreement to facilitate the transfer of German Jews and part of their property to Palestine offered the Zionists an unexpected opportunity to strengthen their demographic position, even though it meant undercutting the worldwide Jewish anti-Nazi boy-cott.[44] The Yishuv was still rather small (278,000 Jews) and substantially outnumbered by the Palestinian Arabs. Never-theless in 1937, the British appeared ready to offer to the Jews a ministate in a partitioned Palestine. But this proposal rapidly vanished from the table as the international situation deteriorated. By May 1939, it was clear that the Balfour Dec-laration was dead and the Zionist enterprise in serious danger of being derailed by Great Britain at the very moment when a deadly trap was closing in on the Jews of Europe. The fore-most leader of Palestinian Jewry, David Ben-Gurion, was fully aware of the defensive and objectively weak position of the Yishuv. However, Zionism and world Jewry had little choice after September 1939 but to support the Allied war effort de-spite increased British hostility to their national aspirations. At the same time, Ben-Gurion was determined to arouse world public opinion against the White Paper policy and to endorse illegal immigration, without renouncing the de facto pact with Great Britain.[45] Despite widespread anger at Britain's restrictions on *aliya* (immigration) and on military organization by the Yishuv, young Palestinian Jews were en-couraged to enlist in the British Army.

The Yishuv and its leadership were nonetheless beset by deep-seated anxieties of impotence, aware of the disparity between the virile self-image of Zionism and its limited ca-pacity to rescue the Jews of Europe. Moreover, by 13 Novem-ber 1942, the earlier reports of the massacres of European Jewry had been reliably confirmed by the arrival of nearly seventy Palestinian Jews held in Europe since the outbreak of the war.[46] They were part of a civilian-exchange agreement with Germans resident in Palestine. The new arrivals came from different parts of Nazi-occupied Europe (including Poland), and their vivid firsthand accounts provided a shock-ing glimpse into the scale of the genocide. Zionist leaders began to wonder if the complete extermination of European Jewry would not mean the end of the movement, as Chaim

Weizmann had already hinted in June 1942. This "terrifying vision" also haunted Ben-Gurion, though he kept it to himself and tried to play down the magnitude of the tragedy in public.[47]

Ben-Gurion nonetheless became increasingly active in pressing the Allies to intervene on behalf of European Jews. He proposed that they offer the Nazis an exchange of Germans held in the Western Hemisphere for Jews in Europe; that neutral countries be encouraged to accept Jews with the promise that the Allies would provide food and guarantee their removal after the war. He wanted bombings of German cities carried out openly as reprisals for the massacre of Jews, together with a propaganda campaign using leaflets over German cities to explain the policy. He thought that warnings to Hitler's allies not to deport or harm their Jews could also be an important deterrent to their further collaboration.[48] Above all, he and other Zionist leaders wished for an easing of the British White Paper restrictions, so that Palestine could absorb more of the survivors. Nor were the death camps ignored.

Chaim Weizmann and Moshe Shertok (Sharett) pressed the British foreign secretary for Allied bombing of the death camp at Auschwitz-Birkenau. Shertok conceded that this might not save too many Jewish lives, but there were still compelling reasons to undertake such an action. In a memorandum of 11 July 1944 that seems to have impressed Eden and Churchill with its cogency, Shertok (a future prime minister of Israel) pointed out that bombing Auschwitz-Birkenau would show "that the Allies waged direct war" on the perpetrators of genocide. It would undermine repeated German assertions "that the Allies are not really so displeased with the work of the Nazis in ridding Europe of the Jews." It would help dissipate skepticism "in Allied quarters with regard to the report of mass extermination perpetrated by the Nazis." Furthermore, it would lend weight to the threat of reprisals against the murderers "by showing that the Allies are taking the extermination of the Jews so seriously as to warrant the allocation of aircraft resources for this particular goal, and thus have a deterrent effect." Finally, it might create some internal German pressure against continuing the massacres.[49]

Despite Churchill's enthusiasm, the British Air Ministry (like its American counterparts) rejected the proposal on technical grounds.[50] The British also rejected the "trucks for blood" deal in 1944 that became known as the Joel Brand affair—something to which Ben-Gurion devoted a great deal of time but which was quickly squashed by the Allies as a Gestapo plot.[51] Brand, a Hungarian Zionist who had met Eichmann in Budapest, traveled to Turkey on orders to present the Jewish Agency with a German proposition to halt the extermination of Hungarian Jewry in exchange for trucks and other equipment. He was arrested by the British on suspicion of being a Nazi agent and no attempt was made to explore the offer or even to play for time. These and other examples underlined the fact that every rescue and aid proposal emanating from or connected to the Yishuv was dependent on Allied approval—a major restriction on the Zionists. For example, the transfer of Transnistrian Jews out of Romania in late 1942 depended on British agreement, which was not forthcoming. A plan to evacuate Jews from Bulgaria to Turkey came closer to success but ultimately failed because of opposition from the British ambassador in Ankara. Where British immigration permits were granted, as in the case of Romanian Jews arriving in Istanbul in 1944, it was due to the cooperation of the local British consulate and of the American War Refugee Board representative, Ira Hirschmann. But such assistance was given only grudgingly, usually where it suited other British military and intelligence operations.

Thus, the Yishuv found itself trapped between a ruthless German annihilation policy and relative Allied indifference or obstruction. The Zionists did not have a state, an army, a government, extensive funds, or any influential allies. They did not control admission to Palestine or to any other country. They did not have the ability to declare war on Germany, nor indeed did they possess any independent means of action, except in the most limited sense. An effective response to the Holocaust was therefore almost wholly dependent on the ability of the Yishuv to persuade the British and the Americans to try to stop the slaughter or provide a refuge for Jews. Ben-Gurion and his colleagues constantly had to take into account these very severe constraints. With one eye on the coming confrontation with the Arabs (which they correctly judged to be inevitable), they sought to strengthen the Yishuv and prepare for the future. As a result, rescue was subordinated to long-range political priorities and to a degree of instrumental thinking that in retrospect sometimes seems chilling.[52] At a Jewish Agency executive meeting on 6 December 1942, Ben-Gurion evoked, for example, the Jews of Poland as "the sacrifices of a nation without a homeland." The only proper response to the Holocaust was "redoubled pressure for Jewish independence."

British responses to the Holocaust were also very much influenced by the Arab-Jewish struggle in Palestine. After 1938, imperial decision makers had become increasingly concerned with their strategic and political position in the Middle East as the world war drew near. Although the British had crushed the Palestinian Arab rebellion by 1939, they resolved to appease Arab aspirations at the expense of the Zionists. Thus, any further Jewish immigration to Palestine was made dependent on Arab acquiescence. To this end, after 1939, a supposedly sympathetic Britain was intensely pressuring European governments during the war to *actively prevent* "illegal" Jewish immigration.[53] British naval forces were diverted to the eastern Mediterranean for the express purpose of intercepting ships carrying such immigrants, who if caught, usually faced deportation and exile. This grim and inhumane policy, backed to the hilt by the army, the Colonial Office, and the Foreign Office, continued (undisturbed by knowledge of the Holocaust) until British withdrawal from Palestine in 1948.

Naturally, if Palestine, which had been expressly given to Britain to help build a Jewish National Home, was a priori excluded, then possibilities for rescue were greatly reduced. So draconian was Britain's policy that by 1945 the miserly quota of seventy-five thousand Jewish immigrants to Palestine throughout the war years had not been achieved.

This obstinacy led to such tragedies as the sinking of the *Struma* refugee ship in February 1942, a disaster that was in large measure the result of British government pressure on Turkey to send the rickety vessel back into the Black Sea, despite all the known risks.[54] It produced responses like the British high commissioner's cable to the Colonial Office in July 1940 about Polish soldiers to be evacuated from southeastern Europe to Palestine, in which he said that "only non-Jews be regarded as acceptable."[55] The plain truth was that *all* branches of the British government were determined to keep the Jews out of their homeland at the very moment that they faced their greatest danger. Almost any argument could be used in this perverse endeavor, including the grossly exaggerated one that some Jewish immigrants might be Nazi agents. And even Jewish and Zionist demonstrations of loyalty to Britain's war against the Nazis did not cut much ice, especially since government officials felt that they could take such support for granted. As one Foreign Office report in 1941 concluded: "When it comes to the point, the Jews will never hamper us to put the Germans on the throne."[56] The contrast with the days of the Balfour Declaration and the First World War, when Great Britain had actively wooed world Jewry (convinced that its friendship was of vital importance to the Allied war effort), could not have been greater.

The scale of the repudiation is the more remarkable since Great Britain was governed during the Second World War by the most powerful prime minister in living memory, Winston Churchill, an ardent pro-Zionist. When in opposition, Churchill had been a fierce critic of the British retreat from its "solemn engagements" given in the Balfour Declaration.

But Churchill's views had no support from his colleagues in February 1940. A year later, he dismissed General A. P. Wavell's objections to arming Palestinian Jews as typical of the strong pro-Arab sentiments of most British Army officers, who had deliberately exaggerated fears of negative repercussions in the Arab world. Churchill felt that "the Arabs, under the impression of recent [British] victories, would not make any trouble now."[57] But in order to avoid an unnecessary confrontation on what to him was a secondary matter, he delayed the project for six months. On 5 July 1942, he intervened in support of Weizmann's request to renew it, writing to the colonial secretary that to indulge the "bias in favour of the Arabs against the Jews" was wrong; indeed, he wanted to make "an example of some of these anti-Semite officers and others in high places" by recall or dismissal.[58]

There were other factors, too, which influenced Churchill. He was convinced that given the growing strength of feeling in the United States for a Jewish army, delay in this matter could damage the British image in America. Moreover, in 1942, when the Yishuv was in direct danger from a German invasion of Palestine by Rommel's Afrika Korps, Churchill thought that "we should certainly give them a chance to defend themselves."[59] But the opposition in Whitehall remained determined and insistent, while the War Office continued to be obstructive. Only Churchill's energetic intervention finally overcame these objections. On 26 July 1944, he wrote to Secretary of War Grigg (who had been firmly opposed): "I like the idea of the Jews trying to get at the murderers of their fellow-countrymen in Central Europe, and I think it would give a great deal of satisfaction in the United States."[60] In a message to Roosevelt on 23 August 1944, to bring him on board, he added that "surely they of all other races have the right to strike at the Germans as a recognisable body."[61] Churchill told the American president (who was basically favorable to the idea) that he had no objection at all to the Jewish brigade flying their own flag, the Star of David, despite "the usual silly objections" that would be raised. "I cannot see why this should not be done. Indeed I think that the flying of this flag at the head of a combat unit would be a message to go all over the world."[62] Such sentiments were consistent with Churchill's long-standing personal support for the creation of a Jewish state, which he repeated to Chaim Weizmann in November 1944. But the army proposal was the only clear instance of Churchill doing anything specific to help the Jews during the Holocaust. This is sobering in light of his enormous contribution to saving Western civilization from Nazi barbarism, and it demonstrates how low the fate of the Jews was on his list of priorities.

Churchill did, however, respond positively to Weizmann's appeal to bomb Auschwitz-Birkenau after Eden had informed him of the matter, replying on 7 July 1944: "Get anything out of the Air Force you can and invoke me if necessary."[63] Unfortunately, Air Ministry officials felt "that this idea would cost British lives and aircraft to no purpose."[64] As Bernard Wasserstein notes, "this was a striking testimony to the ability of the British civil service to overcome ministerial decisions."[65] All too often, ministerial officials in Whitehall had their way in decisions affecting the Jews, when intervention on a higher level might have made a difference. But Churchill, at least, did have the historical imagination to comprehend the magnitude of the tragedy: on 11 July 1944, he wrote to Eden about the Holocaust: "There is no doubt that this is probably the greatest and most horrible crime ever committed in the whole history of the world, and it has been done by scientific machinery by nominally civilised men in the name of a great State and one of the leading races of Europe."[66]

Yet Churchill's statements on the subject were surprisingly rare, considering that he had access to earlier and better information on the massacres of Jews than did any other major Allied leader. The crucial British success in breaking German codes meant that he received regular decryptions of German radio messages, along with intelligence interpretations, soon after becoming prime minister in May 1940. By the summer of 1941, the British knew through their own cryptanalysts of massacres carried out against Jews in Russia by the German Order Police and Waffen-SS. In a speech of 24 August 1941, Churchill actually made an intensely emotional allusion to the "mass murder" and "frightful cruelties" of the Germans, which reflected the information in the reports he had received.[67] However, his emphasis was on the strength of Russian patriotic resistance to the German invaders, not the Jews, whom he never mentioned at all. This pattern continued, despite his access to police decodings. As Richard Breitman has noted, Churchill very seldom went much beyond the limits of the British government consensus about the fate of the Jews in public broadcasts or speeches. An exceptional case was the sympathetic message he sent in November 1941 to the *Jewish Chronicle*, remarking that the Jews had borne "the brunt of the Nazis' first onslaught upon the citadels of freedom and human dignity."[68] They were now suffering beyond endurance, Churchill acknowledged, but their spirit was not broken nor their will to resist. Unfortunately, this statement had a rather limited audience and was only a pale echo of what Churchill already knew about the Nazi killings. Moreover, it was a rare instance of his addressing Jews at all. Churchill was not, for example, interested in meeting with Anglo-Jewish deputations. In this respect, he was even less accessible than Roosevelt.

A good example of this detachment was his lack of any personal response to the desperate appeal written on 16 January 1943 by Lady Reading about "the horrible plight of the Jews." She had implored Churchill to help break asunder "the iron fetters of red tape."[69] How, she asked, could British MPs "stand to show sympathy to the Jewish dead" in the House of Commons while "her officials are condemning these same Jews to die?" "You cannot know of such things. I do not believe you would tolerate them. There are still some 40,000

certificates for Palestine even under the White Paper regulations. Mr Churchill, will you not say they are to be used now,
for any who will escape, man, woman or child. Is it possible, is
it really possible, to refuse sanctuary in the Holy Land?"[70]
The cruel answer is that it was all too possible. Churchill
knew and did little about it, leaving the Foreign Office to send
a characteristically noncommittal reply, invoking the usual
transport difficulties and the military complications involved
in any rescue effort. The consensus in both London and
Washington was adamant that any attempted rescue of Jews
could only complicate or obstruct the war effort.

There is no evidence that Churchill thought otherwise.
Moreover, his foreign secretary, Anthony Eden, who "preferred Arabs to Jews" and was an unshakable anti-Zionist, remained unsympathetic to rescue. His position (shared by the
Foreign Office) was best summed up in his cool reply to
American pressure in March 1943 to help those Jews who
were "threatened with extermination" to get out of southeastern Europe. "If we do that, then the Jews of the world will be
wanting us to make similar offers in Poland and Germany.
Hitler might well take us up on any such offer, and there simply are not enough ships and means of transportation in the
world to handle them."[71]

Eden's bland response was not the result of ignorance. But
as facts accumulated about what was happening to the Jews,
there was also widespread disbelief and a desire on the part of
British officials (like many of their counterparts elsewhere) to
treat the news of mass murder as the unreliable product of
an overheated imagination. A characteristic exemplar of this
proclivity was the chairman of the Joint Intelligence Committee, Victor Cavendish-Bentinck, who agreed with other
officials that the evidence about gas chambers was not to be
trusted, adding in July 1943: "The Poles, and to a far greater
extent the Jews, tend to exaggerate German atrocities in
order to stoke us up."[72] This dismissive and callous attitude is

the more remarkable since a reasonably detailed picture of the death camps, including Auschwitz-Birkenau and its gassing installations, was available to the British government by December 1942 at the latest, if not well before then.

Particularly revealing in this respect was the suspicious reception accorded the eyewitness account of an intrepid Polish underground courier, Jan Karski, who arrived in London in November 1942. Karski, a promising young career diplomat, had soon after the outbreak of war become the liaison between the Polish government-in-exile, based in London, and the resistance organizations in his conquered homeland. In the summer of 1942, this practicing Catholic and ardent Polish patriot had embarked on a highly dangerous mission: with Jewish guides, he had toured the Warsaw ghetto and seen the results of the deportations at first hand. He had visited Izbica Lubelska in eastern Poland and circulated in the vicinity of the Belzec death camp. Karski also accurately identified Treblinka and Sobibór as places of mass execution for Jews. He reported to the British and Americans that of the prewar Polish Jewry of nearly 3.5 million people, "only a small number remain." It was not a question of oppression, Karski emphasized, but "of their complete extermination by all kinds of especially devised and perfected methods of pain and torture."[73]

In describing what went on in Belzec, he specifically mentioned murder by poison gas. Karski repeated word for word the message given to him in Warsaw by a spokesman for the Jewish socialist Bund. "They [in the west] don't believe what they hear. Tell them that *we are all dying*. Let them rescue all those who will still be alive when the Report reaches them. We shall never forgive them for not having supplied us with arms so that we may have died like men, with guns in our hands."[74] Both the anguished Bundist and the Zionist leader who took Karski around the Warsaw ghetto told him that the Jews in Poland were helpless. They could not rely on the Polish underground or the population at large for any help against the Germans. Only the powerful Allied governments could assist effectively, but they must take a series of unprecedented steps: bombing German cities and making it clear that this was in retaliation for the extermination of Jews; using German POWs and German nationals resident in Allied countries as hostages; appealing to the German people through broadcasts and air-dropped leaflets; and spelling out all available data in their possession about Nazi crimes against the Jews.[75]

Karski's mission had an immediate impact on the Polish government-in-exile, which on 10 December 1942 formally appealed to the Allied governments to speak out against the extermination of the Jews in Poland. Indeed, it was the prime mover in the Allied declaration a week later, which publicly condemned Nazi crimes against the Jews for the first time. But proclamations were one thing and actions another. On 18 January 1943, Count Edward Raczynski, in the name of the government-in-exile and also on behalf of Polish Jews, demanded that the Allies bomb Germany in reprisal for the exterminations. The British foreign secretary curtly rejected all demands, offering, as Karski put it, "vague promises to intervene in some neutral countries." In Washington, the Polish courier was received rather more warmly by Roosevelt but without much comprehension of his message, and the practical results were meager. Karski's records of these and other encounters with British and American statesmen, government officials, and high-ranking military personnel are essential reading. He felt with good reason that the testimony in his report of November 1942 should have provided incontrovertible proof of the genocide and led the Allies to immediately undertake special measures to save the European Jews. This did not happen. Instead, he encountered a mixture of political hypocrisy and soulless bureaucracy, narrow national self-interest and sheer indifference in those Western political and military leaders who could have ameliorated the Jewish tragedy in larger or smaller ways.[76] They did not care, or they cast doubt on the extent of the annihilation, or else they saw the Jewish tragedy as being essentially a "Jewish problem," rather than one directly related to the meaning of Western civilization and to humanity as a whole.

8

MODERNITY AND THE NAZI GENOCIDE

Der Tod ist ein Meister aus Deutschland

PAUL CELAN, *"Death Fugue"*

Here in this carload
I am Eve
With my son Abel
If you see my older boy
Cain son of Adam
Tell him that I

DAN PAGIS (written in pencil in a sealed freight car)

In no other place and time has one seen a phenomenon so unexpected and so complex: never were so many human lives extinguished in so short a time, and with so lucid a combination of technological ingenuity, fanaticism and cruelty.

PRIMO LEVI, *The Drowned and the Saved* (1989)

The Nazi genocide has been called "the most spectacular and terrifying instance of industrial killing in this century."[1] It has also been seen in recent years by a growing number of scholars less as a regression to barbarism or as a uniquely horrible event but rather as a characteristic expression of modernity itself. More specifically, the Holocaust has been interpreted as a product of the destructive bureaucratic and technical capacities of modern Western civilization.[2] This sociological approach, exemplified by the work of Zygmunt Bauman, goes beyond the pioneering investigations of Raul Hilberg forty years ago, which first detailed the ice-cold, bureaucratic, and industrial efficiency with which the German genocidal program was carried out; as well as beyond the more controversial theses of Hannah Arendt concerning the conditioned readiness of masses of human beings to abdicate any sense of collective or individual moral responsibility under the pressure of modern totalitarian regimes.[3] For Bauman, the Holocaust is not so much a totalitarian phenomenon as the consequence of an inherent potential of modern life and its organizational culture, dominated by "rational" bureaucracies, "scientific" ideologies, depersonalization, and the extreme functional specialization of industrial society.[4] Not surprisingly, perhaps, this led him to downplay the influence of historical and ideological factors, such as the anti-Jewish hatred that existed in Christian Europe over many centuries.

In this reading, even "scientific" anti-Semitism, while not ignored, is granted only a qualified, purely functional, and limited causative role in the Nazi genocide.[5] Bauman regards modern racism as a desperate attempt to redraw boundaries that had been crossed as a result of the ceaseless flux and dizzying changes of industrial society. It was an equally vain effort to check and reverse the social mobility produced by Jewish emancipation and to keep the Jews once more in "their place." There is certainly some truth in this model, but it ignores the persistence of a host of premodern prejudices, emotions, and hatreds for which the Nazi worldview merely provided an updated pseudoscientific window dressing. Moreover, the Holocaust, while certainly "modern" in some of its organizational and technical features, had equally as many "archaic" attributes, down to and including its primitive methods of killing. Indeed, as many Jews were eliminated by shooting in the horrific pit exterminations on the eastern front as died in the factory-style exterminations at Auschwitz-Birkenau.

The German historians Götz Aly and Susanne Heim, like Bauman, also regard the Holocaust as having been triggered by modern processes of technical rationalization. However, they claim that the mass murder was designed primarily by technocrats within the German intelligentsia who were involved in planning the Third Reich's population policy.[6] The demographic experts were neither fanatical Nazis nor even anti-Semites but essentially opportunist academics and efficient bureaucrats who believed in "modernization" and at the same time wished to advance their personal careers by helping to map out the Nazi "new order" in Europe. They argued that the deportation or murder of the impoverished Jewish masses in overpopulated agrarian Poland would open the door to greater social mobility and future industrial development. The murder of Jews would get rid of unnecessary consumers and be the first step in a broader plan of genocide against other ethnic groups (Gypsies, Russians, Poles, and others), clearing the way for socioeconomic modernization in eastern Europe. Thus, they say, the Jews were not killed because they were Jews or as the result of an "irrational" racist ideology; rather, they were eliminated on utilitarian grounds as *Luftmenschen* who stood in the way of modern, rational, Western technocratic civilization. The young planners of the Third Reich set the agenda in preparing "the decisions of their superiors, who for their part attached great significance to the advice of their experts and expressly urged them to research in freedom."[7]

There are serious problems with such an approach, though few would quarrel with the assumption of complicity of German academic experts, "strategists," and planners in Nazi crimes. But there are too many facts that simply do not square with this theory. There was, for example, little unanimity among the "Jewish" experts in the Reich when proposing solutions for the starving Jews in the Lódz and Warsaw ghettos.[8] Furthermore, there is no indication that Hitler, whose contempt for "experts" of all kinds (even in military matters) was well-known, ever paid the slightest attention to the proposals of low-level planners.[9] Moreover, one needs to distinguish between a modernization strategy and plain straightforward greed in the plundering of Jewish assets, which was indeed an integral part of Nazi anti-Semitic policy during the *Anschluss,* the pogroms of 1938, the "Aryanization" measures, and the subsequent deportations. The massive expropriation of Jewish wealth and property undoubtedly made Nazism more attractive to millions of non-Jews. But what "modernizing" logic underlay the transport in wartime of 2,200 Jews to Auschwitz-Birkenau from the island of Rhodes, two thousand miles away, despite urgent military transport priorities?[10] What economic or political sense did it make to deport half a million Hungarian Jews to Auschwitz-Birkenau in 1944 after the Normandy landings of the Allies and the advances of the Red Army from the east had made Germany's defeat virtually inevitable? If social "modernization" was the Nazi objective, why deport and murder the highly integrated, economically productive Jews of Germany, Austria, Italy, Holland, or France, who were certainly no *Luftmenschen?* The fact that Nazi economists and planners often employed a "utilitarian" language to mask their prejudices against Jews and Poles by framing their policy proposals in terms of productivity, food supply, public health, or "security threats" should not deceive anyone about their underlying racist content. Rationalizations are not the same as causes. Using the label of "modernization" to categorize the Nazi policy of genocidal annihilation in effect flattens out and "normalizes" mass murder as if it were a slightly deviant variant of normal capitalist development.[11]

Genocidal impulses, as we have shown, were inherent in the Nazi movement, ideology, and collective mind-set. In peacetime, it is true that the official goals of the regime were still confined to "racial separation," followed by expulsions. But by 1939 it was already apparent that if a general war broke out, then conditions would exist for the Nazis to "ethnically cleanse" on a grand scale the physically and mentally handicapped, the Gypsies, and, above all, the Jews.[12] The Nazi leadership did not require planning experts to tell them that in wartime "the destruction of the Jews will go hand in hand with the destruction of our enemies."[13] Goebbels, commenting on a Hitler speech in February 1942, added: "The *Führer* realises the full implications of the great opportunities offered by this war."[14]

The war against the partisans was a case in point. The SS leader in charge of this warfare, Erich von dem Bach-Zelewski, observed: "The fight against partisans was gradually used as an excuse to carry out other measures, such as the extermination of Jews and Gypsies, the systematic reduction of the Slavic peoples ... and the terrorisation of civilians by shooting and looting."[15] So, too, social-engineering models were used by planners to give an aura of scientific rationality to genocide. But such camouflage concerns never interfered with the primacy of politics in the Third Reich.[16] Nor did they prevent Hitler from cursorily dismissing pressures from the army or industrialists to delay the deportation of much-needed skilled Jewish workers.[17] Ghettos, too, were created in

Poland on ideological and political grounds even though they disrupted the economy.

When Himmler instructed Rudolf Höss to establish the Auschwitz-Birkenau concentration camp, the reason given was expressly ideological: the need to extirpate the biological roots of Jewry.[18] Invariably, Himmler's orders and those of his speeches that related to the "Final Solution" spoke of the primordial "racial struggle against Jewry," not of economic benefits.[19] Moreover, whenever Jews were used for slave labor, Himmler demanded that they be worked to death or quickly replaced by Poles so that, as he put it on 2 October 1942, "all the Jews would disappear in accordance with the *Führer*'s wish [*dem Wunsche des Führers entsprechend*]."[20]

Nor is there any convincing evidence for the claim of Aly and Heim that the Nazis ultimately planned the *extermination* of the Slavs (or even of all Slavic elites) as part of their demographic and "modernization" program. Slav nations such as Croatia and Slovakia were allies of Nazi Germany, and the Germans envisaged that Croats and Slovaks would dominate and help destroy the Serb and Czech elites. The Ukrainians and Byelorussians (along with the Balts) were not given even the illusion of independence, but they did have a limited, subordinate status as "helpers" of the Germans, especially in killing Jews. Poles, Serbs, and Great Russians, on the other hand, had no rights at all and were subjected to massacres and horrendous injustices but *not* to systematic genocide. As Himmler expressed it in Poznan in 1943: "Whether the other peoples live in comfort or perish of hunger interests me only insofar as we need them as slaves for our culture. Whether or not ten thousand Russian women collapse from exhaustion while digging a tank ditch interests me only insofar as the tank ditch is completed for Germany."[21]

In the logic of Nazi racial imperialism, Russians and Poles were branded as "inferior" and would be reduced to helots of the Reich. But they did not have to die en masse in the name of an apocalyptic, millenarian ideology. Even Nazi officials and certainly soldiers of the Wehrmacht saw something contrary to their self-image as a *Kulturnation* in any effort to exterminate the entire Polish nation. Significantly, Himmler himself did not exclude "Germanizing" those Poles who were considered "racially valuable" elements; though the rest of the Polish people would be enslaved and economically exploited, with the exception of the elites (clergy, intellectuals, army officers), who were ruthlessly eliminated. Similarly, with the Russians and Ukrainians, utilitarian criteria and expediency played a role in Nazi plans. There was to be a controlled form of "ethnic cleansing," and it was indeed anticipated in 1941 that millions of Slavs would perish in Russia as a result of German conquest, colonization, and a deliberate policy of starvation. But the total extermination of entire Slavic populations was neither practicable for the Nazis, nor did it serve any major ideological agenda.

The Slav peoples of Russia were depicted in wartime as racially inferior and sometimes as Asiatic "subhumans" but not as "lice," "vermin," or "bugs" to be collectively disposed of by industrialized mass murder. Nor was there any Slavic counterpart to the pit killings conducted by the Einsatzgruppen. Neither Poles, Serbs, nor Russians (though they were close to the bottom of the racial-biological hierarchy) were branded as a "world enemy" or reviled as an antirace that threatened the very foundations of "Aryan" civilization and humanity itself. The struggle against the eastern Slavs was in Nazi terms essentially a war of *Lebensraum*. Had it been successful, it would probably have led to the uprooting rather than the murder of as many as thirty million Slavs (deported to Siberia) and their replacement by German settlers in western Russia, the Ukraine, and the Caucasus.

However, this racist vision of a great Germanic empire gradually crumbled as the Nazi state became embroiled in a life-and-death struggle from late 1941 onward against a reinvigorated Soviet Russia and the British Empire, newly reinforced by the United States. The military stalemate and the resulting demographic and logistical bottlenecks in early 1942 led to a shift in German policy. In order to make good its manpower losses and preserve its military-industrial complex, Nazi Germany decided to maximize the labor potential of its subject populations. As a result, millions of Soviet POWs (most of whom were later starved to death), Poles, Czechs, and other Europeans were brought into the Reich to work, even though this clearly undermined the Nazi vision of a racially pure *Volksgemeinschaft.*[22] At the same time, Jews were being deported *out* of the central Reich territories to the east, where they would be subjected to conveyor-belt extermination. Thus, the "rational" alternative of economic hyperexploitation was explicitly *rejected* for the Jews.[23]

The significant element of "modernity" in the Nazi genocidal project did not therefore lie in its mythical "economic rationality" or in any link to a breakneck developmental program of social transformation (as occurred in Stalinist Russia) but rather in the methods that it pioneered in killing. At places like Auschwitz-Birkenau, Majdanek, Sobibór, Treblinka, and other death camps, the entire apparatus of the modern German state—the resources of its bureaucracy and military-industrial complex—were put at the disposal of the SS in order to carry out streamlined exterminations. All the skills and techniques of modern technology, of scientific and medical expertise, as well as precise railway scheduling, were enlisted in the service of racial murder. Raul Hilberg, who initiated the study of this administrative process, long ago observed: "The machinery of destruction, then, was structurally no different from organised German society as a whole. The machinery of destruction was the organised community in one of its special roles."[24]

The organization of mass murder involved not only the immediate perpetrators but literally tens of thousands of other Germans: diplomats, lawyers, doctors, accountants, bankers, clerks, and railway workers, without whom the trains to the death camps would not have run. This monstrous machinery of death could not have been unleashed except in a highly organized and bureaucratized society, methodical, perfectionist, and thoroughly *modern* in its deliberate fragmenting of responsibilities and routinizing of operations. Furthermore, it happened in a state that was able to efficiently coordinate countless bureaucrats in relevant Reich ministries, the army, the judiciary, and the medical establishments, as well as Nazi officialdom in the occupied eastern territories, the SS, and the Order Police. Such relentless systematization and its end product—the gas chambers—is what gave the Holocaust its sinister "modern" aura of depersonalized violence.[25] The gas chambers and crematoriums were an industrial method for liquidating human beings on the basis of a daily quota; they demonstrated "the modern world's capability to organise mass death on a new, more advanced and scientifically planned basis."[26]

This streamlined process was also distinctively modern in its ability to draw on state-of-the-art punch-card technology, which enabled the Third Reich to coordinate the rounding up of Jews throughout Europe, their deportation to the camps, and the statistics that measured their agonies during the "Final Solution." Only after the Jews were successfully identified could they be targeted for asset confiscation, deportation, ghettoization, slave labor, and finally extermination. It was custom-designed American IBM technology, as Edwin Black has recently shown, that gave an unprecedented speed and accuracy to the Germans in identifying Jews in censuses, registrations, and racial-ancestry programs, as well as in organizing railway transportation and concentration-camp registrations.[27]

Similarly, mass murder on this scale could not have happened without the trial run, beginning in 1939, of the Nazi "euthanasia" program. The physicians of the Reich collaborated grossly in using poison gas and lethal injections to murder eighty thousand mentally and physically handicapped Germans. This so-called Operation T4 (named for the central office at 4 Tiergarten Strasse, Berlin) had been personally ordered by Hitler. As Henry Friedlander has pointed out, "The success of the euthanasia policy convinced the Nazi leadership that mass murder was technically feasible, that ordinary men and women were willing to kill large numbers of innocent human beings, and that the bureaucracy would cooperate in such an unprecedented enterprise."[28] The same sinister methods that were used in Operation T4 to mask the killing of the handicapped would be applied in the Nazi death camps. SS guards would be dressed in the white uniforms of medical technicians, and the victims were always led to believe that they were being taken to a shower room rather than to a gas chamber.

The German perpetrators who staffed the machinery of destruction, whether in offices or in the camps, were "not a special kind of German" but rather "a remarkable cross section of the German population."[29] Engaged in a vast murder operation, officially shrouded in secrecy, they appeared to be immune from any pangs of conscience. A vocabulary of euphemisms like "evacuation" or "special treatment" shielded them from any guilty feelings or doubts about the justice of their enterprise.[30]

Hans Mommsen has persuasively argued that the use of bureaucratic and technocratic methods repressed any moral inhibitions among the perpetrators, turning the death of Jews into a technical problem of killing capacity. His view of the Holocaust is that it was essentially a rationalized, quasi-automatic process in which the extermination of those "unfit for work" developed a dynamic of its own: "The bureaucratic machinery created by Eichmann and Heydrich functioned more or less automatically; it was thus symptomatic that Eichmann consciously circumvented Himmler's order, at the end of 1944, to stop the Final Solution. There was no need for external ideological impulses to keep the process of extermination going."[31]

But the machinery of death did not exist in an ideological

void. Even a model bureaucrat like Eichmann—though no fanatical anti-Semite—displayed extraordinary zeal in hunting
down Jews. His constant complaints about obstacles in the
fulfillment of death-camp quotas, his impatience with the existence of loopholes such as the free zone in Vichy France, or
the uncooperativeness of the Italians and other German allies
in expediting the rounding up of Jews were not merely driven
by a petty bureaucrat's desire to prove his efficiency. Eichmann was a convinced Nazi who rejoiced in the slaughter of
Jews. The perpetrators—bureaucrats like Eichmann, modernizing technocrats, planners, and professional people—
fitted themselves effortlessly into the prevailing genocidal
ethos because they believed in what they were doing.[32] Their
motives were not always identical to those of the top Nazi decision makers, but there is every reason to think that they in-
ternalized the institutionalized anti-Semitism of the Nazi
regime. It is most unlikely that they would have implemented
mass murder against any arbitrarily designated enemy group.

The so-called functionalist school of historians has long
argued that the "Final Solution" was not the product of any
grand design but that the Nazi regime was administered by "a
maze of competing power groups and rival bureaucracies"
seeking the favor of a distant Führer.[33] In their view, such lack
of coordination and fragmentation of decision making led to
a "cumulative radicalization" of policies, each more arbitrary,
violent, and radical in their implementation than its prede-
cessors.[34] The Nazis, it has been said, had no specific plan to
"solve the Jewish question" in 1933 and simply drifted step by
step down a very twisted road to Auschwitz-Birkenau.[35] Even
the annihilations, according to Martin Broszat, had a largely
improvisatory character and did not derive from a specific
Hitler order or from a clear "will to exterminate" but rather
from a series of local Nazi initiatives aimed at solving local
problems (food supply, logistical difficulties, and so on) on the
eastern front. For Broszat, the Nazis had to find "a way out of
a blind alley" into which they had maneuvered themselves.

Once the practice of liquidation was established, it gained predominance and eventually evolved in an ad hoc manner into a comprehensive program that was subsequently approved by Hitler.[36] This seems plausible enough until one recalls that throughout the history of Nazi Germany, Hitler pursued a modus operandi of deliberate incitement against the Jews while leaving the execution of the policy to subordinates.

Moreover, some functionalist theories tend (perhaps unintentionally) to normalize Nazism by suggesting that its leaders stumbled into the most extreme criminal behavior. They unconvincingly turn Hitler himself into a weak, indecisive, procrastinating leader whose visionary political perspectives on the "Jewish question" had only a minor impact on the practical policy of genocide.[37] The functionalists also downplay the ancient hatred of Jews, its transformation into "scientific" racism, the status, testimony, and suffering of the Jews themselves as a social and national group, the role of bystanders (individuals as well as states), not to mention the ideological motivations and mentality of the perpetrators.

More recent German scholarship has sought to go beyond the earlier abstract debates on "modernity" and the clash between intentionalists (who believe in the centrality of Hitler and a coordinated decision to murder the Jews of Europe) and skeptical functionalists. Ulrich Herbert, for example, while adopting the theory of "cumulative radicalization" and stressing the role of bureaucracy, does not assume that local decisions—whether in Serbia, Lithuania, or Byelorussia—were made outside a context of deeply ingrained anti-Semitism. He believes that the Holocaust was not simply the result of directives from Berlin but of an interaction between the center and an increasingly radicalized periphery.[38] The empirical studies of Dieter Pohl and Thomas Sandkühler, discussing the General Government and Galicia, highlight the importance of the periphery and the pivotal role of the civil administration in pushing vigorously for a radical anti-

Jewish policy.[39] This kind of research into the complex local political process in the German-occupied territories is certainly welcome; unfortunately, some of it tends to blur the decisive role of Hitler, Himmler, and others in Berlin in initiating, centralizing, and unifying the multitude of regional actions that were all part of a much larger and comprehensive "Final Solution." There are other weaknesses in this new trend in scholarship: the voice of the Jewish victims is rarely heard, and there is a tendency to overstate the symmetry between the Holocaust and the "ethnic cleansing" of other groups (especially Slavs) in eastern Europe. Only the Gypsies, as we have shown, offer a serious point of comparison, though their role in Nazi ideology was minimal.

Herbert, like Goldhagen before him, emphasizes both the numbers of the perpetrators involved (more than was previously assumed) and the fact that the murders were frequently carried out in a traditional, even "archaic" way.[40] Much of the Nazi genocide, he reminds us, is not adequately described by the notion of factory-style killing, a so-called clean death by gassing, or the quasi-anonymous process of the German bureaucracy. The massacres of Jews in Lithuania, Poland, and the Balkans as well as the killings by Wehrmacht soldiers and the Einsatzgruppen on the eastern front support this point.[41]

The "hot-blooded" slaughters and "Jew hunts" carried out by Order Police battalions in occupied Poland (described by Christopher Browning and Daniel Goldhagen) present us with a distinctly unmodern side of the Holocaust, one that aligns it more closely with other twentieth-century genocides. No high technology was required for the 40 percent of Holocaust victims who died through malnutrition, famine, and disease in the ghettos, through being worked to death in labor camps, through deportations late in the war that turned into horrific death marches, or through the gruesome executions in pits, trenches, and ravines, using machine guns, rifles, and revolvers. There was nothing particularly modern or civilized about such genocidal acts, any more than there is about those since 1945 in Cambodia, Rwanda, Bosnia, and other "backward" parts of the world. No spectacular industrial measures were needed for this purpose. Yet the moral lesson of the concentration and death camps in particular suggests that what Europe witnessed in the middle of the twentieth century was nonetheless something unprecedented: not so much in the statistics of the dead but in the devilish scale of the sufferings inflicted on the victims and the depravity of their tormentors.[42]

In each of the death camps there were between twenty and thirty-five SS men in charge (a high percentage were German Austrians), assisted by a number of Ukrainian auxiliaries. At Treblinka, the Germans succeeded in their ruse of presenting it as a transit camp (*Durchgangslager*) where Jews were supposedly to be "disinfected" before proceeding on to a labor camp (*Arbeitslager*). Abraham Goldfarb arrived at the camp on 25 August 1942. He relates: "When we reached Treblinka and the Germans opened the freight-car doors, the scene was ghastly. The cars were full of corpses. The bodies had been partially consumed by chlorine. The stench from the cars caused those still alive to choke."[43] The death and destruction had begun when the Jews were still in the freight cars, deprived of air, water, and sanitary facilities, as they rolled toward the extermination camps; purposely overcrowded by the SS personnel, these transports were in fact death traps. Oskar Berger, who had arrived three days earlier, witnessed "hundreds of bodies lying all around" as he disembarked from the train. "Piles of bundles, clothes, valises, everything mixed together. SS soldiers, Germans, and Ukrainians were standing on the roofs of barracks and firing indiscriminately into the crowd. Men, women, and children fell bleeding. The air was filled with screaming and weeping."[44]

From eyewitness testimonies, it is evident that sadism and torture knew no bounds at Treblinka, Sobibór, or Belzec, where the cruelty of security guards—Germans, Latvians,

Lithuanians, and Ukrainians—was notorious.[45] As in other camps, they carried out their duties without question but showed considerable initiative when it came to torturing their victims. A good example was the deputy commandant of Sobibór (where 250,000 Jews died), the Viennese-born Gustav Wagner. Like many of the SS personnel in the camps, he was a veteran of the Schloss Hartheim Euthanasia Institute near Linz, a center for killing off the mentally sick and handicapped. Master Sergeant Wagner was in charge of "selections" and better known to his victims as the "Human Beast." One survivor recalled: "Wagner didn't eat his lunch if he didn't kill daily. With an axe, shovel or even his hands. He had to have blood."[46] Another victim remembered him as an angel of Death, for whom "torturing and killing was a pleasure"— he would snatch babies from their mothers' arms and tear them to pieces in his hands.

Another prize torturer and sadist was Christian Wirth, inspector of the death camps in Poland, who had also previously worked in euthanasia institutions and in 1939 had carried out the first known gassing experiments on German "incurables." At the end of 1941, he had been assigned to begin the extermination of Jews in Chelmno, the first of the Nazi death camps to become operational. During the next eighteen months, he oversaw, together with Odilo Globocnik (former Gauleiter of Vienna), the murder of nearly two million Jews in the death camps of Belzec, Sobibór, and Treblinka. A survivor from Belzec (where at least six hundred thousand Jews were murdered) recalled Wirth as "a tall broad-shouldered man in his middle fifties, with a vulgar face—he was a born criminal. The extreme beast.... Although he seldom appeared, the SS men were terrified of him."[47] Franz Suchamel, who served under him, testified that he could not be surpassed in brutality, meanness, and ruthlessness. "We therefore called him 'Christian the Terrible' or 'The Wild Christian.' The Ukrainian guardsmen called him 'Stuka' [a type of dive-bomber]."[48] At Belzec, in August 1942,

Kurt Gerstein personally witnessed how Wirth and his assistants supervised the journey of the Jews to their destruction:

> They drew nearer to where Wirth and I were standing in front of the death chambers. Men, women, young girls, children, babies, cripples, all stark naked, filed by. At the corner stood a burly SS man, with a loud, priestlike voice. "Nothing terrible is going to happen to you!" he told the poor wretches. "All you have to do is to breathe in deeply. That strengthens the lungs. Inhaling is a means of preventing infectious diseases. It's a good method of disinfection." ... One Jewess of about forty, her eyes flaming like torches, cursed her murderers. Urged on by some whiplashes from Captain Wirth in person, she disappeared in the gas chambers. Many were praying, while others asked: "Who will give us water to wash the dead?"[49]

The Austrian commandant of Treblinka and Sobibór, Franz Stangl, was like Wirth a former policeman and had been superintendent at Schloss Hartheim. He was a highly efficient and dedicated organizer of mass murder, even receiving an official commendation as the "best camp commander in Poland." Unlike Wirth, the soft-voiced Stangl was not a sadist but polite and always impeccably dressed (he attended the unloading of transports at Treblinka dressed in white riding clothes); he took pride and pleasure in his "work," running the camp like clockwork. Stangl never looked at his victims as individuals or even as human beings but rather as "cargo." Regarding the Jews, he told the journalist Gitta Sereny: "They were so weak; they allowed everything to happen, to be done to them. They were people with whom there was no common ground, no possibility of communication— that is how contempt is born. I could never understand how they could just give in as they did."[50] He further recalled:

> I think it started the day I first saw the *Totenlager* [extermination area] in Treblinka. I remember Wirth standing there, next to the pits full of blue-black corpses. It had nothing to do with humanity—it could not have. It was a mass—a mass of rotting

flesh. Wirth said, "What shall we do with this garbage?" I think unconsciously that started me thinking of them as cargo ... It was always a huge mass. I sometimes stood on the wall and saw them in the "tube"—they were naked, packed together, running, being driven with whips.[51]

Rudolf Höss, the commandant of Auschwitz-Birkenau from 1 May 1940 until 1 December 1943, appeared outwardly, like Stangl, to be a kindly, unselfish family man who loved his wife. He, too, took a perfectionist pride in his "work" at what he called the "greatest human extermination centre of all time." In 1944, he was commended by his superiors as a "true pioneer in this field, thanks to new ideas and new methods of education."[52] In his autobiography, Höss emphasized the "strong awareness of duty" that had been inculcated in him by his pious Catholic parents: "Every task had to be exactly and conscientiously carried out." He considered his own compulsion to obey orders and to surrender all personal independence as a hallmark of his own morality and petty-bourgeois decency. "I am completely normal," he observed in his book. "Even while I was carrying out the task of extermination I lived a normal life."[53]

Unlike the "willing executioners" among the Order Police or on the eastern front, Höss embodied the ideal type of the passionless, self-disciplined, disinterested "desk murderer" who never personally attended mass executions or selections for the gas chambers but treated his job as purely administrative. What concerned Höss was the practical and technical questions involving timetables, the size of transports, the types of oven, and the methods of gassing. He took pride in being the first to successfully utilize Zyklon B—like Himmler, the squeamish Höss, who could not bear shootings and bloodshed, found poison gas to be more rational, hygienic, and "humane." Naturally, the totally depersonalized commandant of Auschwitz-Birkenau (for whom obedience and duty were the highest virtues) did not have a moment's hesitation in executing Himmler's orders concerning the "Final Solution."

Like Adolf Eichmann, Höss emphasized in his memoirs that he had no personal hatred of Jews, though he evidently never had any doubts about Hitler's objectives either. Having spent three years in the vast laboratory called Auschwitz-Birkenau, gathering "indelible impressions and ample food for thought," he still could not resolve the thorny question of why "members of the Jewish race go to their deaths so easily."[54] Like Stangl, it never occurred to him that the whole apparatus of torture and death over which he personally presided had been carefully designed to achieve precisely that outcome. No wonder that Höss was so delighted by the grotesque Auschwitz-Birkenau motto *Arbeit macht frei* (Work makes you free) and totally uninterested in its macabre meaning for the victims.

At Auschwitz-Birkenau, there were also other technical perfectionists, like the gifted thirty-two-year-old chief doctor, Josef Mengele, who knew exactly why they were there and how killing Jews could advance their careers. Mengele used Auschwitz-Birkenau inmates as guinea pigs for what he believed was pioneering scientific research into presumed racial differences and physical abnormalities. People afflicted with any sort of deformity were killed on his orders, upon their arrival in the camp, to provide new material for his studies. He also conducted medical experiments on living Jews, especially twins, hoping to find a method of creating a race of blue-eyed Aryans to realize the megalomaniac dreams of Nazi racial science. In a conversation at Auschwitz-Birkenau with an Austrian Christian woman doctor, Dr. Ella Lingens, Mengele said that "there were only two gifted nations in the world—the Germans and the Jews." The question, he told Frau Dr. Lingens, is "which one will dominate?"[55]

Mengele's contribution to the millennial struggle for "domination," like that of other SS doctors, was considerable.

He personally killed many prisoners by injecting them with phenol, gasoline, chloroform, or air; he participated in countless "selections" at the Auschwitz-Birkenau railway junction, sending all those "unfit for work" to the gas chambers with a flick of the hand or the wave of a stick. Children, old people, sick, crippled, or physically weak Jews, as well as pregnant women, were instantly sentenced to death. Yet even Mengele, a music lover and a scientific mind, also had his "compassionate" moments when he gave individual patients the best of care, between "selections."[56]

Such discontinuities and "schizophrenic" attitudes characterized many levels of Nazi behavior, testifying to a high degree of personal fragmentation, an extreme compartmentalization of the private and public spheres, and a constant effort to repress awareness of the genocidal reality that they themselves had created. A good example can be found in the diary of Dr. Johann Paul Kremer, a member of the Auschwitz-Birkenau medical corps. On 5 September 1942, he witnessed a "special action" in the women's camp that he called "the most horrible of all horrors," agreeing with a colleague's description of Auschwitz-Birkenau as the *"anus mundi"*—the asshole of the world. Yet the following day, Kremer followed up his record of a dreadful execution with details of a splendid meal: "Today an excellent Sunday dinner: tomato soup, one half of chicken with potatoes and red cabbage (20 grammes of fat), dessert and magnificent vanilla-cream."[57]

In the inverted logic of the SS world, such seeming anomalies became normal. It was a world where to torture and destroy became a certificate of maturity and the total negation of a fellow person, the royal road to absolute sovereignty over life and death. As Jean Améry, a survivor, once put it: National Socialism was the only political system of the twentieth century that "not only practised the rule of the antiman, as had other Red and White terror regimes also, but had established it as a principle."[58] The camps were the ultimate manifestation of this system, reproducing its structures on a miniature scale but in an amplified way. Freedom, choice, and human solidarity had been virtually abolished, replaced by a Hobbesian war of all against all, with survival against the odds as the sole object. Through hunger, beatings, slave labor, exposure to cold, and endless tortures, the aim was to destroy individual autonomy and reduce human beings to purely animal reactions.[59] Women, who in general were treated less severely by the guards, usually survived the ordeal better than men, proving often to be more practical, psychologically stronger, and more willing to help one another.[60]

Although the crimes committed were appallingly inhuman, the criminals themselves were, as Primo Levi has reminded us, human beings like ourselves—ordinary people who committed extraordinary acts: "They were made of the same cloth as we, they were average human beings, averagely intelligent, averagely wicked: save the exceptions, they were not monsters, they had our faces."[61] Franz Stangl was by all accounts a very good husband and father, just as Rudolf Höss exemplified the German bourgeois virtues of discipline, obedience, and work. Their sleep was never disturbed since they rarely saw any suffering faces, concentrating as they did solely on the organizational task at hand. No doubt their impeccable private lives and the watertight compartmentalizing of their existence blunted any sense of the monstrous evil they were perpetrating.

Adolf Eichmann exemplified to perfection the same modern bureaucratic mentality that focused on technical matters without any concern for ultimate ends—a sphere that belonged solely to the Führer, the party, and the state. Like other "desk murderers," Eichmann was congenitally incapable of accepting any personal responsibility: "I never killed a single one.... I never killed anyone and I never gave the order to kill anyone."[62] Of course, such disclaimers were self-serving falsehoods that permeated the whole of German society from the Nazi leadership, the bureaucracy, the army, and the industrialists down to the smallest cogs in the killing machine. The decision makers and the lower-level perpetrators were undoubtedly aware of the enormity of their crimes, otherwise they would not have sought to obliterate all traces of the gas chambers, crematoriums, and mass executions. The SS was determined that no witnesses should survive to tell the terrible secret of what they had done: hence the insane death marches of 1944–1945 with which the history of the Nazi camps came to an end.

Primo Levi has emphasized how the infernal camp system sought to maximize the degradation of its victims by making them complicit in it. Some individuals, like the Kapos of the labor squads, were indeed seduced by material advantages or fatally intoxicated by the power given to them by their tormentors.[63] As prisoners who were themselves appointed by the SS to ensure absolute control over other inmates, the Kapos tyrannized them with a cruel sadism that matched that of their German masters. Perhaps the most demonic of all Nazi crimes was, however, the delegation by the SS of the filthiest part of their work to the victims themselves: the running of the crematoriums, the extracting of corpses from the gas chambers, and the pulling of gold teeth from the jaws of the victims were tasks assigned to Jews.[64] By making Jewish Sonderkommandos responsible for the ovens, the Nazis could demonstrate that, in Levi's words, "the sub-race, the sub-men bow to any and all humiliation, even to destroying themselves."[65] The insidious message of the SS was that "if we so wish and we do so much, we can destroy not only your bodies but also your souls, just as we have destroyed ours."[66]

Twelve "special squads" succeeded one another at Auschwitz-Birkenau, operating for a few months before they were liquidated. In October 1944, the last squad rebelled against the SS, blew up one of the crematoriums and was wiped out in the only revolt that ever occurred at Auschwitz-Birkenau. To ask why they did not rise up sooner would be to grossly underestimate the hellish sequence of segregation, humiliation, forced migration, total physical exhaustion, and rupture with any kind of normality that had accompanied their arrival in the camps and continued with even greater ferocity thereafter. Millions of young, robust, well-trained Soviet military prisoners behaved no differently when they fell into German hands, and the few non-Jews among the "special squads" behaved exactly like the Jews. The camps were designed to create a debilitating sense of impotence in their victims, to literally reduce them to *Untermenschen* and thereby remake them in the image of Nazi propaganda. The enemy must not only die, but he or she must die in torment. This "useless" cruelty was not of course unique to the Third Reich, but it certainly was a fundamental feature of Hitlerism, which combined extreme irrationality and sadism with a modern, pseudoscientific streak of technical perfectionism.

The question frequently arises as to how far the National Socialist system, the death camps, and the Holocaust were a uniquely *German* genocide? Daniel Goldhagen has no doubts that the mass killings of Jews were not simply a German enterprise but in its essence a German national project. The perpetrators, in his view, are not accurately described as "ordinary men" (the title of Browning's parallel study of the police battalions) or simply as Nazis. They were ordinary Germans. And all of German society was permeated by anti-Jewish policy, with extermination at its very center. "Hundreds of thousands of Germans contributed to the genocide and the still larger system of subjugation that was the vast concentration system."[67] I agree with Goldhagen's general assertion that German anti-Semitic beliefs about Jews "were the central causal agent of the Holocaust" but not with his simplistic explanations of how this came about nor with the exclusive importance he has attached to this factor. I partly agree with his analysis of the camps but question whether all of the perpetrator behavior that Goldhagen brands as distinctively "German" was in fact so unique.

The same combination of murderous anti-Semitism, extreme anti-Communism, brutality, and sadism can be found in the behavior of the Lithuanian, Latvian, Ukrainian, Romanian, and Croat executioners. Polish peasants at Jedwabne in July 1941 also exhibited similar traits when burning their Jewish neighbors alive or hacking them to death. The anti-Jewish dynamic was equally, if not even more, present in the Austrians who, though "German" by language and culture, originated from a very different history, society, and civilization. It was not so much an all-pervasive "eliminationist anti-Semitism" that was peculiar to Germany; rather, it was the integration of anti-Semitism into the radical chiliasm of Nazism, which was able to seize power and mobilize all the material and propaganda resources of a highly organized state toward its imperialist and genocidal objectives. To suggest that virtually all Germans identified with this totalitarian state and its murderous anti-Semitic goals is surely a gross oversimplification since they cannot be regarded as a single, undifferentiated entity.

Moreover, the "camp world," although the largest and most significant institutional creation in Nazi Germany, did have a parallel in the Soviet Union that cannot be ignored. True, there was no precise equivalent of Auschwitz-Birkenau and the industrialized killing process in the Soviet gulag; there were proportionately fewer fatalities, and medical care was less inadequate. Arguably, too, Soviet guards may have been more compassionate than their German counterparts. But for a survivor like Margerete Buber-Neumann who experienced both the German and Russian camps, the experiences seemed largely identical: "I ask myself deep down, which is really worse, the lice-infested corncob-walled cabins in Birma [in Kazakhstan] or the nightmare-order of Ravens-brück."[68] At the 1950 trial of David Rousset, himself an eloquent survivor of the camps, she posed a similar awkward question: "It is hard to decide which is the least humane—to gas people in five minutes or to strangle them slowly, over the course of three months, by hunger."[69]

The Germans were well aware that the Russians had annihilated millions of people through forced labor before they even embarked on their own program of concentration camps, and the SS certainly studied this model closely. While Ernst Nolte's notion that the death camps were a Nazi copy of the gulag "original" is quite false, it is important to realize that Hitler admired Stalin and that both dictators and regimes were in a macabre symbiotic relationship.[70] Nevertheless, there were key differences between the Soviet and Nazi systems. Stalin did not set out to deliberately murder the population of the gulags precisely because he needed a vast slave empire in order to finance the *modernization* of Russia. In other words, unlike the Nazi experiment, there were real economic and utilitarian motives behind the Stalinist projects, however costly and utterly inhuman they may have been.[71] The Soviet camps were undoubtedly used to eliminate political enemies (including many Communists), and millions of innocent people died there; but they were oriented to the production of wealth and the industrialization of a backward country: the mining of gold, the felling of timber for export, and the extraction of minerals were indeed an integral part of the gulags.

Prisoners were not sent to the Soviet labor camps to be transformed into *Untermenschen* and then into corpses, as the SS did with the Jews. Some visits and correspondence with the outside world (while rare) was permitted to inmates, who were not totally cut off from the past, their historic communities, and their personal identities. Such elements were expressly denied to Jews in the Nazi camps, who when they prayed, remembered, and learned did so in defiance of their tormentors. Moreover, as Steven Katz has observed, the Nazis did not even engage in the pretense of ideological "reeducation" that (however cynically) was part of the Stalinist gulag.[72] There was simply no point in reeducating those who were a priori vermin or "lice."

Similarly, sexual perversity, salaciousness, and exploita-

236 · Robert S. Wistrich

tion played a very different role in the Soviet and Nazi camp systems. Women in the gulag could still hope to trade sexual favors for life and survival. Under Nazi rule, such a possibility rarely, if ever, existed, since sexual exchanges between Germans and Jews (or even Poles) constituted "racial crimes." As Katz bluntly puts it: "The SS would sexually assault Jewish women and then murder them. They were obligated to murder them."[73]

More revealing still was the attitude to mothers and children, who even under the Soviet slave-labor system enjoyed some rights. Despite the terrible material conditions, children could come into the world in the gulag, and mothers were not obliged to work during the last month of pregnancy or the first month after their birth. In Auschwitz and other camps, no Jewish child was allowed to live. As one survivor, Olga Lengyel, recalled, "the Germans succeeded in making murderers of even us. To this day the picture of those murdered babies haunts me. Our own children had perished in the gas chambers and were cremated in the Birkenau ovens, and we dispatched the lives of others before their first voices had left their tiny lungs."[74] Katz makes the very important point that in contrast to the Soviet gulag and all known genocides, past and present, only under the Nazi Reich were (Jewish) mothers and children (one million of them) *intentionally, systematically, unrelentingly, and without exception* murdered."[75] This was an absolute *novum* of the Holocaust, which marks it off from other crimes in history and underlines Améry's point that the Reich was a kingdom of night in which the "antiman" reigned supreme. Despite the horrors of the Stalinist gulags, the "class enemies" of the socialist order were never reduced to subhuman vermin outside the realm of human and moral obligation.

Perhaps the closest of all analogies to the Nazi genocide in the twentieth century was the great massacre of the Armenian people by the Turks during the First World War; it destroyed about 40 percent of this ancient national community.

Under the cover of war, able-bodied male Armenians were separated from their families and murdered. The remaining women and children, the old, and the feeble were driven into the Syrian desert on forced marches, deprived of food and water. Many were tortured, raped, and killed both by Turks and by marauding Kurds on the way. This bestial treatment was referred to by the American ambassador to Turkey, Henry Morgenthau, as "the destruction of the Armenian race."

The genocidal actions of the Turkish state in "solving the Armenian question" led to the deaths of between five hundred thousand and one million Armenians—the main body of its population in Asia Minor and the fountainhead of its culture.[76] The lack of Zyklon B, gas chambers, and crematoriums did not hinder the killers from carrying out this harrowing mass murder. The Turks did have at their disposal railways, the telegraph, bureaucratic machinery, and modern propaganda techniques, but the killing itself was still carried out by primitive methods.

The Turkish government's objective was to destroy the Christian Armenian population inside Turkey, which was deemed to be actively seeking full independence or autonomy. The Armenians found themselves stereotyped as an "alien nationality," especially after the Young Turk rulers adopted a xenophobic nationalism intended to underpin their dreams of a new Islamic empire stretching from Anatolia to western China. Moreover, the Armenians were particularly vulnerable because of their territorial concentration in eastern Anatolia, which the new rulers saw as the heartland of the future pan-Turkic state.[77]

Once Turkey had aligned itself with imperial Germany against the czarist Russian Empire during the First World War, the Armenians were quickly branded as Russian spies and secessionists—an internal enemy to be deported, starved, and pitilessly destroyed.[78] Armenians had been traditionally despised by Turkish Muslims as infidels, and they had in the 1890s endured massacres (involving about two hundred thousand victims) which had led them to stockpile weapons in anticipation of a further onslaught. This enabled the Turkish state to rationalize its genocide as a preventive strike against a rebellion by those who were accused (like the Jews in Germany) of "stabbing Turkey in the back" in wartime. Unlike in the Holocaust, however, the killing operations against Armenians were never carried out by specialized perpetrator groups. On the contrary, large segments of the provincial population eagerly participated in regional and local massacres, as well as drowning operations along the Black Sea.[79]

It is certainly legitimate to see the Armenian genocide as prefiguring the Holocaust, in that the decision to slaughter the Armenians was implacably cruel, deliberate, firm, and irrevocable. But there are also many dissimilarities between the two events. The brutish "war against the Armenians" was primarily a geopolitical rather than an ideological crusade. Furthermore, the Armenians were never designated as a "racial" enemy, and the war against them remained strictly territorial, without any world-historical, metaphysical, or ontological implications. Armenians who converted to Islam were spared; the majority of Armenians in Istanbul (numbering up to two hundred thousand) did survive, and there was no international crusade to seek out and annihilate Armenians beyond the borders of Turkey. For the Turks, the Armenians were never perceived as a Satanic force that threatened civilization as a whole, and their murder was not planned as an end in itself. It in no way detracts from the horror and scope of the slaughter to point out that it resulted from motivations significantly different from those that influenced the Nazis.[80]

The comparison of genocides is always a difficult exercise, not rendered any easier by the pretentious or mystical claims to "uniqueness" sometimes made for the Holocaust or by the hostile and often irrational responses to such arguments. In focusing on its historical specificity and singularity in this book, there is no implication at all that other massacres or genocides are in any way less interesting, important, or deserving of attention than the Holocaust. But it is equally clear that no other event of the modern era has so fundamentally challenged the foundations of European civilization—its religious values, legal structures, political ideals, trust in science, and commitment to humanity. The question must therefore be asked: Why has the Holocaust more than other genocides so deeply affected modern consciousness? Why has precisely this tragedy become *the* axial event, sparking a huge and ever-expanding diet of feature films, plays, memoirs, oral histories, TV documentaries, scholarly research, and fiction? I believe that the answer does not lie primarily in various political agendas, in the sensationalist appetite for horror stories, or in the rapacity of a so-called Holocaust industry. Nor can it be adequately explained by the fact that we live in a popular culture where, regrettably, victimhood is a source of empowerment. The avalanche of unadulterated kitsch will doubtless continue to plague us, along with commercial exploitation and political correctness. But the reason for the continuing power of the Holocaust is surely linked to the "big question": why did it happen?

The Holocaust was driven by a millenarian, apocalyptic ideology of annihilation that overthrew all the enlightened and pragmatic assumptions of liberal modernity. This does not in itself make it totally different from all other genocides, but it does highlight the Holocaust as an extreme case. The centrality of anti-Semitism and of the Jews to this cataclysmic event was no accident, and this essential fact helps to explain why it resonates so strongly. For the Holocaust cannot ultimately be divorced from the dominant religious tradition of Western civilization. In the Christian imagination of the West, the Jews are both the "chosen people" and a (reprobate) "witness" to the Christian truth. Their fate therefore has a special religious significance as an expression of God's role in the drama of history and as an emblematic part of the eternal struggle between salvation and damnation. Richard Rubinstein has aptly characterized the Holocaust as a "modern version of a Christian holy war carried out by a neopagan National Socialist state hostile to Christianity," though I do not altogether share his belief that "the Nazis did the dirty work for institutions that were destined to outlast them."[81] Hyam Maccoby put it equally well but somewhat differently when he suggested that the Nazis "expressed in racialist terms the concept of the final overcoming of evil that formed the essence of Christian millenarism. The choice of the Jews as a target arose directly out of centuries of Christian teaching which had singled out the Jews as a demonic people dedicated to evil."[82]

Hitler, masquerading as a Germanic warrior "Christ" (the chosen redeemer of a secular salvationist religion) brought this millenarian tradition to a gruesome end in the death camps—the "sacred altars" of the new political religion called National Socialism. In the camps, the images and chronicles of hell to be found in European art and thought were realized in the most macabre fashion. The cataclysmic black passion of the Death-Head SS units announced the extinction of a God of love, compassion, and mercy. The mass murder of the Jews was in that respect a totalitarian-nihilist assault on the ethics of Christianity, as well as the negation of the abstract monotheism that Judaism had bequeathed to the West. In this transvaluation, "the negation of Judaism had to be transformed into the annihilation of the Jews, this time not spiritually but rather physically, not symbolically but in substance."[83] It is at this metahistorical level—and not in the number of victims or even in its war on secular rationalist modernity, liberalism, and "Judeo-Bolshevism"—that the singularity of the Holocaust asserts itself most sharply. Hitler always regarded the ethics of monotheism as the curse of Western civilization, especially the fifth commandment, "Thou shalt not kill." The Nazi ideology whose realization climaxed with Auschwitz-Birkenau had to target the Jews as its victims of choice precisely because it had selected death over life and human sacrifice as the road to redemption.

NOTES

1. ANTI-SEMITISM AND THE JEWS

1. On the Armenian genocide, see Vahakn N. Dadrian, "The Convergent Aspects of the Armenian and Jewish Cases of Genocide," *Holocaust and Genocide Studies* 3.2 (1996): 151–69, and Robert F. Melson, *Revolution and Genocide: On the Origins of the Armenian Genocide and the Holocaust* (Chicago, 1992), 145–47, for estimated casualties and pp. 247–57 on similarities and differences. For the wider issues and problems of methodology and comparison, see Leo Kuper, *Genocide: Its Political Use in the Twentieth Century* (New Haven, 1981); R. J. Rummel, *Death by Government, Genocide, and Mass Murder* (New Brunswick, 1994); Yehuda Bauer, "Holocaust and Genocide: Some Comparisons," in Peter Hayes, ed., *Lessons and Legacies: The Meaning of the Holocaust in a Changing World* (Evanston, 1991), 34–46; and Alan S. Rosenbaum, ed., *Is the Holocaust Unique?* (Boulder, 1996), 101–99.

2. Robert Conquest, *The Great Terror: A Reassessment* (New York, 1990); Robert Conquest, *The Harvest of Sorrow: Soviet Collectivization and the Terror-Famine* (New York, 1986), 217–330. For the differences, see Steven T. Katz, "Auschwitz and the Gulag: A Study in 'Dissimilarity,'" in Alan Berger, ed., *Proceedings of the Holocaust Scholars Conference* (Lewiston, Me., 1992), 71–89, and

his essay "Mass Death under Communist Rule and the Limits of 'Otherness,'" in Robert S. Wistrich, ed., *Demonizing the Other: Antisemitism, Racism, and Xenophobia* (Amsterdam, 1999), 267–93. Stephane Courtois et al., eds., *The Black Book of Communism* (New York, 1997), highlights the scale of mass killing under Communist regimes in the twentieth century.

3. Götz Aly, *"Final Solution": Nazi Population Policy and the Murder of the European Jews* (London, 1999); Michael Burleigh, *The Third Reich: A New History* (London, 2000), 486–573. See also Richard C. Lukas, *The Forgotten Holocaust: The Poles under German Occupation, 1939–1944* (Lexington, Ky., 1986), 1–39.

4. Angus Fraser, *The Gypsies* (Cambridge, 1996); Donald Kenrick and Gratton Puxon, *The Destiny of Europe's Gypsies* (New York, 1972), 76–186; Ian Hancock, *The Pariah Syndrome: An Account of Gypsy Slavery and Persecution* (Ann Arbor, 1988). A comprehensive comparative perspective can be found in Wolfgang Wippermann, *"Wie die Zigeuner": Antisemitismus und Antiziganismus in Vergleich* (Berlin, 1997).

5. Ian Hancock, "Gypsy History in Germany and the Neighbouring Lands: A Chronology to the Holocaust and Beyond," *Nationalities Papers* 19.3 (winter 1991); 395–412; Henry R. Huttenbach, "The Romani Porajmos: The Nazi Genocide of Europe's Gypsies," ibid., 373ff.; Sybil Milton, "Gypsies and the Holocaust", *The History Teacher* 24.4 (August 1991): 1–13.

6. Yehuda Bauer, "Gypsies," in *Encyclopedia of the Holocaust* (New York, 1990), 2:634–38, Fraser, *Gypsies,* 260; Kenrick and Puxon, *Destiny,* 140ff.

7. Michael Zimmermann, *Rassenntopie und Genozid: Die nationalsozialistische "Lösung der Zigeunerfrage"* (Hamburg, 1996), 297ff., and *Verfolgt, vertrieben, vernichtet. Die nationalsozialistische Vernichtungspolitik gegen Sinti und Roma* (Rulda, 1989), 61–83.

8. Klaus Fischer, *The History of an Obsession: German Judeophobia and the Holocaust* (London, 1998), 81–153.

9. Jakob Wassermann, *Mein Weg als Deutscher und Jude* (Berlin, 1921); Fischer, *History,* 174–75.

10. Yirmiyahu Yovel, *Dark Riddle: Hegel, Nietzsche, and the Jews* (Cambridge, 1998), 127–29.

11. See Jacob Golomb and Robert S. Wistrich, eds., *Nietzsche: Godfather of Fascism?* (Princeton, 2001), introduction.

12. Good examples of this annexation are Alfred Bäumler, *Nietzsche als Philosoph und Politiker* (Leipzig, 1931), and Alfred Rosenberg, *Friedrich Nietzsche* (Munich, 1944).

13. For an imaginative and controversial elaboration, see George Steiner's novel, *The Portage to San Cristóbal of A.H.* (London, 1981), 120, and his essay, "The Long Life of Metaphor: An Approach to 'the Shoah,'" *Encounter* (February 1987): 55–61, as well as Ron Rosenbaum, *Explaining Hitler: The Search for the Origins of His Evil* (New York, 1998), 307–18.

14. Ernst Piper, "Alfred Rosenberg—der Prophet des Seelenkrieges," in Michael Ley and Julius H. Schoeps, eds., *Der Nationalsozialismus als politische Religion* (Frankfurt, 1997), 107–25.

15. Hermann Rauschning, *The Voice of Destruction* (New York, 1940), 235–42.

16. Jacob Katz, *Out of the Ghetto: The Social Background of the Emancipation of the Jews* (New York, 1978), 191–219.

17. James Parkes, *The Conflict of the Church and Synagogue* (Cleveland, 1961), 151–270; Rosemary Ruether, *Faith and Fratricide: The Theological Roots of Anti-Semitism* (New York, 1971); Alan Davies, ed., *Antisemitism and the Foundations of Christianity* (New York, 1979); Edward H. Flannery, *The Anguish of the Jews* (New York, 1985), 47–144; and most recently James Carroll, *Constantine's Sword: The Church and the Jews* (Boston, 2001), 67–342. All of the above are Christian scholars.

18. Ruether, *Faith*, 113; Carroll, *Constantine's Sword*, 92–93. See also Hyam Maccoby, *The Sacred Executioner: Human Sacrifice and the Legacy of Guilt* (London, 1982), 146.

19. Maccoby, *Sacred Executioner*, 121–33.

20. Joshua Trachtenberg, *The Devil and the Jews: The Medieval Conception of the Jew and Its Relation to Modern Antisemitism* (New Haven, 1943), 11–56; Robert S. Wistrich, *Antisemitism: The Longest Hatred* (New York, 1992), 13–42.

21. Ibid.

22. Trachtenberg, *Devil*, 124–39; Gavin Langmuir, "Historiographic Crucifixion," in *Les Juifs au regard de l'histoire: mélanges en l'honneur de Bernhard Blumenkranz* (Paris, 1985), 109–27; Rainer Erb, ed., *Die Legende vom Ritualmord: Zur Geschichte der Blutbeschuldigung gegen Juden* (Berlin, 1993).

23. See Wistrich, *Demonizing the Other*, 1–12.

24. Heiko A. Oberman, *The Roots of Antisemitism in the Age of Renaissance and Reformation* (Philadelphia, 1984), 117.
25. Martin Luther, "Von den Juden und ihren Lügen," *Luthers Reformations-Schriften* 20 (1890), 1861–2026.
26. Henri Zukier, "The Transformation of Hatred: Antisemitism as a Struggle for Group Identity," in Wistrich, *Demonizing the Other*, 118–30.
27. Y.-M. Yerushalmi, "L'Antisemitisme racial est-il apparu au XXe siècle? De la 'limpieza de sangre' espagnole au nazisme: continuités et ruptures," *Esprit* (March–April 1993), 5–35.
28. Ibid. See also Henry Kamen, *Inquisition and Society in Spain in the Sixteenth and Seventeenth Centuries* (Bloomington, 1985), 6–43, 62–133; Ben-Zion Netanyahu, *The Origins of the Inquisition in Fifteenth Century Spain* (New York, 1995), 207–512, 925–1094.
29. B. D. Weinryb, *The Jews of Poland* (Philadelphia, 1973), 185–95; Jaroslaw Pelenski, "The Cossack Insurrections in Jewish-Ukrainian Relations," in Peter Potichnyj and Howard Aster, eds., *Ukrainian-Jewish Relations in Historical Perspective* (Edmonton, 1988).
30. Jay R. Berkowitz, *The Shaping of Jewish Identity in Nineteenth-century France* (Detroit, 1989), 71.
31. Pierre Sorlin, *"La Croix" et les Juifs (1880–1889)* (Paris, 1967); Stephen Wilson, *Ideology and Experience: Antisemitism in France at the Time of the Dreyfus Affair* (East Brunswick, N.J., 1982), 456–584; Pierre Birnbaum, *"La France aux Français": Histoire des haines nationalistes* (Paris, 1993), 29–82, 102–16, 187–220.
32. Richard I. Cohen, "Recurrent Images in French Antisemitism in the Third Republic," in Wistrich, *Demonizing the Other*, 183–95; Zeev Sternhell, *La Droite révolutionnaire, 1885–1914* (Paris, 1978), 177–244; Pierre Birnbaum, *"La République Juive" de Léon Blum à Pierre Mendes-France* (Paris, 1988), and *The Jews of the Republic* (Stanford, 1996), 136–58, 301–17.
33. Paul W. Massing, *Rehearsal for Destruction: A Study of Political Antisemitism in Imperial Germany* (New York, 1949); Uriel Tal, *Yahadut ve-Natzrut be-Raykh ha-Sheni* [Judaism and Christianity in the Second Reich] (Jerusalem, 1975), 185–234; F. Stern, *The Politics of Cultural Despair: A Study of the Rise of German Ideology* (Berkeley, 1961), 267–98; Robert S. Wistrich, *Socialism and the*

Jews: The Dilemmas of Assimilation in Germany and Austria-Hungary (London, 1982).

34. W. Boehlich, ed., *Der Berliner Antisemitismusstreit* (Frankfurt, 1965), 5–51, 77–90, 222–35; P. G. J. Pulzer, *The Rise of Political Antisemitism in Germany and Austria* (Cambridge, Mass., 1988), 71–120; Werner Jochmann, *Gesellschaftskrise und Judenfeindschaft in Deutschland, 1870–1945* (Hamburg, 1988), 30–98.

35. George L. Mosse, *The Crisis of German Ideology: Intellectual Origins of the Third Reich* (New York, 1971), 280–317. Jochmann, *Gesellschaftskrise,* 99–170; Shulamit Volkov, "The Written Matter and the Spoken Word: On the Gap Between pre-1914 and Nazi anti-Semitism," in F. Furet, ed., *Unanswered Questions: Nazi Germany and the Genocide of the Jews* (New York, 1989), 33–53; Daniel Goldhagen, *Hitler's Willing Executioners: Ordinary Germans and the Holocaust* (New York, 1996), 49–128; and Robert S. Wistrich, "Helping Hitler," *Commentary* (July 1996), 27–31, for a critique.

36. Theodor Fritsch, *Antisemiten-Katechismus* (Leipzig, 1883), cited in Massing, *Rehearsal,* 306; Theodor Fritsch, *Handbuch der Judenfrage* (Leipzig, 1936); Jacob Katz, *From Prejudice to Destruction: Antisemitism, 1700–1933* (Cambridge, Mass., 1982), 304–78, esp. 311, 315; Lucy Dawidowicz, *The War Against the Jews, 1933–45* (London, 1983), 96.

37. Paul de Lagarde, *Deutsche Schriften* (Göttingen, 1904), 217–47; Stern, *Politics of Cultural Despair,* 3–36.

38. Eugen Dühring, *Die Judenfrage als Rassen-Sitten -und Culturfrage* (Karlsruhe, 1881), 46–72; Uriel Tal, *Christians and Jews in Germany: Religion, Politics and Ideology in the Second Reich* (Ithaca, 1975), 223–82; originally published as Tal, *Yahadut ve-Natzrut be-Raykh ha-Sheni.*

39. Houston S. Chamberlain, *Die Grundlagen des neunzehnten Jahrhunderts* (Munich, 1909), 1:323–546, and *Briefwechsel mit Kaiser Wilhelm II* (Munich, 1928). See also Geoffrey C. Field, *Evangelist of Race: The Germanic Vision of Houston S. Chamberlain* (New York, 1981).

40. Celia S. Heller, *On the Edge of Destruction: Jews of Poland Between the Two World Wars* (New York, 1980), 50–57; Ezra Mendelsohn, *The Jews of East Central Europe Between the World Wars* (Bloomington, 1983), 40.

41. Elias Heifetz, *The Slaughter of the Jews in the Ukraine* (New York, 1920), 1–20, 41–74; J. Lestchinsky, *Twishn Lebn un Toit* (Vilna, 1930); 1:19–53. See also Baruch Ben-Anat, "Peraot Ukraina, 1919–1921," *Kivunim* 47.10 (December 1996): 105–39 (in Hebrew).

42. Robert S. Wistrich, *Revolutionary Jews from Marx to Trotsky* (London, 1976), 1–22.

43. For Communist attitudes toward the Jews in the Soviet Union, see Edmund Silberner, *Kommunisten zur Judenfrage* (Darmstadt, 1983), 138–210.

44. Alfred Rosenberg, *Der Staatsfeindliche Zionismus,* 2d ed. (Munich, 1938); Adolf Hitler, *Mein Kampf* (Boston, 1943), 324–25; Robert Wistrich, *Hitler's Apocalypse: Jews and the Nazi Legacy* (New York, 1985), 154–73.

45. Mendelsohn, *Jews of East Central Europe,* 23–30, 68–71, 100–107; David Vital, *A People Apart: The Jews in Europe 1789–1939* (Oxford, 1999), 837–96.

46. Edward Wynot, " 'A Necessary Cruelty': The Emergence of Official Antisemitism in Poland," *American Historical Review* 76.4 (October 1971): 1035–58; Jerzy Holzer, "Polish Political Parties and Antisemitism," *Polin* 8 (1994): 200–205; Szymon Rudnicki, *Obóz Narodowo Radykalny i Geneza i dzialalnosc* (Warsaw, 1985).

47. Yfaat Weiss, "Polish and German Jews Between Hitler's Rise to Power and the Outbreak of the Second World War," *Leo Baeck Yearbook* (henceforth *LBIYB*) 44 (1999): 205–23; Emmanuel Melzer, "Antisemitism in the Last Years of the Second Polish Republic," in Y. Gutman et al., eds, *The Jews of Poland Between Two World Wars* (Hanover, N.H., 1989), 126–37; William W. Hagen, "Before the 'Final Solution': Towards a Comparative Analysis of Political Antisemitism in Interwar Germany and Poland," *The Journal of Modern History* 68 (June 1996): 351–81.

48. Ezra Mendelsohn, "Interwar Poland: Good for the Jews or Bad for the Jews?" in C. Abramsky et al., eds., *The Jews in Poland* (Oxford, 1986), 130–39.

49. Norman Davies, *God's Playground: A History of Poland* (Oxford, 1981), 2:240–66; Emmanuel Meltzer, *Ma'avak Medini Be Malkodet: Yehudei Polin, 1935–1939* (Tel Aviv, 1982), trans. as *No Way Out: The Politics of Polish Jewry, 1935–1939* (Cincinnati,

1997); Pawel Korzec, *Juifs en Pologne: la question Juive pendant l'entre-deux-guerres* (Paris, 1980), 165–98, 263ff.

50. Anna Landau-Czajka, "The Ubiquitous Enemy: The Jew in the Political Thought of Radical Right-Wing Nationalists in Poland, 1926–1939," *Polin* 4 (1989): 169–203, and "The Image of the Jew in the Catholic Press during the Second Republic," *Polin* 8 (1994); Israel Gutman, "The Popular Image of the Jew in Modern Poland," in Wistrich, *Demonizing the Other*, 257–66.

51. Ronald Modras, *The Catholic Church and Antisemitism in Poland, 1933–1939* (London, 1994), 315, 345–46; Edward Wynot, "The Catholic Church and State, 1935–1939," *Journal of Church and State* 15 (1973): 223–40.

52. Bernard Wasserstein, *Britain and the Jews of Europe, 1939–1945* (London, 1979), 17–21.

53. Henry Feingold, "Was There Communal Failure? Some Thoughts on the American Jewish Response to the Holocaust," *American Jewish History* 81.1 (autumn 1993): 60–80. See also Henry Feingold, *Bearing Witness: How America and Its Jews Responded to the Holocaust* (Syracuse, N.Y., 1995), 169–201, 225–76.

54. Richard Bolchover, *British Jewry and the Holocaust* (Cambridge, 1993), 103–20; also Tony Kushner, *The Persistence of Prejudice: Anti-Semitism in British Society During the Second World War* (Manchester, 1989), 78–105, and *The Holocaust and the Liberal Imagination* (Oxford, 1994), 146–72.

55. Abraham Brumberg, "The Bund and the Polish Socialist Party in the Late 1930s," in Gutman, *Jews of Poland*, 75–96; Jerzy Holzer, "Relations Between Polish and Jewish Left-wing Groups in Interwar Poland," in Abramsky, *Jews in Poland*, 140–46.

56. Emanuel Ringelbaum, *Polish-Jewish Relations During the Second World War*, ed. and annotated by Joseph Kermish and Shmuel Krakowski (Evanston, 1992), 7–8.

57. Ibid., 39.

58. Ibid., 53. Ringelbaum reproached the Poles for not actively opposing the impression that "the entire Polish nation of all classes approved of the behaviour of the Polish anti-Semites."

59. Mordekhai Tenenbaum-Tamaroff, *Dapim min hadlekhah* (Tel Aviv, 1947), 49–50.

60. Karski's report on Polish Jewry under Nazi and Soviet occupa-

tion is reprinted in Norman Davies and Antony Polowsky, eds., *Jews in Eastern Poland and the U.S.S.R., 1939–46* (London, 1991). See esp. 269.

61. Jan Blónski, *Biedni Polacy patrza na ghetto* (The poor Poles look at the ghetto) (Cracow, 1994), reprints Kossak-Szczucki, "Protest," in full. See also Antony Polonsky, "Beyond Condemnation. Apologetics and Apologies: On the Complexity of Polish Behavior Toward the Jews During the Second World War," in *Studies in Contemporary Jewry* (Oxford, 1997), 13:190–224.

62. Jan T. Gross, *Neighbors: The Destruction of the Jewish Community in Jedwabne, Poland* (Princeton, 2001), 90–104.

63. See Jan Gross, *Upiorna dekada: trzy eseje o stereotypach na temat Zydów, Polaków, Niemców, Kommunistów, 1939–1948* (Cursed decade: three essays on stereotypes about Jews, Poles, Germans, and Communists) (Cracow, 1998).

64. Gross, *Neighbours,* 105–10.

65. Ibid., 54–71. The quote is on 65.

2. FROM WEIMAR TO HITLER

1. Jochmann, *Gesellschaftskrise,* 132–70.

2. See Hans Mommsen, *The Rise and Fall of Weimar Democracy* (Chapel Hill, 1996).

3. H. A. Winkler, "Anti-Semitism in Weimar Society," in Herbert A. Strauss, ed., *Hostages of Modernization: Studies in Modern Antisemitism, 1870–1939* (Berlin, 1993), 196–205.

4. Jochmann, *Gesellschaftskrise,* 171–94.

5. Werner T. Angress, "Juden im politischen Leben der Revolutionszeit," in Werner E. Mosse and Arnold Paucker, eds., *Deutsches Judentum in Krieg und Revolution, 1916–1923* (Tübingen, 1971), 235–51.

6. Ibid., 254–308.

7. Ernst Schulin, *Walther Rathenau: Repräsentant, Kritiker, und Opfer seiner Zeit* (Göttingen, 1979); Peter Loewenberg, *Fantasy and Reality in History* (New York, 1995), 108–18.

8. Yitzhak Arad et al., eds., *Documents on the Holocaust* (Jerusalem, 1981), 15–18.

9. Robert S. Wistrich, "Georg von Schoenerer and the Genesis of Modern Austrian Antisemitism," in Strauss, *Hostages,* 675–88.

10. Robert S. Wistrich, *The Jews of Vienna in the Age of Franz Joseph* (Oxford, 1989), 211.

11. Brigitte Hamann, *Hitler's Vienna: A Dictator's Apprenticeship* (New York, 1999), 244–45, 251–53.

12. Robert S. Wistrich, "Karl Lueger and the Ambiguities of Viennese Antisemitism," *Jewish Social Studies* 45 (1983): 251–62; Richard S. Geehr, *Karl Lueger: Mayor of Fin de Siècle Vienna* (Detroit, 1990), 171–207.

13. Hamann, *Hitler's Vienna*, 273–303.

14. *Mein Kampf,* 120. For other influences on Hitler's anti-Semitism stemming from sources such as Lanz von Liebenfels and Guido von List, see Jackson Spielvogel and David Redles, "Hitler's Racial Ideology: Content and Occult Sources," *Simon Wiesenthal Centre Annual (SWC)* (1986): 227–46; also Nicholas Goodrick-Clarke, *The Occult Roots of Nazism: Secret Aryan Cults and Their Influence on Nazi Ideology; The Ariosophists of Austria and Germany, 1890–1935* (New York, 1992), 33–48, 90–122, 192–204.

15. Hamann, *Hitler's Vienna,* 24–27, 38–39, 62–67; Paul Lawrence Rose, *Wagner: Race and Revolution* (London, 1992), 147, 181–83; Joachim Köhler, *Wagner's Hitler: The Prophet and His Disciple* (Cambridge, 2000), 191–208, 269–95; T. C. W. Blanning, "Hitler, Vienna, and Wagner," *German History* 18.4 (2000): 487–94; Saul Friedländer and Jörn Rüsen, eds., *Richard Wagner im Dritten Reich* (Munich, 2000), esp. the essay by Paul L. Rose, pp. 283–308.

16. Margaret Brearley, "Hitler and Wagner: The Leader, the Master, and the Jews," *Patterns of Prejudice* 22.2 (1988): 3–21.

17. Wistrich, *Antisemitism,* 57.

18. *Mein Kampf,* 55.

19. Ibid.

20. Ibid., 60–62.

21. Hamann, *Hitler's Vienna,* 347–59. See also Ian Kershaw, *Hitler, 1889–1936: Hubris* (London, 1999), 36–69, on his period as a dropout.

22. *Mein Kampf,* 59.

23. Ibid., 512. Arad, *Documents,* 445–48.

24. *Mein Kampf,* 445–48.

25. Ibid., 65.

26. Klaus Vondung, *Magie und Manipulation: Ideologische Kult und politische Religion des Nationalsozialismus* (Göttingen, 1971); James

Rhodes, *The Hitler Movement: A Modern Millenarian Revolution* (Stanford, 1980), 29–84, and Ley and Schoeps, *Nationalsozialismus,* 151–85, 229–60.

27. Wistrich, *Hitler's Apocalypse,* 27–47.
28. *Mein Kampf,* 772.
29. Hitler to Chvalkovsky, 21 January 1939, in *Documents on German Foreign Policy, 1918–1954, Series D* (Washington, D.C., 1949–1964), 190–95 (henceforth *DGFP*).
30. Werner Maser, ed., *Hitler's Letters and Notes* (New York, 1974), 215.
31. Ibid.
32. Gerhard L. Weinberg, ed., *Hitler's Zweites Buch: Ein Dokument aus dem Jahre 1928* (Stuttgart, 1961), 22–23.
33. Ibid., 222.
34. Wistrich, *Hitler's Apocalypse,* 43–44.
35. Alex Bein, "Der Jüdische Parasit-Bemerkungen zur Semantik der Judenfrage," *Vierteljahrshefte für Zeitgeschichte* (1965), 121–49 (henceforth *VJfZ*).
36. Philippe Burrin, "Nazi Antisemitism: Animalization and Demonization," in Wistrich, *Demonizing the Other,* 223–33.
37. Randall T. Bytwerk, *Julius Streicher* (New York, 1983); Kershaw, *Hitler,* 179, 560, 563–64; Fred Hahn, *Lieber Stürmer! Leserbriefe an das NS-Kampfblatt 1924 bis 1945* (Stuttgart, 1978), 84ff.
38. Robert G. Waite, *Hitler: The Psychopathic God* (New York, 1978), 448.
39. Karl Dietrich Bracher, *The German Dictatorship* (London, 1991), 109–33, 195–213; Jochmann, *Gesellschaftskrise,* 117–54.
40. Jochmann, *Gesellschaftskrise,* 265ff.; Silberner, *Kommunisten,* 268–70.
41. Norman Cohn, *Warrant for Genocide: The Myth of the Jewish World Conspiracy and the Protocols of the Elders of Zion* (London, 1970), 138–63, 187–213.
42. Walter Laqueur, *Weimar: A Cultural History* (London, 1974), 78–109; Anton Kaes et al., eds., *The Weimar Republic Sourcebook* (Berkeley and Los Angeles, 1994), 119–44; Robert S. Wistrich, *Weekend in Munich: Art, Propaganda and Terror in the Third Reich* (London, 1996), 56ff.
43. Bracher, *German Dictatorship,* 210–12; Winkler, "Anti-Semitism," 201ff.; Burleigh, *Third Reich,* 106–13. See also G. J. Giles, *Students and National Socialism in Germany* (Princeton, 1985), 44–90.

44. Richard Hamilton, *Who Voted for Hitler?* (Princeton, 1982), 355–419; Thomas Childers, *The Nazi Voter: The Social Foundations of Fascism in Germany, 1919–1933* (Chapel Hill, 1983), 142–269.

45. Bracher, *German Dictatorship,* 252–68. Henry A. Turner, *Hitler's Thirty Days to Power: January 1933* (London, 1996), 135–83, shows that his victory was by no means inevitable.

46. On the rampant anti-Semitism in the German medical community, see Robert Proctor, *Racial Hygiene: Medicine under the Nazis* (Cambridge, Mass., 1988), 131–76.

47. "Racial Hygiene in Germany," *The Times* (London), 7 April 1933.

48. Entry of 10 January 1939 in Victor Klemperer, *Tagebücher 1933–1941* (Berlin, 1995), 1:456–57. The first volume was translated into English under the title *I Shall Bear Witness* and appeared in London in 1998.

49. Ibid., 457. For a perceptive review of the second volume, see Daniel Johnson, "What Victor Klemperer Saw," *Commentary* (June 2000), 44–50.

50. On German Zionism, see Robert Weltsch, *Ja-Sagen zum Judentum* (Berlin, 1933), and his *Die deutsche Judenfrage: Ein kritischer Rückblick* (Königstein, 1981), 73–82. See also Jehuda Reinharz, ed., *Dokumente zur Geschichte des deutschen Zionismus, 1882–1933* (Tübingen, 1981), 470–549, for the reactions of German Jewry and German Zionists. The most comprehensive analysis of the general Zionist response is in Daniel Frankel, *Al pnei Tehom: Ha Mediniut Ha-Tsionit ve-she'elat yehudei Germania, 1933–1938* (Jerusalem, 1994), 63–154. On Nazi policy toward Zionism and Palestine, see David Yisraeli, "The Third Reich and Palestine," *Middle Eastern Studies* 7.3 (October 1971): 343–53, and his *Ha-Reich ha Germani ve-erets Yisrael* (Ramat Gan, 1974). See also Francis R. Nicosia, *The Third Reich and the Palestine Question* (London, 1985), and his "The End of Emancipation and the Illusion of Preferential Treatment: German Zionism, 1933–1938," in *LBIYB* (1991), 243–65.

51. Hjalmar Schacht, *Abrechnung mit Hitler* (Hamburg, 1949), 59ff. See also his *76 Jahre meines Lebens* (Hamburg, 1953), 44ff. Avraham Barkai, *Vom Boykott zur "Entjudung": Der wirtschaftliche Existenzkampf der Juden in Dritten Reich, 1933–1943* (Frankfurt, 1988),

is the best scholarly account of the dispossession of German Jewry.

52. Uwe Dietrich Adam, *Judenpolitik im Dritten Reich* (1972), 72–144. O. D. Kulka, "Da'at Ha-Kahal be-Germania hanatsionalsot-sialistit ve-ha-beiya ha-yehudit," *Zion* 40.3–4 (1975); 186–290, is the most detailed study of German public opinion. On the Lutherans, see Richard Gutteridge, "German Protestantism and the Jews in the Third Reich," in O. D. Kulka and Paul Mendes-Flohr, eds., *Judaism and Christianity under the Impact of National Socialism* (Jerusalem, 1987), 251–70. On Catholics, see G. Lewy, *The Catholic Church and Nazi Germany* (New York, 1965), 268–308; Konrad Riepgen, "German Catholicism and the Jews," in Kulka and Mendes-Flohr, *Judaism*, 197–226; Giovanni Miccoli, *I Dilemmi e il silenzio di Pio XII: Vaticano, Seconda Guerra mondiale e Shoah* (Milan, 2000), 118–200; Michael Phayer, *The Catholic Church and the Holocaust, 1930–1965* (Bloomington, 2000), 67–81.

53. Jeremy Noakes and Geoffrey Pridham, eds., *Documents on Nazism, 1919–1945* (London, 1974), 1:462.

54. Karl Schleunes, *The Twisted Road to Auschwitz: Nazi Policy Towards German Jews, 1933–1939* (Urbana, 1970), 148–49.

55. Adam, *Judenpolitik*, 114–44; Hermann Graml, *Antisemitism in the Third Reich* (Oxford, 1992), 120–29.

56. Norman H. Baynes, ed., *The Speeches of Adolf Hitler* (London, 1942), 1:732–34; Max Domarus, ed., *Hitler: Reden und Proklamationen, 1932–1945* (Würzburg, 1962), 1:537.

57. Domarus, *Hitler,* 1:537.

58. See Abraham Margaliot, "The Reaction of the Jewish Public in Germany to the Nuremberg Laws," *Essays in Holocaust History* (Jerusalem, 1979), 41.

59. Ibid., 50.

60. "Isolation of Jews in Germany: Effect of New Laws," *The Times* (London), 18 September 1935.

61. Margaliot, "Reaction," 50ff.

62. For example, Georg Kareski's interview in Goebbels's newspaper, *Der Angriff,* 23 December 1935. See ibid., 50.

63. Elie Ben Elissar, *La Diplomatie du IIIe Reich et les Juifs* (Paris, 1969), 163–84; Duff Hart-Davis, *Hitler's Olympics: The 1936 Games* (London, 1986), 66–88, 138–40.

64. Helmut Krausnick and Martin Broszat, *Anatomy of the SS State* (London, 1973), 51ff.

65. Gerhard Botz, "The Dynamics of Persecution in Austria, 1938–1945," in Robert S. Wistrich, ed., *Austrians and Jews in the Twentieth Century* (London, 1992), 199–219.

66. See Herbert Rosenkranz, *Verfolgung und Selbstbehauptung: Die Juden in Österreich, 1938–1945* (Vienna, 1978), and Doron Rabinovici, *Instanzen der Ohnmacht: Wien, 1938–1945—Der Weg zur Judenrat* (Frankfurt, 2000), for the subsequent dispossession, persecution, deportation, and murder of Austrian Jewry.

67. "Berlin Outbreak of Jew-baiting," *The Daily Telegraph*, 16 June 1938.

68. David S. Wyman, *Paper Walls: America and the Refugee Crisis, 1938–1941* (New York, 1985), 50; Joshua B. Stein, "Great Britain and the Evian Conference of 1938," *The Wiener Library Bulletin*, new series, 29.37–38 (1976).

69. "Nations Take Their Stand on Refugees," *Daily Express*, 8 July 1939; Paul R. Bartrop, *Australia and the Holocaust, 1933–1945* (Melbourne, 1994), 61–78; Irving Abella and Harold Troper, *None Is Too Many: Canada and the Jews of Europe* (New York, 1983), 19–37, 51–66.

70. On American immigration policy between 1933 and 1945, see Arthur Mosse, *While Six Million Died* (New York, 1968); Saul S. Friedman, *No Haven for the Oppressed: United States Policy Towards Jewish Refugees, 1933–45* (Detroit, 1973); Monty Noam Penkower, *The Jews Were Expendable: Free World Diplomacy and the Holocaust* (Urbana, 1983); David S. Wyman, *The Abandonment of the Jews: America and the Holocaust* (New York, 1984).

71. *The Times* (London), 16 July 1938.

72. Golda Meir, *My Life* (London, 1975), 127.

73. *Völkischer Beobachter*, 1 February 1939. Also, N. H. Baynes, *Speeches*, 1:738.

3. PERSECUTION AND RESISTANCE

1. Helmut Heiber, "Der Fall Grünspan," VJfZ, 5 (1957): 134–72; Michael R. Marrus, "The Strange Story of Herschel Grynszpan," *American Scholar* 57.1 (1988): 69–79; Gerald Schwab, *The Day the Holocaust Began: The Odyssey of Herschel Grynszpan* (New York, 1990).

2. "Germany's Day of Wrecking and Looting," *Manchester Guardian*, 11 November 1938.

3. Ibid.

4. Noakes and Pridham, *Documents on Nazism*, 2, Doc. 424.

5. Ibid.

6. Kulka, "Da'at Ha-Kahal," 232–42; Jörg Wollenberg, ed., *The German Public and the Persecution of the Jews, 1933–1945* (Atlantic Highlands, N.J., 1996), 19.

7. Saul Friedländer, *Nazi Germany and the Jews*, vol. 1: *The Years of Persecution, 1933–1939* (New York, 1997), 278.

8. Schleunes, *Twisted Roads*, 247.

9. See the stenographic report on the meeting of 12 November 1938 under Goering's chairmanship reproduced in Michael Berenbaum, ed., *Witness to the Holocaust* (New York, 1997), 55–68. See also Peter Loewenberg, "The Kristallnacht as a Public Degradation Ritual," in *LBIYB* 32 (1987): 309–23.

10. Berenbaum, *Witness*, 67.

11. Ibid., 60–61.

12. Graml, *Antisemitism*, 142–44; Wistrich, *Hitler's Apocalypse*, 83–87.

13. Schleunes, *Twisted Road*, 165; Helmut Genschel, *Die Verdrangung der Juden aus der Wirtschaft im Dritten Reich* (Göttingen, 1966), 299–30.

14. Berenbaum, *Witness*, 55.

15. Friedländer, *Nazi Germany*, 1:284–300.

16. *Das Schwarze Korps*, 24 November 1938.

17. Ian Kershaw, "The Persecution of the Jews and German Popular Opinion in the Third Reich," *LBIYB* 26 (1981): 261ff.

18. Hitler to Chvalkovsky, *DGFP*, 190–95.

19. Domarus, *Hitler*, 2:1058.

20. Hans Mommsen, "The Realization of the Unthinkable: The Final Solution of the Jewish Question," in G. Hirschfeld, ed., *The Politics of Genocide* (London, 1986), 97–114.

21. Baynes, *Speeches*, 1:740.

22. *DGFP, D*, 5:921–25 (memo of Schacht, 16 January 1939).

23. Ibid., D, 4:336–41.

24. Wistrich, *Hitler's Apocalypse*, 85.

25. Himmler and Heydrich later preferred the term *the wish of the Führer* (*des Führers Wunsch*) when transmitting unwritten orders

for the "Final Solution." See Gerald Fleming, *Hitler und die Endlösung* (Munich, 1982), 64.

26. Burleigh, *Third Reich*, 571ff.

27. Ernst Klee, "Euthanasie," in *NS-Staat* (Frankfurt, 1983); Paul Weindling, *Health, Race, and German Politics Between National Unification and Nazism, 1870–1945* (Cambridge, 1989); Michael Berenbaum, ed., *A Mosaic of Victims: Non-Jews Persecuted and Murdered by the Nazis* (New York, 1990); Lukas, *Forgotten Holocaust*; Richard Plant, *The Pink Triangle: The Nazi War Against Homosexuals* (New York, 1986); and Henry Friedlander, *The Origins of the Nazi Genocide: From Euthanasia to the Final Solution* (Chapel Hill, 1995), 246–302.

28. Elke Froehlich, ed., *Die Tagebücher von Joseph Goebbels: Sämtliche Fragmente* (Munich, 1987), 3:628.

29. Ibid., 612.

30. Stig Hornshoj-Möller, *"Der ewige Jude": Quellenkritische Analyse eines antisemitischen Propagandafilms* (Göttingen, 1995), 3–23.

31. Arad, *Documents*, 173–77. For Nazi ghettoization policy in Poland between 1939 and 1941, see Christopher R. Browning, *The Path to Genocide: Essays on Launching the Final Solution* (Cambridge, 1993), 28–56.

32. For a comprehensive study, see Isaiah Trunk, *Judenrat* (New York, 1972), 259–450, and for his description of the ghetto police, 475–547; Philip Friedman, *Roads to Extinction* (New York, 1980), 539–53; Aharon Weiss, "Jewish Leadership in Occupied Poland: Postures and Attitudes," *Yad Vashem Studies* 12 (1977): 335–65, and "Judenrat," in *Encyclopaedia of the Holocaust*, 1:762–67.

33. Raul Hilberg, *The Destruction of the European Jews* (Chicago, 1967), 664–68. See also his *Perpetrators, Victims, Bystanders: The Jewish Catastrophe, 1933–1945* (London, 1995).

34. Hilberg, *Perpetrators*, 16–17.

35. Hannah Arendt, *Eichmann in Jerusalem: A Report on the Banality of Evil* (London, 1994 [1963]), 125. See also Richard I. Cohen, "Breaking the Code: Hannah Arendt's *Eichmann in Jerusalem* and the Public Polemic," *Michael* 13 (1993), 29–85.

36. Raul Hilberg et al., eds. *The Warsaw Ghetto Diary of Adam Czerniakow* (New York, 1979), 70.

37. Rumkowski's addresses "Work Protects Us from Annihilation"

(2 February 1942) and "Give Me Your Children," in Beren-
baum, *Witness,* 81–86. See also Primo Levi, *The Drowned and the Saved* (London, 1999), 44–51.

38. *Scroll of Agony: The Warsaw Diary of Chaim A. Kaplan* (New York, 1954), 129.

39. Ibid., 130.

40. Ibid., 244–45 (diary entry of 20 February 1941).

41. Ibid., 202–3 (2 October 1940). In this same entry, Kaplan ob-
served that never before in Jewish history "did we have so cruel and barbaric an enemy," nor one so evil "that it would forbid an entire people to pray."

42. Dawidowicz, *War,* 312–18, See Shimon Huberbrand, *Kiddush Hashem: Jewish Religious and Cultural Life in Poland During the Holocaust* (New York, 1987), 175–221, for religious practice.

43. Janusz Korczak, *Ghetto Diary* (New York, 1978), 79–189; Joanna Michlic-Coren, "Battling Against the Odds: Culture, Education and the Jewish Intelligentsia in the Warsaw Ghetto, 1940–1942," *East European Jewish Affairs (EEJA)* 27 (1997):77–92.

44. Dawidowicz, *War,* 417.

45. E. Klee et al., eds., *"Those Were the Days": The Holocaust Through the Eyes of the Perpetrators and Bystanders* (London, 1991), 28; Dinah Porat, "The Holocaust in Lithuania: Some Unique Aspects," in D. Cesarani, ed., *The Final Solution* (London, 1994), 159–74.

46. " 'They Shall Not Take Us Like Sheep to the Slaughter!' Proclamation by the Jewish Pioneer Youth Group in Vilna," in Arad, *Documents,* 433.

47. Ibid. See also Avraham Tory, *Surviving the Holocaust: The Kovno Ghetto Diary* (Cambridge, Mass., 1990), notes by Dina Porat. The diary, written originally in Yiddish, provides a powerful picture of life in the Kovno ghetto, suspended between hope and despair. On the Jewish resistance in Vilna, see Y. Arad, *Vilna ha-
yehudit be-ma'avak u ve-klyon* (Tel Aviv, 1976). On Jewish resistance in general, see Lucien Steinberg, *Jews Against Hitler* (London, 1978).

48. See Ber Mark, *Uprising in the Warsaw Ghetto* (New York, 1975), 97–195, for the documents. See also Y. Gutman, *The Jews of Warsaw, 1939–1943: Ghetto, Underground, Revolt* (Bloomington, 1982).

49. Arad, *Documents,* 315–16. For the objectives, appeals, and reports

of the Jewish underground, see ibid, 293–309. For SS General Stroop's final report after crushing the revolt, see ibid., 312–13.

50. See Reuben Ainzstein, *Jewish Resistance in Nazi Occupied Eastern Europe* (London, 1974), 279–462, for the Jewish partisans; see 463–550 on the fighting ghettos of Minsk, Vilna, and Białystok; see 551–670 on the Warsaw ghetto uprising, and see 714–816 on the revolts in Treblinka, Sobibór, and Auschwitz-Birkenau. See also Steinberg, *Jews Against Hitler,* 167–292; S. Krakowski, *Leḥima yehudit be-Polin neged ha-natzim* (Jerusalem, 1977)—a study of Jewish armed resistance in Poland; Dov Levin, *Fighting Back: Lithuanian Jewry's Armed Resistance to the Nazis, 1941–1944* (New York, 1985), 167–228; N. Tec, *Defiance: The Bielski Partisans. The Story of the Largest Armed Resistance by Jews During World War II* (Oxford, 1993); Arno Lustiger, ed., *Zum Kampf auf Leben und Tod: Das Buch vom Widerstand der Juden, 1933–1945* (Cologne, 1994).

51. J. N. Porter, ed., *The Jewish Partisans: A Documentary History of Jewish Resistance in the Soviet Union During World War II* (Lanham, Md., 1982); J. Kagan and D. Cohen, *Surviving the Holocaust with the Russian Jewish Partisans* (London, 1998), 162–224.

52. Henri Michel, "Jewish Resistance and the European Resistance Movement," *Yad Vashem Studies* 7 (1968): 7–16; M. Novitch, *Le Passage des barbares: contribution à l'histoire de la déportation et de la resistance des Juifs grecs* (Nice, 1962); Annie Latour, *The Jewish Resistance in France* (New York, 1981); Gitta Amipaz-Silber, *La Résistance Juive en Algérie, 1940–1942* (Jerusalem, 1986), 62–150; Dan Michman, ed., *Belgium and the Holocaust: Jews, Belgians, Germans* (Jerusalem, 1998), 3–40; Steinberg, *Jews Against Hitler,* 81–138.

53. See René Cassin, *Les Hommes partis de rien* (Paris, 1974), 136; Henri Amouroux, *Les Passions et les haines, Avril–Décembre 1942* (Paris, 1981); A. Rayski, *De Gaulle et les Juifs (1940–1944)* (Paris, 1994).

54. O. D. Kulka, "The Reichsvereinigung of the Jews in Germany (1938/9–1943)," in I. Gutman et al., eds., *Patterns of Jewish Leadership in Nazi Europe, 1933–1945* (Yad Vashem, 1979), 45–58; Konrad Kwiet and Helmut Eschwege, *Selbstbehauptung und Widerstand: Deutsche Juden im Kampf um Existenz und Menschenwürde, 1933–1945* (Hamburg, 1984).

55. See the essays by Herbert Freeden, Hajo Bennett, Joseph Walk,

and others in A. Paucker, ed., *Die Juden im Nationalsozialistischen Deutschland, 1933–1943* (Tübingen, 1986). Also Arno Herzberg, "The Jewish Press under the Nazi Regime: Its Mission, Suppression, and Defiance," *LBIYB* 36 (1991): 367–88; A. Paucker, "Resistance of German and Austrian Jews to the Nazi Regime, 1933–1945," *LBIYB* 40 (1995): 13–14; and Paucker's *Jewish Resistance in Germany: The Facts and the Problems* (Berlin, 1991), 5–6.

56. Paucker, *Jewish Resistance* 5–6. The Zionist youth movement in Germany also became strongly antifascist. See Chaim Schatzker, "The Jewish Youth Movement in Germany in the Holocaust Period," *LBIYB* 32 (1987): 157–82, and 33 (1988): 301–25; and Jehuda Reinharz, "Hashomer Hatsair in Germany," part 2, "Under the Shadow of the Swastika, 1933–1938," *LBIYB* 32 (1987): 183–229.

57. Paucker, *Jewish Resistance,* 9, 12.

58. E. Silberner, "Die Kommunistische Partei Deutschlands zur Judenfrage," *Jahrbuch des Instituts für Deutsche Geschichte* 8 (1979): 283–334.

59. Paucker, *Jewish Resistance,* 12

4. The "Final Solution"

1. Aly, *Final Solution,* and "The Planning Intelligentsia and the 'Final Solution,' " in M. Burleigh, ed., *Confronting the Nazi Past: New Debates on Modern German History* (London, 1996), 140–53. For a critique of Aly's earlier functionalism, see Browning, *Path to Genocide,* 59–76.

2. Richard Breitman, *The Architect of Genocide: Himmler and the Final Solution* (London, 1991), 112–120.

3. Himmler's reflections on the treatment of "alien races" can be found in Berenbaum, *Witness,* 74–76.

4. See also Christopher R. Browning, *Nazi Policy, Jewish Workers, German Killers* (Cambridge, 2000), 13–14. Hitler read Himmler's memorandum on 25 May 1940, confirming the guidelines, which he found "very good and correct."

5. Arad, *Documents,* 216–18; Browning, *Path to Genocide,* 18–20, 23–27, 127–28; Breitman, *Architect,* 121–31.

6. Hilberg, *Destruction,* 260–61; Arad, *Documents,* 217, Breitman, *Architect,* 121, 124–25.

7. Leni Yahil, "Madagascar—Phantom of a Solution for the Jewish Question," in B. Vago and G. L. Mosse, eds., *Jews and Non-Jews in Eastern Europe* (New York, 1974), 315–40; see also Magnus Brechtken, *"Madagaskar für die Juden": Antisemitische Idee und Politische Praxis, 1885–1945* (Munich, 1997), 295, who argues that the Madagascar Plan was intended as a "death sentence" for European Jewry.

8. Arad, *Documents,* 376.

9. Ibid., 416–17.

10. Ibid., 416.

11. Ibid., 398–400.

12. Dawidowicz, *War,* 163–64. See also Jürgen Förster, *Das Unternehmen "Barbarossa" als Eroberungs- und Vernichtungskrieg* (Stuttgart, 1987); Hannes Heer, "Killing Fields: Die Wehrmacht und der Holocaust," in H. Heer and K. Naumann, eds., *Vernichtungskrieg: Verbrechen der Wehrmacht, 1941 bis 1944* (Hamburg, 1995), 57–77, and "Die Logik des Vernichtungskrieges: Wehrmacht und Parisanen Kampf," 104–156, and his *Tote Zonen: Die deutsche Wehrmacht an der Ostfront* (Hamburg, 1999) and *The German Army and Genocide,* ed. Hamburg Institute for Social Research (New York, 1999).

13. Omer Bartov, *The Eastern Front, 1941–1945: German Troops and the Barbarization of Warfare* (London, 1985), 106–56, and *Hitler's Army: Soldiers, Nazis, and War in the Third Reich* (New York, 1991), 106–86. On Manstein, see Robert Wistrich, *Who's Who in Nazi Germany* (London, 1995), 166–67.

14. Omer Bartov, "Savage War," in Burleigh, *Confronting the Nazi Past,* 125–39.

15. Andreas Hillgruber, "Die 'Endlösung' und das deutsche Ostimperium als Kernstück des rassenideologischen Programms des Nationalsozialismus," *VfZ* 20 (1972): 133–53; Eberhard Jäckel, *Hitler's World View: A Blueprint for Power* (Harvard, 1981); Wistrich, *Hitler's Apocalypse,* 67–68, 114–15.

16. F. Halder, *Kriegstagbuch, 1939–1942* (Stuttgart, 1962–1964), 2: 336–37; Dawidowicz, *War,* 161.

17. Dawidowicz, *War,* 157.

18. Hilberg, *Destruction,* 262.

19. Arad, *Documents,* 376–78; see also Jürgen Förster, "The Wehrmacht and the War of Extermination against the Soviet Union,"

Yad Vashem Studies 14 (1981): 7–34; for the execution of these orders and treatment of Soviet POWs, see Christian Streit, *Keine Kameraden, die Wehrmacht, und die sowjetischen Kriegsgefangenen, 1941–1945* (Stuttgart, 1978), 88–89, 253ff.

20. *Eichmann Interrogated:Transcripts from the Archives of the Israeli Police*, ed. Jochen von Lang and Claus Sibyll (New York, 1983), 75.
21. Wistrich, *Hitler's Apocalypse*, 188.
22. Philippe Burrin, *Hitler et les Juifs* (Paris, 1989), 138.
23. Ibid., 139–40.
24. Krausnick, "Persecution of the Jews," 85.
25. Ibid., 111.
26. See Breitman, *Architect*, 90, 139–41, 152–3, 199; Browning, *Nazi Policy*, 45–46.
27. Christopher R. Browning, *Fateful Months: Essays on the Emergence of the Final Solution* (New York, 1985), 30–31.
28. Michael Tregenza, "Belzec Death Camp," *The Wiener Library Bulletin*, new series (1977): 30: 41–42, 8–24; Yitzhak Arad, *Belzec, Sobibór, Treblinka. The Operation Reinhard Death Camps* (Bloomington, 1999), 23–29, 68–74.
29. Hilberg, *Destruction*, 564–66; Rudolf Höss, *Commandant of Auschwitz* (London, 1959). Deborah Dwork and Robert Jan van Pelt, *Auschwitz: 1270 to the Present* (New York 1996), 236–353.
30. Arad, *Documents*, 247–48. See Christian Gerlach, "Die Wannsee-Konferenz, das Schicksal der deutschen Juden und Hitlers Grundsatzentscheidung, alle Juden zu ermordern" *Werkstattgeschichte* 18 (1997): 29–30, notes that Frank's speech virtually parrots Hitler's remarks four days earlier, which Gerlach regards as the crucial moment in formalizing the "Final Solution."
31. Arad, *Documents*, 249.
32. Berenbaum, *Witness*, 165–71. For the background, see Gerlach, "Wannsee-Konferenz," 7–44; tr. in *Journal of Modern History* 12 (1998): 759–812.
33. Arad, *Documents*, 251.
34. Ibid. On Luther, see Christopher Browning, *The Final Solution and the German Foreign Office* (New York, 1978), 76–81, 115–24, 158–61.
35. Arad, *Documents*, 258–60.
36. Jeremy Noakes, "The Development of Nazi Policy Towards the

German 'Mischlinge,' 1933–1945," *LBIYB* 34 (1989): 291–354; Adam, *Judenpolitik*, 316–33.

37. About 520,000 Jews were murdered in Galicia, which together with the Lublin district has been the object of a number of important regional case studies. See Dieter Pohl, *Von der Judenpolitk zum Judenmord: Der Distrikt Lublin des Generalgouvernements 1933–1944* (Frankfurt, 1993) and *Nationalsozialistische Judenverfolgung in Ostgalizien 1941–1944* (Munich, 1997), 267–356. See also Thomas Sandkühler, "Endlösung," in *Galizien* (Bonn, 1996), 166–289, and his article in Ulrich Herbert, ed., *National Socialist Extermination Policies: Contemporary German Perspectives and Controversies* (New York, 2000), 104–27.

38. Letter from Minsk, dated 16 December 1941; *Documents*, 408–9.

39. Arad, *Documents*, 394.

40. Ibid., 395.

41. Daniel Carpi, "The Mufti of Jerusalem, Amin el-Husseini, and His Diplomatic Activity during World War II (October 1941–July 1943)," *Studies in Zionism* (summer 1983): 101–31; Philip Mattar, *The Mufti of Jerusalem: Al-Hajj Amin al-Husayni and the Palestinian National Movement* (New York, 1991), 99–107. For a translation of his articles into Hebrew, see Zvi Elpeleg, *Me-Nekudat Reuto shel Ha-Mufti* (In the Eyes of the Mufti), (Tel Aviv, 1995), and *The Grand Mufti, Haj Amin al-Hussaini, Founder of the Palestinian National Movement* (London, 1994).

42. *DGFP*, series D, 13:201.

43. Ibid., 202.

44. Ibid., 203.

45. Ibid.

46. Ibid., 204.

47. Ibid. For the Mufti's ringing endorsement of Hitler's attitude to the Palestine question, see *DGFP*, vol. 11 (London, 1961), 1153–54; for his anti-Semitism and implication in the "Final Solution," see Joseph Schechtman, *The Mufti and the Fuehrer* (New York, 1965), 154–58, which included transferring Jewish children to Poland where they would be under the Nazis' "active supervision"; also Wistrich, *Hitler's Apocalypse*, 169–70, and Daniel Carpi, "The Diplomatic Negotiations over the Transfer

of Jewish Children from Croatia and Turkey to Palestine in 1943," *Yad Vashem Studies* 12 (1977): 109–24.

48. Gerlach, "Wannsee-Konferenz," 25–28.

49. Ibid. For a critique of Gerlach's theses, see Browning, *Nazi Policy*, 26–57.

50. Burrin, *Hitler et les Juifs*, 140–42.

51. Ibid., 141.

52. According to secret SD reports, the German public interpreted Hitler's speech to mean "that very soon the last Jew would be driven off European soil." See O. D. Kulka, "Public Opinion in Nazi Germany: The Final Solution," *The Jerusalem Quarterly* 26 (winter 1983): 36.

53. Louis Lochner, ed., *The Goebbels Diaries, 1942–43* (New York, 1948), 114.

54. Ibid., 138.

55. Krausnick, "Persecution of the Jews," 120.

56. Ibid.

57. Hilberg, *Destruction*, 454–56, for the background.

58. Mario D. Fenyo, *Hitler, Horthy, and Hungary: German-Hungarian Relations* (New Haven, 1972), 129.

59. Arad, *Documents*, 344–45.

60. Ibid.

61. Ibid. See Breitman, *Architect*, 242–43.

62. Arad, *Documents*, 344. Burleigh, *Third Reich*, 659–61.

63. Berenbaum, *Witness*, 177ff. See also Bradley Smith and Agnes Peterson, eds., *Heinrich Himmler: Geheimreden 1933 bis 1945* (Frankfurt, 1974).

64. Yehuda Bauer, *Jews for Sale? Nazi-Jewish Negotiations, 1933–1945* (New Haven, 1994), 102–15.

65. *Le Testament politique de Hitler* (Paris, 1959), 89.

66. *Nazi Conspiracy and Aggression* (Washington, D.C. 1946), 6:260–63.

67. Ibid.

68. Dawidowicz, *War*, 18.

5. BETWEEN THE CROSS AND THE SWASTIKA

1. *Mein Kampf,* 206.
2. *Die Rede Adolf Hitlers in der ersten grossen Massenversammlung* (Munich, 1925), 8.
3. Ernst Boepple, ed., *Adolf Hitlers Reden* (Munich, 1933), 55–56.
4. *Mein Kampf,* 336. Speech of 12 April 1922, in Eberhard Jäckel and Axel Kuhn, eds., *Hitler: Sämtliche Aufzeichnungen, 1905–1924* (Stuttgart, 1980), 623.
5. Klaus Scholder, "Judentum und Christentum in der Ideologie and Politik des Nationalsozialismus, 1919–1945" in Kulka, and Mendes-Flohr, *Judaism and Christianity,* 183–96; and his *A Requiem for Hitler* (London, 1989), 140–81.
6. Speech in Munich, 17 December 1922, in Jäckel and Kuhn, *Hitler,* 770.
7. Ibid.
8. Ibid., 623.
9. Ibid.
10. Baynes, *Speeches,* 1:20 (12 August 1922).
11. Friedrich Heer, *Der Glaube des Adolf Hitler: : Anatomie einer politischen Religiosität* (Munich, 1968); Robert Wistrich, *Between Redemption and Perdition* (London, 1990), 55–70.
12. Friedrich Heer, *Gottes erste Liebe* (Munich, 1968).
13. *Mein Kampf,* 564–65. Dinter, a notorious anti-Semite, founded the *Geistchristliche Religionsgemeinschaft,* which sought to present Nazism as a second Protestant Reformation. See Kershaw, *Hitler,* 298.
14. Kershaw, *Hitler,* 269. Wistrich, *Who's Who,* 161–63.
15. G. Pridham, *Hitler's Rise to Power: The Nazi Movement in Bavaria, 1923–33* (London, 1973), 146–83; Ian Kershaw, *Der Hitler-Mythos* (Stuttgart, 1980), 37.
16. *Mein Kampf,* 65.
17. Baynes, *Speeches,* 1:42 (10 April 1923).
18. *Mein Kampf,* 687; E. Calic, ed., *Conversations with Hitler* (New York, 1971), 51; Kershaw, *Hitler,* 154–55.
19. Margerete Plewnia, *Auf dem Weg zu Hitler: Der völkische Publizist Dietrich Eckart* (Bremen, 1970), 94–112.
20. *Auf Gut Deutsch* (Munich) 1 (1919): 18.
21. *Auf Gut Deutsch,* 2 (1919): 554. See also Dietrich Eckart, *Der Bol-*

shchewismus von Moses bis Lenin: Zwiegespräch zwischen Adolf Hitler und mir (Munich, 1924). The first to grasp the significance of this text and Eckart's influence on Hitler was Ernst Nolte, "Eine Frühe Quelle zu Hitlers Antisemitismus," Historische Zeitschrift 192 (1961): 584–606.

22. John Conway, "The German Church Struggle and Its Aftermath," in Abraham Peck, ed., Jews and Christians after the Holocaust (Philadelphia, 1982), 42; Gutteridge, "German Protestantism," 227–50; Theodore S. Hamerow, On the Road to the Wolf's Lair: German Resistance to Hitler (Cambridge, Mass., 1999), 12–13, 52–54, 60–63, 95–96, 146–49, 151–58; Klaus Scholder, The Churches and the Third Reich (London, 1987), 1:99–119, 127–45, 189–218.

23. Doris L. Bergen, Twisted Cross: The German Christian Movement in the Third Reich (Chapel Hill, 1996), 61–100.

24. Eberhard Bethge, Dietrich Bonhoeffer: Theologe, Christ, Zeitgenosse (Munich, 1967), 323, 557–59; Hamerow, On the Road, 160–62, 204–8.

25. Robert Michael, "Theological Myth, German Antisemitism, and the Holocaust: The Case of Martin Niemöeller," Holocaust and Genocide Studies 2.1 (1987): 105–22.

26. Klauss Scholder, Die Kirchen und das Dritte Reich: Vorgeschichte und Zeit der Illusionen, 1918–1934 (Frankfurt, 1977), 1:116–23; Hamerow, On the Road, 195–202; Ronald J. Rychlak, Hitler, the War, and the Pope (Huntingdon, Ind., 2000), 43–69.

27. Konrad Repgen, "Zur Vatikanischen Strategie beim Reichskonkordat," VJfZ 31 (1983): 506–35.

28. Miccoli, I Dilemmi, 286.

29. B. Stasiewski, Akten deutscher Bischöfe über die Lage der Kirche, 1933–1945, vol. 1: 1933–1934 (Mainz, 1968), 101ff.

30. Faulhaber's sermons on the Bible appeared in English as Judaism, Christianity, and Germany (New York, 1935). His published papers were edited by Ludwig Volk, Akten Kardinal von Faulhaber, 1917–1945 (Mainz, 1978).

31. Ibid., 184–85; see also Phayer, Catholic Church, 15ff.

32. Scholder, "Judaism and Christianity," 191.

33. "Mit Brennender Sorge," Acta Apostolicae Sedis 29 (1937): 145–67; for Faulhaber's draft, see Dieter Albrecht, Der Notenwechsel zwis-

chen dem Heiligen Stuhl und der Deutschen Reichsregierung, Veröffentlichungen der Kommission für Zeitgeschichte, 1:402–43 (henceforth VKZ).

34. Miccoli, *I Dilemmi,* 174–75, 178; Repgen, "Zur Vatikanischen Strategie," 209–10.
35. Ludwig Volk, ed., *Akten deutscher Bischöfe über die Lage der Kirche, 1933–1945,* vol. 6: *1943–1945,* VKZg, Reihe Z: Quellen (Mainz, 1983), 34:675n1.
36. Miccoli, *I Dilemmi,* 351.
37. Ibid., 189.
38. Ibid., 499n309; Volk, *Akten Kardinal,* doc. 799, p. 944.
39. Miccoli, *I Dilemmi,* 195.
40. Heinrich Portmann, *Kardinal von Galen: Ein Gottesmann seiner Zeit,* 16th ed. (Münster, 1978), 334–66.
41. Burleigh, *Third Reich,* 262, 400–402.
42. H. R. Trevor-Roper, ed., *Hitler's Table Talk, 1941–1944* (London, 1973), 78–79.
43. Ibid., 6–7.
44. Ibid.
45. Ibid.
46. Ibid., 7.
47. Ibid., 79.
48. Ibid.
49. Ibid., 78.
50. Ibid., 143.
51. Ibid., 314.
52. Ibid.
53. See Alfred Rosenberg, *Der Mythus des 20 Jahrhunderts* (Munich, 1939), and Ernst Piper's essay on Rosenberg in Ley and Schoeps, *Nationalsozialismus,* 107–25.
54. Donald J. Dietrich, "Catholic Resistance in the Third Reich," *Holocaust and Genocide Studies* 3.2 (1988): 171–76. See also Heinz Boberach, ed., *Berichte des SD und der Gestapo über Kirchen und Kirchenvolk in Deutschland, 1934–1944* (Mainz, 1971), which is a source of great importance covering ten years of Nazi rule and the reports the regime received from its agents concerning the Christian churches in Germany.
55. Trevor-Roper, *Hitler's Table Talk,* 722.

56. Heinz-Albert Raem, *Pius XI und der Nationalsozialismus: Die En-zyklika "Mit Brennender Sorge" vom 14 März 1937* (Paderborn, 1979).

57. *Actes et documents du saint siège relatifs à la Seconde Guerre Mondiale*, 11 vols. (Vatican City, 1965–1981), (henceforth *Adss*); *Lettres de Pie XII aux évêques Allemands, 1939–1945* (Vatican City, 1993), 419. See also the summary (at times tendentious) of Pierre Blet, *Pie XII et la Seconde Guerre Mondiale d'après les archives du Vatican* (Paris, 1997).

58. G. Passelecq and B. Suchecky, *L'encyclique cachée de Pie XI: une occasion manquée de l'église face à l'antisémitisme* (Paris, 1995), 320ff.; Giovanni Miccoli: " 'Chiesa Cattolica, Questione Ebraica' e Antisemitismo fra Ottocento e Novecento nella Recente Storiografia," in Giacomo Martina and Ugo Dovere, eds., *I grandi problemi della storiografia civile e religiosa* (Rome, 1999), 323–54.

59. *Adss*, 9:170, doc. 82.

60. Owen Chadwick, *Britain and the Vatican During the Second World War* (Cambridge, 1986), 205.

61. Burzio to Maglione, 9 March 1942, in *Adss*, vol. 8, doc. 298; see also Livia Rothkirchen, "The Churches and the 'Final Solution' in Slovakia," in Kulka and Mendes-Flohr, *Judaism and Christianity*, 413–41.

62. Gerhart Riegner, *A Warning to the World: The Efforts of the World Jewish Congress to Mobilise the Christian Churches Against the Final Solution*. Lecture at Hebrew Union College, Cincinnati, 17 November 1983.

63. Chadwick, *Britain*, 211–12. *Adss*, 8:758.

64. Chadwick, *Britain*, 213. *Adss*, 8:676, 679, doc. 507. Only three days earlier, a report from Scavizzi to the secretary of state had informed him that more than two million Jews had been killed. *Adss*, 8:669–70, doc. 496.

65. Chadwick, Britain. On 26 September 1942, Taylor reported to the Vatican on mass deportations and execution of Jews at special killing centers. *Foreign Relations of the United States* (*FRUS*), (Washington, D.C. 1961), 3:772. The Polish ambassador to the Vatican, Kazimierz Papée, had also confirmed that Jews were being murdered in camps all over Poland. *Adss*, 8: 497.

66. Chadwick, *Britain*, 215.

67. Ibid.

68. Ibid.
69. Ibid.
70. Ibid. See *Adss,* 8:666, for the confirmation to the Vatican by Count Malvezzi of the Institute for Industrial Research that "systematic massacres" of the Jews in Poland were happening daily and took on the "most fearful and incredible proportions" (Montini's notes, 18 September 1942, doc. 493).
71. A pastoral letter by the Slovak bishops, published on 26 April 1942, had blamed the Jews for Christ's horrible death on the cross. While observing that Jews were also human beings, it did not oppose the "legal actions of the government in taking steps to eradicate the evil influence of the Jews." Rothkirchen, "Churches," 417–18.
72. Sidor to Maglione, *Adss,* 8:541–44, doc. 383.
73. Ibid., note of Tardini, 597–98, doc. 426. "Ma che non possa tener a freno un sacerdote, chi lo può capite?"
74. Menahem Shelah, "The Catholic Church in Croatia, the Vatican, and the Murder of Croatian Jews," In Yedua Bauer et al., eds., *Remembering for the Future* (Oxford, 1988), 266–80; Jonathan Steinberg, "Types of Genocide? Croatians, Serbs, and Jews, 1941–5," in Cesarani, *Final Solution,* 175–93.
75. Shelah, "Catholic Church," 270; Phayer, *Catholic Church,* 31–40, is highly critical of the Vatican for ignoring the moral issues raised by the genocide in Croatia. So, too, is John Morley, *Vatican Diplomacy and the Jews During the Holocaust, 1939–1943* (New York, 1980), 165, who emphasizes that the Croatian perpetrators depicted themselves "as loyal to the Church and to the Pope."
76. *Adss,* 7:166, doc. 7, Christmas broadcast of Pius XII, 24 December 1942. See also Robert S. Wistrich, "The Pope, the Church, and the Jews," *Commentary* (April 1999), 22–28.
77. Chadwick, *Britain,* 218.
78. *Adss,* 9:170, doc. 82. See also 2:323–9.
79. *Adss,* Ibid., vol. 2.
80. Ibid., 2:324.
81. Pius XII to von Preysing, 22 April 1940, in Ibid., 2:138–42, doc. 45.
82. Pius XII's speech was reprinted in *The Tablet* (London), 12 June 1943.

83. The entire speech as broadcast on Vatican Radio was published in *The Tablet*, 9 June 1945, under the heading "The Catholic Church and the Third Reich: Pope Pius XII Surveys an Heroic History."

84. Ibid.

85. Ibid.

86. Susan Zuccotti, "Pope Pius XII and the Holocaust: The Case in Italy," in I. Herzer et al., eds., *The Italian Refuge: Rescue of Jews During the Holocaust* (Washington, D.C., 1989), 254–70, and *Under His Very Windows: The Vatican and the Holocaust in Italy* (2001), chap. 13–16, which I read in manuscript.

87. *Adss*, 9:506ff., doc. 368; Miccoli, *I Dilemmi*, 250–62; Phayer, *Catholic Church*, 97–104; Susan Zuccotti, *The Italians and the Holocaust: Persecution, Rescue, and Survival* (New York, 1987) chap. 6.

88. *Adss*, 9:506ff., doc. 368; Morley, *Vatican Diplomacy*, 180–81.

89. *Adss*, 8:296, doc. 165; see also Michael R. Marrus and Robert O. Paxton, *Vichy France and the Jews* (Stanford, 1985) 201–2; Miccoli, *I Dilemmi*, 391–97.

90. *Adss*, 9:459, doc. 317; Miccoli, *I Dilemmi*, 401ff.; Susan Zuccotti, "The Italian Racial Laws, 1938–1945,"in J. Frankel, ed., *Studies in Contemporary Jewry* (New York, 1997) 8:133–52.

91. Emil Fackenheim, *The Jewish Return into History: Reflections in the Age of Auschwitz and a New Jerusalem* (New York, 1978), 76.

6. Collaboration Across Europe

1. L. Dobroszycki and S. Gurock, eds., *The Holocaust in the Soviet Union* (New York, 1993), 3–73; Y. Arad, "The Holocaust of Soviet Jewry in the Occupied Territories of the USSR," *Yad Vashem Studies* 21 (1991): 1–47; John Garrard, "The Nazi Holocaust in the Soviet Union: Interpreting Newly Opened Russian Archives," *EEJA* 25.2 (winter 1995): 3–40; Zvi Gitelman, ed., *Bitter Legacy: Confronting the Holocaust* (Bloomington, 1997).

2. Martin Dean, *Collaboration in the Holocaust: Crimes of the Local Police in Belorussia and Ukraine, 1941–44* (London, 2000).

3. Ibid., 60–76, 101.

4. Ibid., 75–6.

5. John A. Armstrong, *Ukrainian Nationalism* (New York, 1963), 46–47, 101–75; Hryhory Kostiuk, *Stalinist Rule in the Ukraine*

(London, 1960), 47–59; Conquest, *Harvest of Sorrow,* 219–21, and for the huge losses under Soviet domination, 306. See also Katz, "Mass Death," in Wistrich, *Demonizing the Other,* 272–76; for the Jewish factor, see especially Taras Hunczak, "Ukrainian-Jewish Relations During the Soviet and Nazi Occupations," in Yuri Boshyk, ed., *Ukraine During World War II: History and Aftermath* (Edmonton, 1986), 39–57.

6. Taras Hunczak, "A Reappraisal of Symon Petliura and Ukrainian-Jewish Relations, 1917–21, *Jewish Social Studies* 3 (1969): 163–83; J. Klier and Shlomo Lambroza, eds., *Pogroms: Anti-Jewish Violence in Modern Russian History* (Cambridge, 1992), 293–372; Ben-Anat, "Peraot Ukraina," 105–39.

7. Alexander Dallin, *German Rule in Russia 1941–1945* (New York, 1957), 107–67; A. F. Vysotsky et al., eds., *Nazi Crimes in Ukraine, 1941–44: Documents and Materials* (Kiev, 1987).

8. Avraham Tory, *Surviving,* 4–12; Porat, "Holocaust in Lithuania," in Cesarani, *Final Solution,* 159–74.

9. Porat, "Holocaust in Lithuania," 162–66.

10. Steinberg, "Types of Genocide?"175ff. For the German "Final Solution" in Serbia and the first use of gas vans, see Browning, *Fateful Months,* 39–85.

11. Steinberg, "Types of Genocide?" 176–77.

12. Menahem Shelah, "Croatia," *Encyclopaedia of the Holocaust,* 324–25.

13. Ibid.

14. Stepinac to Maglione, 24 March 1943, *Adss,* 9, annexe 2, 221–24, and summary of his protests by the Secretariat of State, 224–29; Morley, *Vatican Diplomacy,* 147–65.

15. Marcone to Maglione, 8 March 1943, Adss, 9, annexe 1, 219–21, doc. 130; on Pavelić, B. Krizman, *Pavelic izmedju Hitlera i Musolinija* (Zagreb, 1980); for the Serb standpoint concerning Ustashe crimes, see Vladimir Dedijer, *Jasenovac—Das Jugoslawische Auschwitz und der Vatican* (Freiburg, 1988), 76–200.

16. Arendt, *Eichmann,* 190; on massacres of Jews by the Romanian army and police on Soviet territory, see Hilberg, *Destruction,* 200–201.

17. Eugen Weber, "Romania," in H. Rogger and E. Weber, eds., *The European Right* (Berkeley, 1966), 501–74; Emanuel Turczynski, "The Background of Romanian Fascism," in Peter F. Sugar, ed.,

Native Fascism in the Successor States, 1918–1945 (Santa Barbara, 1971), 101–12; B. Vago, *The Shadow of the Swastika: The Rise of Fascism and Anti-Semitism in the Danube Basin, 1936–39* (London, 1975), 55–65, 128–29; Leon Volovici, *Nationalist Ideology and Anti-Semitism: The Case of Romanian Intellectuals in the 1930s* (Oxford, 1991), 45–158.

18. Vago, *Shadow,* 21–72.
19. Arendt, *Eichmann,* 191. For the stark details concerning Romanian massacres, see Radu Ioanid, *The Holocaust in Romania: The Destruction of Jews and Gypsies under the Antonescu Regime, 1940–1944* (Chicago, 2000).
20. J. Ancel, "The Romanian Way of Solving the 'Jewish Problem' in Bessarabia and Bukovina, June–July 1941," *Yad Vashem Studies* 19 (1988): 187–232.
21. Randolph L. Braham, *The Politics of Genocide: The Holocaust in Hungary* (New York, 1981), 743–809, 1113–20, and "The Holocaust in Hungary: A Retrospective Analysis," in David Cesarani, ed., *Genocide and Rescue: The Holocaust in Hungary, 1944* (Oxford, 1997), 29–46.
22. Seredi supported the anti-Jewish laws and welcomed the removal of the "wickedly destructive influence" of Hungarian Jews. Quoted in Yehuda Bauer, *A History of the Holocaust* (New York, 1982), 315–16. The papal nuncio in Hungary, Angelo Rotta, had to fight hard against such obstacles in his efforts to rescue Jews. See Phayer, *Catholic Church,* 106–9.
23. Robert S. Wistrich, "The Jews and Nationality Conflicts in the Habsburg Lands," *Nationalities Papers* 22.1(1994): 119–39.
24. N. Katzburg, *Hungary and the Jews: Policy and Legislation, 1920–1943* (Ramat Gan, 1981), 262–84; Randolph L. Braham, "Hungary: Jews During the Holocaust," in *Encyclopaedia of the Holocaust,* 698–702.
25. Nicholas Kállay, *Hungarian Premier* (London, 1954), 75–76; Fenyo, *Hitler, Horthy, and Hungary,* 72–78.
26. Fenyo, *Hitler, Horthy, and Hungary,* 168ff. In a conversation with Kállay in Rome on 2 April 1943, Pope Pius XII thanked him "for having succeeded in keeping Hungary from such [Nazi] inhumanity." The pope, according to Kállay, deplored the brutal German policy toward Jews.

27. Randolph L. Braham, "The Rightists, Horthy, and the Germans: Factors Underlying the Destruction of Hungarian Jewry" in Vago and Mosse, *Jews and Non-Jews,* 137–56.
28. Nevertheless, the Allied response has been much attacked. See J. S. Conway, "Between Apprehension and Indifference: Allied Attitudes to the Destruction of Hungarian Jewry," *Wiener Library Bulletin,* new series, 27.30–31 (1973–1974): 37–48; Wyman, *Abandonment of the Jews,* 237–41; for the pope's telegram to Horthy, see Rychlak, *Hitler,* 222.
29. On Szálasi and the consequences of the coup on 15 October 1944, see C. A. Macartney, *October Fifteenth: A History of Hungary, 1929–1945* (New York, 1957).
30. On Rotta, see Phayer, *Catholic Church,* 106–9, and many relevant documents in *Adss* relating to Hungary in 1944. Also Leni Yahil, "Raoul Wallenberg: His Mission and His Activities in Hungary," *Yad Vashem Studies* 15 (1983): 7–54.
31. For the Swiss press, David Kranzler, *The Man Who Stopped the Trains to Auschwitz: George Mantello, El Salvador, and Switzerland's Finest Hour* (Syracuse, N.Y., 2000), 122–43. See also Theo Tschuy, *Dangerous Diplomacy* (Grand Rapids, Mich., 2000), 52ff., 146–207, for the story of the Swiss diplomat Carl Lutz, who saved thousands of Hungarian Jews in Budapest; on the darker aspects of indirect Swiss involvement in the Holocaust, see Alfred Häsler, *The Lifeboat Is Full: Switzerland and the Refugees, 1933–1945* (New York, 1969), 33–153; Georg Kreis, ed., *Switzerland and the Second World War* (London, 2000), 103–57.
32. Bauer, *Jews for Sale?* 70–71.
33. *Ibid.,* 74–82, 98–99; Weissmandel's accusations in *Hametzar* (New York, 1960) concerning the "betrayal" of European Jewry by world Jewry and the Zionist movement are refuted by Shabtai Teveth, *Ben-Gurion and the Holocaust* (New York, 1996), 112–30.
34. Bauer, *Jews for Sale?* 98ff.
35. N. Oren, "The Bulgarian Exception: A Reassessment of the Salvation of the Jewish Community," *Yad Vashem Studies* 7 (1968): 83–106; F. B. Chary, *Bulgarian Jews and the Final Solution* (Pittsburgh, 1972), 35–100; Avraham Ben-Yakov, "Bulgaria," in *Encyclopaedia of the Holocaust,* 263–88.

36. Michael Bar-Zohar, *Ha Rakevot yatsou raiqot: Ha-Hatzala Hanoezet shel yehudei Bulgaria me ha-hashmada* (Beyond Hitler's grasp: The heroic rescue of Bulgaria's Jews) (Or Yehuda, 1999), in Hebrew, 107–19, 133–37.

37. Chary, *Bulgarian Jews,* 90ff., 129–83.

38. Arendt, *Eichmann,* 187–88, Chary, *Bulgarian Jews,* 153–54.

39. Leni Yahil, *The Rescue of Danish Jewry: Test of a Democracy* (Philadelphia, 1969), 31–83, 382–95.

40. Tatiana Brustin-Berenstein, "The Historiographic Treatment of the Abortive Attempt to Deport the Danish Jews," *Yad Vashem Studies* 40 (1986): 181–218; Hans Kirchhof, "Denmark: A Light in the Darkness of the Holocaust," *Journal of Contemporary History* 30 (1995): 431–79.

41. On the evolution of Swedish reactions, see the extensive documentation in Steven Koblik, *The Stones Cry Out: Sweden's Response to the Persecution of the Jews* (New York, 1988), 167–293; Paul A. Levine, *From Indifference to Activism: Swedish Diplomacy and the Holocaust, 1938–1944* (Uppsala, 1996), points to the positive change in Swedish attitudes in 1942. See also Hannu Rautkallio, *Finland and the Holocaust* (New York, 1987), for the rescue of Finland's Jews.

42. H. J. Boas, *Religious Resistance in Holland* (London, 1945); J. M. Snoek, *De Nederlandse Kerken en de Joden 1940–1945* (The Hague, 1990), 73–99.

43. Jacob Presser, *The Destruction of the Dutch Jews* (New York, 1969); Leni Yahil, "Methods of Persecution, A Comparison of the 'Final Solution' in Holland and Denmark," *Scripta Hierosolymitana Studies in History* 23 (1972): 298ff.; J .C. H. Blom, "Persecution of the Jews in the Netherlands in a Comparative International Perspective," *Dutch Jewish History* (Jerusalem, 1989), 2:273–90, and "Oorlogsdocumentatie '40–45," *Derde Jahrboek* (Amsterdam, 1989), 9–66; Guus Meershoek, "De Amsterdamse hoofscommissaris en de deportatie van de Joden," *Derde Jahrboek* (Amsterdam, 1992), 9–44. Also by the same author, *Dienaren van het gezag: De Amsterdamse politie tijdens de bezetting* (Amsterdam, 1999) (Servants of the authorities: the Amsterdam police during the occupation) (Amsterdam, 1999).

44. Louis de Jong, "Jews and Non-Jews in Nazi Occupied Holland," in Max Beloff, ed., *On the Track of Tyranny* (London, 1960),

139–55; Gerhard Hirschfeld, *Nazi Rule and Dutch Collaboration: The Netherlands under German Occupation, 1940–1945* (Oxford, 1988); also Louis de Jong, *Het Koninkrijk der Nederlanden tijdens de Tweede Wereldoorlog*, vols. 1–14 (The Hague, 1969–1991), which contains a great deal of information about the fate of Dutch Jewry in the Second World War.

45. Joseph Michman, "The Controversial Stand of the Joodse Raad in the Netherlands," *Yad Vashem Studies* 10 (1974): 9–68; Dan Michman, "De oprichting van de 'Joodsche Raad voor Amsterdam vanvit een vergelijkend perspectief,' " *Derde Jahrboek* (Amsterdam, 1992), 75–101.

46. Maxime Steinberg, *L'Etoile et le fusil*, vol. 1: *La Question Juive, 1940–1942* (Brussels, 1983), 83–84, points out that many of the Ostjuden did not register as required by the authorities, which gave them a better chance of survival than in neighboring Holland.

47. R. van Doorslaer *et al.*, eds., *Les Juifs de Belgique: de l'immigration au génocide, 1925–1945* (Brussels, 1994); Martin Conway, *Collaboration in Belgium: Léon Degrelle and the Rexist Movement* (New Haven, 1993); Maxime Steinberg, "The Judenpolitik in Belgium Within the West European Context: Comparative Observations," in Michman, *Belgium and the Holocaust*, 199–214.

48. Pierre Pierrard, *Juifs et Catholiques Français* (Paris, 1970); Pierre Birnbaum, *Antisemitism in France* (Oxford, 1992), 109–99; Marrus and Paxton, *Vichy France*, 27–53.

49. The relevant German documents are in Serge Klarsfeld, ed., *Die Endlösung der Judenfrage in Frankreich* (Paris, 1977), 13–229; Joseph Billig, *La Solution finale de la question Juive* (Paris, 1977); G. Wellers, A. Kaspi, and S. Klarsfeld, *La France et la question Juive* (Paris, 1981); see also Paul Webster, *Pétain's Crime: The Full Story of French Collaboration in the Holocaust* (London, 1990); Jacques Adler, *The Jews of Paris and the Final Solution* (New York, 1987), 223–40.

50. Richard H. Weisberg, *Vichy Law and the Holocaust in France* (Amsterdam, 1996), 37–158.

51. Jean Laloum, *La France antisémite de Darquier de Pellepoix* (Paris, 1979); on Vallat, see Marrus and Paxton, *Vichy France*, 73–120, and 281–340 for Darquier.

52. Marrus and Paxton, *Vichy France*, 106ff.

53. P. Laborie, *L'Opinion Français sur Vichy* (Paris, 1990); Susan Zuccotti, *The Holocaust, the French, and the Jews* (New York, 1993), 138–56.

54. For German intentions and French police collaboration, see the documents in Klarsfeld, *Endlösung,* 50–66, 75–195; also John P. Fox, "How Far Did Vichy France 'Sabotage' the Imperative of Wannsee?" in Cesarani, *Final Solution,* 194–214.

55. Marrus and Paxton, *Vichy France,* 261.

56. Ibid., 269 (*FRUS,* 1942, 2:710, 26 August 1942).

57. Ibid., 269 (*Jewish Telegraphic Agency,* 14 September 1942); also Geoffrey Warner, *Pierre Laval and the Eclipse of France* (London, 1968), and Fred Kupferman, *Pierre Laval* (Paris, 1976).

58. M. Marrus, "French Churches and the Persecution of Jews in France, 1940–1944," *Remembering for the Future* (1988) 307–46.

59. Serge Klarsfeld, *Le Mémorial de la déportation des Juifs en France* (Paris, 1978). Many thousands of Jews were also assisted and hidden by members of the French population, especially in the countryside. One Protestant village, Le Chambon-sur-Lignon, smuggled several thousand Jews to safety.

60. Renée Poznanski, *Les Juifs en France pendant la Seconde Guerre Mondiale* (Paris, 1997), 351 ("le gouvernement allemand les réclame, mais dans l'intention bien arrêtée de les exterminer impitoyablement et méthodiquement"); on Jewish responses, see Richard I. Cohen, *The Burden of Conscience: French Jewish Leadership During the Holocaust* (Bloomington, 1987), 185–92, and Lucien Lazare, *La résistance Juive en France* (Paris, 1988).

61. Philippe Garnier, ed., *Une certaine France: l'antisémitisme, 40–44* (Paris, 1975); Jean-Pierre Azéma and François Bédarida, eds., *La France des années noires* (Paris, 1993), 2 vols.; Pierre Drieu la Rochelle, *Journal, 1939–1945* (Paris, 1992), 54–59. This diary of a leading French collaborator illustrates well enough the pervasive and paranoid anti-Semitism of the time, though it is still relatively mild when compared to the racist ravings of Louis-Ferdinand Céline or Lucien Rebatet's *Les Décombres* (Paris, 1942).

62. *Mein Kampf,* 637.

63. Wolfgang Schieder, ed., *Faschismus als soziale Bewegung: Deutschland und Italien im Vergleich* (Göttingen, 1983); George L. Mosse with Robert S. Wistrich, eds., *International Fascism* (London, 1979), introduction by George Mosse, 1–38.

64. E. R. von Starhemberg, *Between Hitler and Mussolini* (London, 1942), 92–93; Meir Michaelis, *Mussolini and the Jews: German-Italian Relations and the Jewish Question, 1922–1945* (Oxford, 1978), 69.

65. Leon Poliakov and Jacques Sabille, *Jews under the Italian Occupation* (Paris, 1954), 49–180; Menahem Shelach, *Heshbon Damim* [*Blood Account*]: *Hatzaalat Yehudei Croatia al yiday ha-Italkim* (Tel Aviv, 1986), 51–156, on the rescue of Croatian Jewry by the Italians; Zuccotti, *Italians and the Holocaust;* Jonathan Steinberg, *All or Nothing: The Axis and the Holocaust, 1941–43* (London, 1991); and Daniel Carpi, *Between Mussolini and Hitler: The Jews and the Italian Authorities in France and Tunisia* (Hanover, N.H., 1994), 102–35, 241–49.

66. Steinberg, *All or Nothing,* 168–80, pointedly highlights the stark contrast between the humanitarian and relatively liberal attitudes of the Italian Army and those of the Wehrmacht.

67. Ibid. For the historical background, see the essays in Robert S. Wistrich and Sergio della Pergola, eds., *Fascist Antisemitism and the Italian Jews* (Jerusalem, 1995), 13–96.

68. Renzo de Felice, *Storia degli ebrei Italiani sotto il fascismo* (Turin, 1972); Nicola Caracciolo, *Gli ebrei e Italia durante la guerra 1940–45* (Rome, 1986), 42–43, quotes a survivor, Blanka Stern, who escaped to Italy: "the Germans had psychological ways of making us Jews into an inferior race, not human anymore, people without rights. When we arrived in Italy the people gave us back our sense of being human." This is a fascinating book of interviews.

69. Lochner, *Goebbels Diaries*, 241.

70. On the "Final Solution" in Italy, see de Felice, *Storia,* 389–91; F. Folkel, *La Risiera di San Sabba* (Milan, 1979); Liliana Picciotto Fargion, "The Anti-Jewish Policy of the Italian Social Republic (1943–1945), in *Yad Vashem Studies* 17 (1986): 18–49.

7. Britain, America, and the Holocaust

1. Wyman, *Abandonment of the Jews,* xv. See Peter Novick, *The Holocaust in American Life* (Boston, 1999), 47–59, for a contrary view.

2. Ibid., 124–37.

3. David Wyman, "Why Auschwitz Was Never Bombed," *Commen-*

tary 65 (May 1978): 37–46; Richard S. Levy, "The Bombing of Auschwitz Revisited: A Critical Analysis," *Holocaust and Genocide Studies* 10 (1996): 267–98.

4. Meyer Weinberg, *Because They Were Jews: A History of Anti-Semitism* (New York, 1986), 214.

5. Leo Ribuffo, "Henry Ford and *The International Jew*," *American Jewish History* 69 (June 1980): 437–77; Robert Singerman, "The American Career of *The Protocols of the Elders of Zion*," *American Jewish History* 70 (September 1981): 48–78; Albert Lee, *Henry Ford and the Jews* (New York, 1980), 29–31, 46–51.

6. Leo Ribuffo, *The Old Christian Right: The Protestant Far Right from the Great Depression to the Cold War* (Philadelphia, 1983).

7. Ralph L. Kolodny, "Catholics and Father Coughlin: Misremembering the Past," *Patterns of Prejudice* 19.4 (1985): 15–25.

8. Richard Breitman and Alan M. Kraut, *American Refugee Policy and European Jewry, 1933–1945* (Bloomington, 1987), 70–73.

9. Weinberg, *Because They Were Jews*, 220ff.; Wyman, *Abandonment*, 14–15.

10. Quoted in Melvin J. Urofsky, *We Are One! American Jewry and Israel* (New York, 1978), 49; Fred L. Israel, ed., *The War Diary of Breckinridge Long: Selections from the Years 1939–1944* (Lincoln, Nebr., 1966); Breitman and Kraut, *American Refugee Policy*, 112–45.

11. Wasserstein, *Britain*, 244–49.

12. The report suggested *inter alia* that "we may as well take down the plaque from the Statue of Liberty and black out the 'lamp beside the golden door,'" ibid., 294.

13. Wyman, *Abandonment*, 210–15.

14. Feingold, "Was There Communal Failure?" 60ff.; Haskell Lookstein, *Were We Our Brothers' Keepers? The Public Response of American Jews to the Holocaust, 1933–1945* (New York, 1986).

15. Alex Grobman, "Reactions of American Jewry Through the American and Jewish Press, 1939–1942," M.A. thesis (Hebrew University of Jerusalem, 1978); Rafael Medoff, *The Deafening Silence: American Jewish Leaders and the Holocaust* (New York, 1987).

16. See Yitshaq Ben-Ami, *Years of Wrath, Days of Glory* (New York, 1982); Wyman, *Abandonment*, 90–92, 253–54.

17. Wyman, *Abandonment*, 345–47.

18. Aaron Berman, *Nazism, the Jews and American Zionism, 1933–1948* (Detroit, 1990), 80–89.

19. Aaron Berman, "Rescue Through Statehood: The American Zionist Response to the Holocaust," in Cesarani, *Final Solution,* 228–45; Monty Penkower, *The Jews Were Expendable,* 2d ed. (Detroit, 1988), 92.

20. Berman, *Nazism,* 86–87.

21. The Riegner telegram is in Berenbaum, *Witness,* 252–54; for the British response, see Wasserstein, *Britain,* 168–69; on the American reaction, Wyman, *Abandonment,* 42–43, 128–29. Also Walter Laqueur, *The Terrible Secret* (London, 1980), 79–83, and Penkower, *Jews,* 64–70.

22. Wyman, *Abandonment,* 90, estimates the crowd at forty thousand, a record at Madison Square Garden.

23. Stephen J. Whitfield, "The Politics of Pageantry, 1936–1946," *American Jewish History* 84.3 (September 1996): 221–51; at 242. Ben Hecht wrote the script, Billy Rose produced, Moss Hart directed, and Kurt Weill created the score. Paul Muni and Edward G. Robinson were the narrators. These stars were among the most prominent artists and entertainers of Jewish origin in America.

24. Wasserstein, *Britain,* 189–94; Penkower, *Jews,* 98–121.

25. Wasserstein, *Britain,* 196. For Canadian attitudes regarding Bermuda, see Abella and Troper, *None Is Too Many,* 126–47.

26. Wasserstein, *Britain,* 201.

27. Ibid. For the American side, see Wyman, *Abandonment,* 104–23, 341–43. It should be noted that in 1942, publicity, protest, and calls for action regarding the Holocaust (especially by Christian church leaders and MPs) were much more vocal in Britain than in the United States. A year later, the position was reversed. See Tony Kushner, "Rules of the Game: Britain, America, and the Holocaust in 1944," in *Holocaust and Genocide Studies* 5 (1990): 381–403.

28. Feingold, *Politics of Bearing Witness,* 169–201.

29. Wyman, *Abandonment,* 288–307; Martin Gilbert, *Auschwitz and the Allies: The Politics of Rescue* (London, 1983), 307–17.

30. Gilbert, *Auschwitz,* 316–27.

31. Ibid., 216, 245.

32. Berenbaum, *Witness,* 296–304, for the documents.
33. Ibid., 298–300.
34. Ibid., 304 (McCloy's letter of 14 August 1944).
35. Richard Breitman, "The Allied War Effort and the Jews, 1942–3," *Journal of Contemporary History* 20 (1985), 135–57, and *Official Secrets: What the Nazis Planned, What the British and Americans Knew* (London, 1999), 88–109, on the British, and 228–30 for a comparison between Roosevelt and Churchill.
36. Breitman, *Official Secrets,* 192ff.
37. Gilbert, *Auschwitz,* 184.
38. Quoted in Marrus and Paxton, *Vichy France,* 196.
39. Ibid., 196–97.
40. Joseph Heller, "Roosevelt, Stalin, and the Palestine Problem at Yalta," *Wilson Library Bulletin,* new series, 30.41–42 (1977): 25–35.
41. Ibid.
42. Quoted by Berman, "Rescue Through Statehood," 237.
43. Ibid., 239.
44. Yisraeli, "Third Reich," 343ff.; Y. Gelber, "Hamediniut Hatzionit Veheskem Haha'avarah," *Yalkut Moreshet* 18 (1974): 23–100; Edwin Black, *The Transfer Agreement* (New York, 1984), 146–53, 166.
45. David Ben-Gurion, *Ba ma-arakhah* (Tel Aviv, 1949), 3:14.
46. On the responses of the Yishuv and the Zionist movement to the Shoah, see Yoav Gelber, "Zionist Policy and the Fate of European Jewry, 1939–1942," *Yad Vashem Studies* 13 (1979): 169–209; Dina Porat, "Palestinian Jewry and the Jewish Agency: Public Response to the Holocaust," in R. Cohen, ed., *Vision and Conflict in the Holy Land* (New York, 1990), 246–73; Dina Porat, *The Blue and Yellow Stars of David: The Zionist Leadership in Palestine and the Holocaust, 1939–1945* (Cambridge, Mass., 1990), 239–62; the more partisan and tendentious Tom Segev, *The Seventh Million: The Israelis and the Holocaust* (New York, 1993), 97–110; on Mapai, see Y. Weitz, *Muda'ut ve hoser onim: Mapai lenokhah hashoah, 1943–45* (Aware but helpless: Mapai and the Holocaust) (Jerusalem, 1994).
47. Shabtai Teveth, *Ben-Gurion: The Burning Ground, 1886–1948* (Boston, 1987), 854–60, and *Ben-Gurion and the Holocaust,* 221–60; see also Tuvia Friling, "Ben-Gurion and the Holocaust

of European Jewry, 1939–1945: A Stereotype Re-examined," *Yad Vashem Studies* 18 (1988): 199–232, for context and perspective.

48. Chaim Barlas, *Hatzalah Bimei Shoah* (Tel Aviv, 1975), 293–95; Berenbaum, *Witness*, 296ff.; Gilbert, *Auschwitz*, 299–322; and Wasserstein, *Britain*, 309ff.

49. Quoted in Teveth's *Ben-Gurion and the Holocaust*, 212–13.

50. Gilbert, *Auschwitz*, 285, 304ff., 319; Wasserstein, *Britain*, 313–20.

51. See Alex Weissberg, *Desperate Mission: Joel Brand's Story* (New York, 1958), and Brand's own Hebrew memoir, *Beschlichut Nidonim Lemavet* (Tel Aviv, 1956); J. S. Conway, "The Holocaust in Hungary: Recent Controversies and Reconsiderations," in Randolph Braham, ed., *The Tragedy of Hungarian Jewry* (New York, 1986), 1–33; Gilbert, *Auschwitz*, 217–28, 240–44, 253–55; and Bauer, *Jews for Sale?* 172–95.

52. Idith Zertal, "The Poisoned Heart: The Jews of Palestine and the Holocaust," *Tikkun* 2.1 (1988): 79–83, is vehemently critical; for more nuanced verdicts, see Dina Porat, "Ben-Gurion and the Holocaust," in R. Zweig, ed., *David Ben-Gurion: Politics and Leadership in Israel* (London, 1991), 145–70; and Tuvia Friling, *Hetz ba-arafel: David Ben-Gurion, Hanhagat Ha-yishuv ve-nisionot Hatzalah be-Shoah* (Arrow in the dark: David Ben-Gurion, the Yishuv leadership, and rescue efforts during the Shoah) (Beer-Sheva, 1998), 2.657ff.

53. Wasserstein, *Britain*, 45, 66–69.

54. Ibid., 143–52.

55. Ibid., 145.

56. Ibid., 37.

57. Quoted by Martin Gilbert in "The Most Horrible Crime: Churchill's Prophetic, Passionate, and Persistent Response to the Holocaust," *The Times Literary Supplement*, 7 June 1996, 3–5.

58. Wasserstein, *Britain*, 280.

59. Ibid., 275–79.

60. Gilbert, "Most Horrible Crime"; for the other side of the coin and a much more critical view, see Michael J. Cohen, "Churchill and the Jews: The Holocaust," *Modern Judaism* 6.1 (February 1986): 27–49.

61. Ibid.

62. Ibid.

63. Gilbert, *Auschwitz*, 270.
64. Ibid., 305.
65. On the mind-set of British officialdom, Wasserstein, *Britain*, 350–55.
66. Quoted in Breitman, *Official Secrets*, 209.
67. Ibid., 93; Gilbert, "Most Horrible Crime," 4.
68. Breitman, *Official Secrets*, 106.
69. Ibid., 171.
70. Ibid.
71. Wasserstein, *Britain*, 188.
72. Breitman, *Official Secrets*, 119. He shows that the British government and its intelligence services knew about the Holocaust earlier than previously assumed. This information included reports about Auschwitz and the death-camp system in Poland well before the summer of 1944, contrary to what Martin Gilbert had imagined twenty years ago. See Barbara Rogers, "British Intelligence and the Holocaust: *Auschwitz and the Allies* Re-examined," *The Journal of Holocaust Education* 8.1 (summer 1999): 89–106.
73. Laqueur, *Terrible Secrets* 229–38; Thomas E. Wood and Stanislaw M. Jankowski, *Karski: How One Man Tried to Stop the Holocaust* (New York, 1994) 117–19, 142–47; Gilbert, *Auschwitz*, 93–95; Breitman, *Official Secrets*, 146–50; and the documents in Berenbaum, *Witness*, 256–61.
74. Berenbaum, *Witness*, 249–50. See also the heart-rending appeal of Shmuel Zygelbojm, the Jewish representative on the Polish National Council based in London, on 246–47. In protest against the indifference of a world "which witnessed the extermination of the Jewish people without taking any steps to prevent it," he committed suicide in London during the autumn of 1942.
75. Laqueur, *Terrible Secret*, 236.
76. Ibid., 121, and E. Raczynski, *In Allied London* (London, 1962). See also the two comprehensive volumes by David Engel, *In the Shadow of Auschwitz: The Polish Government-in-Exile and the Jews, 1939–1942* (Chapel Hill, 1987), 157–213, and *Facing a Holocaust: The Polish Government-in-Exile and the Jews, 1943–1945* (Chapel Hill, 1993), 15–167; on Karski's mission to the United States, see Engel, *Facing a Holocaust*, 2:89–94.

8. MODERNITY AND THE NAZI GENOCIDE

1. Omer Bartov, *Murder in Our Midst: The Holocaust, Industrial Killing, and Representation* (New York, 1996), 4.

2. Zygmunt Bauman, *Modernity and the Holocaust* (Oxford, 1989), is perhaps the best articulated of these efforts. For an interesting critique, see Hans Mommsen, "Nationalsozialismus als vorgetäuschte Modernisierung," in Walter H. Pehle, ed., *Der historische Ort des Nationalsozialismus* (Frankfurt, 1990), 31–46.

3. Hannah Arendt, *Totalitarianism* (New York, 1968).

4. For the role of medicine and science, see Robert J. Lifton, *The Nazi Doctors: Medical Killing and the Psychology of Genocide* (New York, 1986); Benno Müller Hill, *Murderous Science* (Oxford, 1988).

5. Bauman, *Modernity*, 33.

6. See Wolfgang Schneider, ed., *Vernichtungspolitik: Eine Debatte über den Zusammenhang von Sozialpolitik und Genozid im nationalsozialistischen Deutschland* (Hamburg, 1991), for a discussion of Aly and Heim's themes.

7. Götz Aly and Susanne Heim, "Die Ökonomie der Endlösung?" in *Beiträge zur nationalsozialistischen Gesundheits und Sozialpolitik* (Berlin, 1987) 5:14.

8. Browning, *Path to Genocide*, 59ff., points out that initially the arguments of "productionists" in favor of economic self-sufficiency in the ghettos had the upper hand.

9. Ulrich Herbert, "Racism and Rational Calculation: The Role of 'Utilitarian' Strategies of Legitimation in the National Socialist Weltanschauung," *Yad Vashem Studies* 24 (1994): 133.

10. Michael Burleigh, "A Political Economy of the Final Solution? Reflections on Modernity, Historians, and the Holocaust," *Patterns of Prejudice* 30.2 (1996): 29–41.

11. Dan Diner, "Rationalization and Method: Critique of a New Approach in Understanding the 'Final Solution,'" *Yad Vashem Studies* 24 (1994): 87.

12. Peter Longerich, *Politik der Vernichtung: Eine Gesamtdarstellung der nationalsozialistischen Judenverfolgung* (Munich, 1998).

13. Lochner, *Goebbels Diaries*, 102.

14. Ibid.

15. Quoted in Matthew Cooper, *The Phantom War* (London, 1979),

57. See also Yehoshua Büchler, "The Extermination of the Jews Disguised as Anti-Partisan Warfare in the Occupied Areas of the Soviet Union 1941–1942," M.A. thesis in Hebrew (Hebrew University of Jerusalem, 1989).

16. See Tim W. Mason, "The Primacy of Politics—Politics and Economics in National Socialist Germany," in Henry A. Turner, ed., *Nazism and the Third Reich* (New York, 1972), 175–200.

17. Albert Speer, *The Slave State: Heinrich Himmler's Masterplan for SS Supremacy* (London, 1981), 251.

18. Höss, *Commandant of Auschwitz,* 206.

19. Smith and Peterson, *Heinrich Himmler,* 201.

20. Helmut Heiber, ed., *Reichsführer! Briefe an und von Himmler* (Stuttgart, 1970), 190.

21. *Trial of the Major War Criminals before the International Military Tribunal* (Nuremberg, 1948), 29:123.

22. Ulrich Herbert, "Arbeit und Vernichtung: Ökonomisches Interesse und Primat der Weltanschauung im Nationalsozialismus," in Dan Diner, ed., *Ist der nationalsozialismus Geschichte?* (Frankfurt, 1987), 198–236.

23. Browning, *Paths to Genocide,* 59–85.

24. Raul Hilberg, *The Destruction of the European Jews,* 3 vols. (New York, 1985), 3:994.

25. See Bauman, Chap. 4, on "the uniqueness and normality of the Holocaust."

26. Mark Levene, "Is the Holocaust Simply Another Example of Genocide?" *Patterns of Prejudice* 28.2 (1994): 3–26, at 23.

27. Edwin Black, *IBM and the Holocaust: The Strategic Alliance Between Nazi Germany and America's Most Powerful Corporation* (London, 2001).

28. Friedlander, *Origins of Nazi Genocide,* 284.

29. Christopher Browning, "The Revised Hilberg," *Simon Wiesenthal Centre Annual* (1986), 291.

30. Hilberg, *Destruction,* 669.

31. Hans Mommsen, "The Realisation of the Unthinkable: The 'Final Solution of the Jewish Question' in the Third Reich," in his *From Weimar to Auschwitz: Essays in German History* (Cambridge, 1991), 224–53, at 250.

32. David Bankier, "On Modernisation and the Rationality of Extermination," *Yad Vashem Studies* 24 (1994): 109–29.
33. Michael Marrus, *The Holocaust in History* (London, 1988), 40.
34. Ian Kershaw, *The Nazi Dictatorship: Problems and Perspectives of Interpretation* (London, 1993), 85–86, for a discussion of Hans Mommsen's work, which first popularized this term.
35. Schleunes, *Twisted Road*, viii.
36. Martin Broszat, "Hitler und die 'Endlösung': Aus Anlass der Thesen von David Irving," *VfZ* 25.4 (1977): 739–75.
37. Mommsen, "Realisation of the Unthinkable," 232–33.
38. Herbert, *National Socialist Extermination Policies*, 1–52, editor's introduction.
39. Ibid., 83–127, for the articles by Pohl and Sandkühler.
40. Ibid., 37.
41. See Porat, "Holocaust in Lithuania" and Steinberg, "Types of Genocide" in Cesarani, *Final Solution;* Mark Mazower, *Inside Hitler's Greece: The Experience of Occupation, 1941–1944* (London, 1993), and Jonathan Steinberg, "The Holocaust, Society, and Ourselves," *The Jewish Quarterly* 153 (spring 1994): 46–50. See also the new book by Jan T. Gross, *Neighbors: The Destruction of the Jewish Community in Jedwabne, Poland* (Princeton, 2001).
42. Tzvetan Todorov, *Facing the Extreme: Moral Life in the Concentration Camps* (London, 1999), 289–90.
43. Arad, *Belzec*, 84.
44. Ibid.
45. Ibid., 67.
46. Wistrich, *Who's Who*, 269.
47. Ibid., 278–79, for a short biography of Wirth.
48. Arad, *Belzec*, 183.
49. Bauer, *History of the Holocaust*, 210–11.
50. Wistrich, *Who's Who*, 241–42. See also Gitta Sereny, *Into That Darkness: An Examination of Conscience* (London, 1977). This is the only case in which a death-camp commandant ever revealed his feelings in lengthy interviews.
51. Quoted in Arad, *Belzec*, 186.
52. Wistrich, *Who's Who*, 123–24.
53. Höss, *Commandant of Auschwitz*.
54. Todorov, *Facing the Extreme*, 170.

55. Martin Gilbert, *The Holocaust: The Jewish Tragedy* (London, 1986), 582.

56. Todorov, *Facing the Extreme,* 142; Primo Levi, *The Drowned and the Saved* (London, 1989), 56, already noted that in the camps compassion and brutality "can coexist in the same individual and in the same moment, despite all logic."

57. "Diary of Johann Paul Kremer," in J. Bezwinska and D. Czech, eds., *KL Auschwitz, Seen by the SS* (New York, 1984), 214–15.

58. Jean Améry, *At the Mind's Limits* (London, 1999), 31. These are reflections by a survivor on Auschwitz-Birkenau and its realities.

59. Bruno Bettelheim, *The Informed Heart* (Glencoe, Ill., 1960), 109.

60. Todorov, *Facing the Extreme,* 78.

61. Levi, *Drowned,* 202.

62. Todorov, *Facing the Extreme,* 152.

63. Levi, *Drowned,* 30ff.

64. Ibid., 34.

65. Ibid., 35.

66. Ibid., 37.

67. Goldhagen, *Hitler's Willing Executioners,* 8.

68. Margerete Buber-Neumann, *Déportée à Ravensbrück* (Paris, 1988), 53.

69. David Rousset et al., eds., *Pour la vérité sur les camps concentrationnaires* (Paris, 1990), 183.

70. For Nolte's views, see his "A Past That Will Not Pass Away," *Yad Vashem Studies* 19 (1988): 71. This issue reproduces the main documents of the German "battle of the historians" (*Historikerstreit*) in the 1980s.

71. Steven T. Katz, *The Holocaust and Comparative History.* Leo Baeck Memorial Lectures, vol. 37 (New York, 1993), 3–29.

72. Ibid., 20–21.

73. Ibid., 22.

74. Olga Lengyel, *Five Chimneys: The Story of Auschwitz* (New York, 1947), 110–11.

75. Katz, *Holocaust,* 24.

76. The figures for the total number of Armenian deaths vary enormously. Katz gives a minimum of 476,000 and a high of 776,000 fatalities (ibid., 17). Some Armenian historians speak of more than a million deaths. Robert F. Melson estimates that between

1915 and 1918, one million out of two million Armenians were killed. See his "The Armenian Genocide" in Rosenbaum, *Is the Holocaust Unique?* 89. He adds that between 1918 and 1923 half a million more Armenians perished at Turkish hands.

77. Pierre Papazian, "A 'Unique Uniqueness'?" *Midstream* (April 1984), 14–18, and the responses by Yehuda Bauer, Helen Fein, George M. Kren, Leon H. Rappoport, and Nora Levin (19–25).

78. Melson, "Armenian Genocide," 92–93.

79. Vahakn N. Dadrian, "The Comparative Aspects of the Armenian and Jewish Cases of Genocide," in Rosenbaum, *Is the Holocaust Unique?* 104–5.

80. Katz, *Holocaust,* 6–17.

81. Richard L. Rubinstein, "Religion and the Uniqueness of the Holocaust," in Rosenbaum, *Is the Holocaust Unique?* 11–18.

82. Maccoby, *Sacred Executioner,* 175.

83. Uriel Tal, "On the Study of the Holocaust and Genocide," *Yad Vashem Studies* 13 (1979): 45.

INDEX

Africa, 51, 58, 90–91, 171, 175, 194, 197
Aly, Götz, 214, 217
American Jews, 23, 68, 69, 71, 144, 188, 191–92, 193, 196, 198
Anschluss (1938), 72, 130, 215
anti-Semitism: as central to Holocaust, 239–40; distinctive features to Hitler's, 37–38; extremist post-World War I, 43–44; historical roots of, 1, 3, 6–27; and Hitler worldview, 35–42; Jewish response to, 23–25; Marr's term for, 16–17; and modernity of Holocaust, 222, 223, 233–34; post-World War I, 19–27; pre-World War I, 1, 3, 6–18; as psychopathic disease, 77; rational, 40; "scientific," 213–14; secularization of, 14. *See also specific nation or topic*
Arendt, Hannah, 75, 155, 213
Armenian people, 236–38
Auschwitz-Birkenau (Silesia): Allied bombing of, 188, 195–96; Belgium Jews in, 169; British knowledge about, 208; climax of Nazi ideology in, 240; commandant of, 228–29; as death camp, 100; as embodiment of Holocaust, 100; establishment of, 217; and "Final Solution," 222; French Jews in, 172, 174, 175, 177; gassing in, 100, 158, 177, 228–29; Gypsies in, 4–5; Hungarian Jews in, 160, 195, 215; Italian Jews in, 183; killing methods at, 219; and modernity of Holocaust, 214, 215, 219, 222, 228–29, 234, 236; mothers and children at, 236; resistance and revolts in, 80, 82, 232–33; Roman Jews in, 145; Russian POWs in, 4; Salonika Jews in, 177; scientific research at, 229–30; "special squads" at, 232–33
Austria: annexation of, 56; anti-Semitism in, 36, 56, 123; Catholic reactions to Nazi policies in, 123, 132;

Christian Socialists in, 123; collaboration in, 177; deportation of Jews in, 97, 103, 104, 113; emigration of Jews in, 38, 50, 56, 65–66; expropriation of Jewish property in, 56; and "Final Solution," 104, 108, 177; Hitler as youth in, 37–38, 123; and Hitler's anti-Semitism, 36; Hitler's return to, 56; Jewish population in, 36, 56, 72; Jews in pre-World War I, 37–38

Babi Yar massacres, 92–93
Balfour Declaration, 19–20, 199, 203
Baltic states, 5, 20–21, 72, 93–94, 108, 149. *See also specific state*
Bavaria, 33, 34, 35, 44, 121–22, 124. *See also* Munich, Germany
Belgium, 50, 57, 83, 84, 138, 141, 169
Belzec (Poland), 100, 208, 225–27
Ben-Gurion, David, 185, 192, 199, 200, 201, 202
Bermuda Conference (1943), 193–94, 198
Bertram, Adolf, 130, 131, 136–37
Biltmore Hotel (New York City): conference at, 192–93
blood libel, 12, 42
blood purity, 14, 49
"blood and soil" doctrines, 126
Bohemia, 13, 98, 103, 104, 141
Bolsheviks, 19, 40–41, 43, 94–97, 125–26, 132–33, 134, 147, 153. *See also* Communism; Marxism; Soviet Union
Bormann, Martin, 65, 132, 136
Browning, Christopher, 224, 233
Bulgaria, 163–65, 201

capitalism, 17, 36, 110, 111, 125–26, 156
Casablanca Conference (1943), 197
Catholic Church/Catholicism: and anti-Semitism, 14, 16, 22, 25, 26, 122–23, 128; concordat (1933) between Nazis and, 127–28, 135, 136, 145; detente

ABOUT THE AUTHOR

Robert Wistrich is Neuberger Professor of modern European and Jewish history at the Hebrew University of Jerusalem. He previously held the Chair for Jewish Studies at University College, London, as well as guest professorships at Harvard, Brandeis, and Oxford Universities, and at the Institute of Advanced Study in the Netherlands (NIAS). An editor of East European Jewish Affairs and a regular contributor to the *Times Literary Supplement,* Professor Wistrich is widely recognized as one of the world's foremost authorities on the history of modern Jewry and anti-Semitism. He is the author of many highly regarded books, including the award-winning *Socialism and the Jew, The Jews of Vienna in the Age of Franz Joseph, Antisemitism: The Longest Hatred, Revolutionary Jews from Marx to Trotsky, Trotsky: Fate of a Revolutionary, Who's Who in Germany, Hitler's Apocalypse: Jews and the Nazi Legacy, Between Redemption and Perdition: Antisemitism and Jewish Identity,* and *Weekend in Munich: Art, Propaganda and Terror in the Third Reich.* He also scripted, edited, and presented several acclaimed documentary films for British television, including *The Longest Hatred* and *Good Morning, Mr. Hitler.*

A NOTE ON THE TYPE

The principal text of this Modern Library edition
was set in a digitized version of Janson, a typeface that
dates from about 1690 and was cut by Nicholas Kis,
a Hungarian working in Amsterdam. The original matrices have
survived and are held by the Stempel foundry in Germany.
Hermann Zapf redesigned some of the weights and sizes for
Stempel, basing his revisions on the original design.

Printed in the United States
by Baker & Taylor Publisher Services